From Twitter to Capitol Hill

Critical Media Literacies Series

Series Editor

William M. Reynolds (*Georgia Southern University, USA*)

Editorial Board

Peter Appelbaum (*Arcadia University, USA*)
Jennifer Beech (*University of Tennessee – Chattanooga, USA*)
Eleanor Blair (*Western Carolina University, USA*)
Ana Cruz (*St. Louis Community College, USA*)
Venus Evans-Winters (*Illinois State University, USA*)
Julie C. Garlen (*Georgia Southern University, USA*)
Nicholas Hartlep (*Berea College, Kentucky, USA*)
Mark Helmsing (*George Mason University, USA*)
Sherick Hughes (*University of North Carolina – Chapel Hill, USA*)
Danielle Ligocki (*Oakland University, USA*)
John Lupinacci (*Washington State University, USA*)
Peter McLaren (*Chapman University, USA*)
Yolanda Medina (*Borough of Manhattan Community College/CUNY, USA*)
Brad Porfilio (*Seattle University, USA*)
Jennifer Sandlin (*Arizona State University, USA*)
Julie Webber (*Illinois State University, USA*)
Handel Kashope Wright (*The University of British Columbia, Canada*)
William Yousman (*Sacred Heart University, USA*)

VOLUME 10

The titles published in this series are listed at *brill.com/cmls*

From Twitter to Capitol Hill

*Far-Right Authoritarian Populist Discourses,
Social Media and Critical Pedagogy*

By

Panayota Gounari

BRILL

LEIDEN | BOSTON

Cover illustration: Collage by Thanassis Gounaris

All chapters in this book have undergone peer review.

The Library of Congress Cataloging-in-Publication Data is available online at https://catalog.loc.gov

Typeface for the Latin, Greek, and Cyrillic scripts: "Brill". See and download: brill.com/brill-typeface.

ISSN 2666-4097
ISBN 978-90-04-42830-0 (paperback)
ISBN 978-90-04-42831-7 (hardback)
ISBN 978-90-04-51047-0 (e-book)

Copyright 2022 by Koninklijke Brill NV, Leiden, The Netherlands.
Koninklijke Brill NV incorporates the imprints Brill, Brill Nijhoff, Brill Hotei, Brill Schöningh, Brill Fink, Brill mentis, Vandenhoeck & Ruprecht, Böhlau Verlag and V&R Unipress.
All rights reserved. No part of this publication may be reproduced, translated, stored in a retrieval system, or transmitted in any form or by any means, electronic, mechanical, photocopying, recording or otherwise without prior written permission from the publisher. Requests for re-use and/or translations must be addressed to Koninklijke Brill NV via brill.com or copyright.com.

This book is printed on acid-free paper and produced in a sustainable manner.

Advance Praise for
From Twitter to Capitol Hill

"The book provides several contributions—most centrally, it describes and applies Gounari's original framework for discourse analysis. It contains an excellent case study that is not only very convincing and well-done, but also that uses a text (Trump's speech to his followers on January 6, 2021) that is extremely pertinent and interesting to see analyzed in this way. Gounari also ties the controversy over Critical Race Theory directly into her argument for the importance of a critical pedagogy that places historicity as central. This is commendable not just in terms of introducing a vision for critical pedagogy that centers history, but also in specifically tying it so directly and meaningfully into current controversies. The Critical Race Theory issue is huge, and the author's response to it via critical pedagogy is one of the most compelling recent arguments for critical pedagogy I have come across."
– **Jeremiah Morelock, Boston College**

"It is an important and original critical investigation in the field. There is a massive amount of original, highly relevant conceptualization and critique through a well measured but critical writing. I was very intrigued with several aspects of the book including the theoretical synergy between discourse studies, populism, and social media. Similarly, the stuff on synthesising discourse historical approach and one dimensional discourse model was very refreshing and original."
– **Majid Khosravinik, University of Newcastle**

"*From Twitter to Capitol Hill* is timely, urgent, and essential. Gounari systematically analyzes the structure of right-wing authoritarianism, showing how it recuperates familiar elements of fascism while also exploiting 21st century mediascapes. This book explains clearly how capitalism's one-dimensional discourse is being weaponized against social solidarity in the present, and argues compellingly for a return to critical pedagogy's radical roots in response. Gounari's incisive exposé of the grim nexus of neoliberal economies of communication and the mediatization of racism is truly indispensable reading for all scholars, educators, and activists committed to dialogue and justice in these difficult times."
– **Noah De Lissovoy, Professor, Cultural Studies in Education, University of Texas at Austin**

To my parents
Tassos and Nacy

Contents

Preface XI
Acknowledgments XVIII
List of Figures XXI

Introduction 1
1   Far-Right Populist Authoritarianism   4

1 Far-Right Authoritarian Populism, Fascism, New Fascism, Trumpism 14
1   Introduction   14
2   A New Fascism?   17
3   Fascism, Neofascism, Far Right and Trumpism   23
4   Conclusion   33

2 One-Dimensional Discourse, Authoritarianism and Social Media: A Theoretical Framework 39
1   Introduction   39
2   What Is One-Dimensional Discourse?   41
3   Features of One-Dimensional Discourse   44
4   (Social) Media   53
5   From Mediatization to (Social) Mediatization   55
6   Conclusion   60

3 From Twitter to Capitol Hill: One-Dimensional Discursive Extremism and the Language of Digital Aggressiveness 66
1   Introduction   66
2   Critical Discourse Analysis/Studies (CDA/S) and the Discourse-Historical Approach (DHA)   68
3   From Twitter to Capitol Hill   71
4   Trump's Speech at the Ellipse-Save America Rally   80
5   One-Dimensional Discourse and the Language of Total Administration   85
6   Discursive Themes/Argumentative Constructions   86
7   Conclusion   93

4 Against Critical Pedagogy: For a Critical Pedagogy with a Radical Political Project 100
1   Introduction   100

CONTENTS

2 Historical Roots and Main Concepts of Critical Pedagogy: Making the Pedagogical Political 103

3 Critical Pedagogy: Where Are We Today? 109

4 Moving Forward 113

5 Emergency Time as a Pedagogical Project: Historical Thinking and Critical Consciousness 132

1 'Actions Committed in the Past' 132

2 Emergency Time: Unsettled Accounts with History 138

3 History: A Critical Public Pedagogy Project of Recontextualization 148

4 Making the Pedagogical Historical and the Historical Pedagogical 152

Appendix A: Trump's Last Two Tweets on January 8th, 2021 161

Appendix B: Twitter Blog Post on the Permanent Suspension of Donald Trump's Account, January 8th, 2021 162

Appendix C: Donald Trump Talking to Reporters after the Charlottesville Rally 165

Index 167

Preface

As a female, foreign-born scholar living in the United States at a time of capitalist restoration, the apogee of the privatization and corporatization of education, and coming out of four years of far-right authoritarian populism, never-ending racism, anti-blackness, immigrant backlash, and violent manifestations of patriarchy as recorded in the *#metoo* movement, I have often felt demoralized. In the current context, it feels, at times, that academic writing might be an exercise in futility. After all, the world has been in a downward spiral for too long now, and words cannot change society. Or can they?

There is a plethora of academic work out there, that keeps piling up, becoming part of the academic market of published commodities that sustains a particular division of labor. The work we actually do in institutions of higher education is highly stratified, and highly inequitable as evidenced, for example, in labor statuses and hierarchies between full time vs. part time, tenured vs. non-tenured, White vs. faculty of color, female vs. male scholars and the ever-looming job precarity. There are increasing calls for quantity at the expense of quality and depth, and a mechanization of the intellectual process, in an attempt to quantify our output (articles, books, etc.) as a commodity. For instance, "more than a half of all published journal articles in the social sciences are never quoted. Many articles are never read by anyone except the 'anonymous peer reviewers' and copy editors" (Eriksen, 2001, p. 92). It is obvious that only a small fraction of articles' and books' contents manages to find their way into our disciplinary discourses. So why is this vast amount of scholarly work produced (under the pressure to publish or perish) if not to meet particular institutional requirements? Or, maybe, to feed the vanity of actually holding a research agenda, often for the sake of simply holding it? Why do we write?

In the *Tyranny of the Moment* Thomas Eriksen claims that "when growing amounts of information are distributed at growing speed, it becomes increasingly difficult to create narratives, orders, developmental sequences. The fragments threaten to become hegemonic. This has consequences for the ways we relate to knowledge, work and lifestyle in a wide sense" (Eriksen, 2001, pp. 109–110). The fragmentation of narratives and knowledge further forces academics into silos and prevents them from reading each other (because they are competing or underestimate their colleagues' work, or they simply don't have the time) and from coming together and working as a collective. It also generates competitiveness, overblown egos and narcissism, and abusive individuals who survive and thrive in enabling academic environments. A form of dehumanizing authoritarianism manifests in academic intellectual production. The neoliberal model is colonizing time, space, and our very minds, deprioritizing or even abolishing what makes us human.

And this brings me to a second aspect of academic labor, that is dehumanization. This dehumanization has roots in the very structure of our institutions of higher education and is weaponized in the labor we are expected to offer, the demands put upon us, the abuse we are often subject to, by more powerful colleagues, particularly as women in the academy; at times, it comes with the disillusionment about the kinds of relationships and solidarity that we hope to find; the kind of alliances we seek to forge; the struggle to see ourselves beyond the personal, to engage in socially committed scholarship in a landscape of pathological ambition, commodification, intensification and mechanization of academic labor and the obliteration of space and time; Time to invest in thinking deeply. Our minds have slowly been colonized by technocratic concerns, the automation and instrumentalization of an educational system that has handed off its role and responsibility to the market.

All this is to say that the conditions in which we currently exist, live, breathe, labor, and write can be traumatizing both on the professional and individual level. With the COVID-19 pandemic, trauma has been further intensified. The world is a painful place to exist, to think to create, to labor; To learn and to teach. Challenges include extreme austerity, privatization of public resources, environmental destruction, corporatism, financial annihilation of working and middle classes; exploitation, social immiseration, oppression, racism and authoritarianism, surveillance, and increased militarization. Capitalism and its neoliberal iterations breed destructiveness and death and resonate with the notion of 'social necrophilia.' The metaphor comes from Erich Fromm, Frankfurt School philosopher, social psychologist, and psychoanalyst. In his seminal work on the *Anatomy of Human Destructiveness*, Fromm (1973) defines necrophilia as "the passionate attraction to all that is dead, decayed, putrid, sickly; it is the passion to transform that which is alive into something unalive; to destroy for the sake of destruction; the exclusive interest in all that is purely mechanical. It is the passion to tear apart living structures" (Fromm, 1973, p. 369). Social necrophilia in the capitalist context is the blunt organized effort on the part of a hegemonic political and financial system to implement economic and social policies that result in the physical, material, social and financial destruction of human beings, particularly the most vulnerable, and their environment: policies that promote death, whether physical or symbolical. Or both. In this landscape, we are trying to find ways to do meaningful research. Research that could make a difference—even the smallest.

Can scholars who are engaged in social research be traumatized by the social issues and injustices they study? How does being immersed in and

PREFACE   XIII

studying far-right extremism and neo-Nazi politics, discourses and practices register in the researcher's psyche? Can we be traumatized by our work when it entails researching and unveiling the dehumanization of human beings and our societies? What are the effects on the researcher who tries to uncover layers of symbolic and material violence in an effort to understand and, hopefully, help change social reality?

These are some of the questions that have been weighing heavily on my mind, for over a year now, while being immersed in the land of authoritarianism and far-right populism and extremism for the purposes of this book. I recently stumbled upon an article by James Robins in *The New Republic* that captures in its title exactly this struggle, albeit for historians: Can historians be traumatized by history? Robins (2021) discusses the profound effects secondhand experience of past horrors could have for historians, and the ways in which bearing witness to atrocities can cause what clinical psychologists Karen Saakvitne and Laurie Anne Pearlman called in 1995 'vicarious trauma.' While scholars can be traumatized, their trauma doesn't even start to compare with the physical and psychological trauma entire groups of people have suffered, as a result of the inhumane and unjust practices we study. That said, for any scholar who is honestly invested in the study of social problems and their real material consequences on human beings, and who is trying to produce a form of socially committed scholarship, the process could be traumatizing and demoralizing. Going through material where different groups of people are stripped off their humanity, where their human existence in cancelled, and they are annihilated as historical subjects, is not a simple exercise in rhetoric, neither a good sad story to tell. Our work is not exhausted in narratives. Narratives create and sustain relationships of power and give shape to material practices. This is one reason why we write.

Far-right populism, authoritarian politics and deep conservativism are proving to be surprisingly stubborn and powerful. From Europe and the rise of neo-fascist parties to the United States with Trumpism and the Alt-right, to Latin America, and many other places around the world, reactionary forces have been rolling back social welfare provisions and rights achieved in the 60s and 70s by the labor and other progressive social movements, creating a landscape of precarity, disposability, fear, insecurity, and violence.

At the same time, these forces have seized mainstream discourse in order to make fascism relevant again. Hegemony, as the organization of consent to achieve leadership of a class alliance is shifting back to what Arendt (1971) called its usual 'implements': raw physical violence, teargas, water cannons, beatings, and deadly violence. The state's repressive apparatus (army, police, prisons) is unapologetically taking again center stage in ways that are reminiscent of fascist regimes. More and more people embrace this kind of politics giving power and an unprecedented dynamic to authoritarianism. There is a social, political, and psychological dimension in authoritarianism. The latter is embodied as the desire for fascism and the development of what Wilhelm Reich discussed in the *Mass Psychology of Fascism* (1949/1980) and Adorno et al. have presented in *The Authoritarian Personality* (2019), both classic books in understanding authoritarian and fascistic tendencies and what makes people susceptible to such ideologies.

I have been preoccupied and deeply disturbed by the meteoric rise and proliferation of far-right extremist ideologies and politics, particularly the past ten years. Living through four years of Trump administration and witnessing the rise of Trumpism, as an embodiment of far-right populism, further pushed me to start thinking about the reasons behind the revival of authoritarian, neo-Nazi, and fascist ideologies. At the same time, I witnessed the rise, legitimation, and criminal activity of the Greek neo-Nazi party Golden Dawn in my home country, Greece. These two moments 'read' against a broader landscape of authoritarian politics, have deeply troubled me, and kept me up at night. As a critical linguist and educator, I sought to find answers in the fields I know better: critical applied linguistics and critical education. The starting point of this book was "the awareness of a social and political problem that possesses linguistic aspects" (Reisigl, 2008, p. 100). How have far-right politics and ideologies been shaped into discourses? What are the characteristics of these discourses? How have far-right extremist discourses been embodied in and generated a language of aggressiveness and in what ways has their linguistic realization contributed towards the popularity and rise of far-right extremist movements? How has far-right authoritarianism impacted the educational landscape? What might be the sites where authoritarian politics are realized more effectively and why? The Capitol insurrection crystallized for me a connection often impossible to make between discourses, and social practices realized and materialized in actual social events. Prompted by the plethora of news stories and preliminary reports on the insurrection, I started delving more into social media corpora only to confirm the central role they have been playing in the rise of Trumpism, as well as in the revival of far-right extremism and white supremacism. The well-known, from Critical Discourse Studies (CDS) literature, 'dipole' of 'we' vs 'they,' an essential discursive feature of far-right populist discourses, emerged in the data in full glory. Social media discourses further embodied many characteristics of authoritarianism.

To move forward with this work, I had to start backwards: to look into the past, to understand far-right populism and authoritarianism historically, as the grounds for apprehending contemporary authoritarian populist discourses.

PREFACE

The journey down history lane took me, naturally, to Nazi Germany of the early 1940's where, I was, once again, faced with the realization, that the history of humanity is the 'Magna Carta of barbarism' (Ortega y Gasset, 1930), the history of atrocities (Castoriadis, 2000, p. 26). History, however, is also time filled with possibility and a lens through which we can envision the new. History is also the present we live and, as James Baldwin has powerfully argued in his 1965 essay *Unnameable Objects, Unspeakable Crimes,*

> the great force of history comes from the fact that we carry it within us, are unconsciously controlled by it in many ways, and history is literally present in all that we do. It could scarcely be otherwise, since it is to history that we owe our frames of reference, our identities, and our aspirations.

It is part of our historical vocation to live in history with optimism. Despite the darkness of this historical period, we traverse and the heavy shadow it casts in contemporary human societies, I have often taken refuge in Antonio Gramsci's 'pessimism of the intellect' and 'optimism of the will.' I think it is this 'optimism of the will' that should be keeping scholars working for social change and visiting and challenging dangerous spaces. Despite what comes across as hopelessness for humanity, this book is, at its core, a project of hope; of an educated hope. This is another reason why we write.

Reading down a forum thread on Iron March, the neo-Nazi platform (that I present in detail in Chapter 3), I came across user Ethno Nationalist (1D40) who was writing to another member about his college experience: "We're actually starting off with 'The Authoritarian Personality' and Adorno's anti-racist, psychoanalyctic nonsensence [sic] and other Frankfurt school rubbish. They start early to feed the agenda in university it seems." I want to make it clear upfront that this book is inspired by and unapologetically draws on 'Frankfurt school rubbish.'

I think of this book in terms of sociopolitical, epistemological, and strategic factors, as Ricento (2000) has suggested. The sociopolitical factors have to do with the capitalist crises across the globe, as well as the rise of authoritarianism and far-right populism in the United States and in many places around the world. The shifting sociopolitical landscape compels researchers and educators to see our work always in connection with the real world. To cite the great sociologist C. Wright Mills, as researchers, we must translate private troubles into public issues and vice versa.

In terms of epistemology, I strive to ground my work historically and understand the paradigm of knowledge and research, as well as recent shifts that include both new critical lenses, as well as distortions. In my own work, I am trying to use lenses that move away from a narrow, reductionistic framework and easy solutions and slogans. I want, instead, to build my analyses around historical and larger structural, sociopolitical considerations. I am further assisted to do so by the critical tools coming out of linguistics, particularly Critical Discourse Studies.

Finally, the strategic factors have to do with the implicit and explicit rationale behind undertaking particular kinds of research in critical pedagogy and critical language studies. Writing has unavoidably a pedagogical dimension. To this last point, I think of my research as militant in the sense that I have a clear linguistic, educational, and political project and I strive to use my writing as a tool and a weapon. As a tool, my research serves to delve deeper into the educational and linguistic issues at hand, to analyze, understand and question them, but also to communicate with my readers in an honest and meaningful way. As a weapon, I see my writing as an active intervention, a social critique that strives to illuminate human realities and understandings with the goal of educational and social change. In my research, education, both as a site of labor and as an object of inquiry, is a core institution, not because schools change society but, rather, because schools can shape, inform, and mobilize subjectivities, collective identities and shape critical consciousness. At the same time, all inter-related processes, practices, and ideologies in schools and in society are embodied and enacted in language and discourses. I explore and critically analyze these discourses as part of a historical discursive analysis that serves as a core methodological tool in my work. As C. Wright Mills has astutely observed

> Scholarship is a choice of how to live as well as a choice of career [...] What this means is that you must learn to use your Me experience in your intellectual work: continually to examine and interpret it. In this sense craftsmanship is the center of yourself and you are personally involved in every intellectual product upon which you may work. To say that you can 'have experience' means, for one thing, that your past plays into and affects your present, and that it defines your capacity for future experience. (Mills, 1959/2000, p. 196)

As academics and educators, we are constantly called to confront and address crises coming in waves. From the neoliberal assault against education, to authoritarianism and the far-right populist insurgence to the COVID-19 pandemic, our shifting landscape often affects our labor but also our research in detrimental ways. In trying to work through all this, I am constantly rethinking

PREFACE   XVII

and reflecting on my own position as a scholar-educator. In times of crisis, scholars-educators must be in the first line of defense and critique. As our societies become laboratories for the fierce implementation of neoliberal policies, that have generated more repression, human immiseration, dehumanization and authoritarianism, our schools and classrooms are sites where we reflect, reject and rebel. This is why we write.

References

Arendt, H. (1971). *On violence*. Harcourt Brace & Company.

Baldwin, J. (1966). Unnameable objects, unspeakable crimes. In Ebony (Ed.), *The White problem in America* (pp. 173–181). Johnson.

Castoriadis, C. (2000). *The rise of insignificance*. Ypsilon Books.

Eriksen, J. (2001). *The Tyranny of the moment*. Pluto Press.

Fromm, E. (1973). *The anatomy of human destructiveness*. Holt, Rinehart & Winston.

Mills, C. W. (2000). *The sociological imagination*. Oxford University Press. (Original work published 1959)

Reich, W. (2007). *The mass psychology of fascism* (3rd ed.). Farrar, Straus & Giroux. (Original work published 1946)

Reisigl, M. (2008). Analyzing political rhetoric. In R. Wodak & M. Krzyzanowski (Eds.), *Qualitative discourse analysis in the social sciences* (pp. 96–120). Palgrave Macmillan.

Ricento, T. (2000). Historical and theoretical perspectives in language policy and planning. *Journal of Sociolinguistics, 4*(2), 196–213.

Robbins, J. (2021, February 16). Can historians be traumatized by history? *The New Republic*. https://newrepublic.com/article/161127/can-historians-traumatized-history?fbclid=IwAR1ZPJF7NzJtVouZa6NydcLwQTS-NDLxFkW9rnND6r3uNm7_hn9EQQ9tvOs

Sandlin, J. A., Schultz, B. D., & Burdick, J. (2010). Understanding, mapping, and exploring the terrain of public pedagogy. In J. A. Sandlin, B. D. Schultz, & J. Burdick (Eds.), *Handbook of public pedagogy: Education and learning beyond schooling* (pp. 1–6). Routledge.

Ortega y Gasset, J. (1964). *The revolt of the masses*. W.W. Norton. (Original work published 1930)

Acknowledgments

Who writes a book during a global pandemic? This work has been the product of rolling lockdowns since March 2020 with the onset of the COVID-19 pandemic. An otherwise traumatic year that brought me tremendous loss and grief, offered me a silver lining: The opportunity to be away from Boston and work remotely from my hometown, Athens Greece during the academic year 2020–2021.

This work is dedicated to my parents Tassos and Nacy. I was yearning for my father to be around when this book is published. While he did not live to see the final product, I will never forget how ecstatic he was when I had told him that I had a book contract. A dedicated progressive educator and a disciplined and extremely well-read scholar and historian, he found refuge in writing his entire life. With many books under his belt, and always with a manuscript 'in progress,' he has always been a role model for me. My mother has always been open-minded and supportive of my most crazy ideas and aspirations since I was a kid; she taught me that everything was possible. Both my parents, as educators rising out of their working-class families, always fought to give us the opportunities they did not have—always with their unconditional love.

My sister Georgia and my brother Thanassis are the closest people to me, and they have supported me all my life, always bringing me a sense of belonging. I have missed them tremendously the last twenty-five years and I never know how we will make up for all that time lost. The three of us are one. My inspiration and strength come from Nicolas and Daphne, the lights of my life. Since they came to this world, they have brought me joy and excitement only, and I can now dream of a future we are all part of. I hope I can leave a better world for them to grow and pursue their dreams, or at least try to.

Crossing paths with George Grollios from the Aristotle University of Thessaloniki was a catalyst in my intellectual development. George and I collaborated in editing and authoring books in Greek on critical and liberatory education. As a more experienced and senior academic, he has modelled for me what it means to do honest, politically engaged, solid, intellectual work. I am forever grateful to him for his friendship, solidarity, and generosity. Through George, I was fortunate to meet a group of amazing colleagues with whom I have developed strong friendships: Kostas Skordoulis, Periclis Pavlidis, and Tassos Liambas. A few Greek female academics have modeled for me what it means to survive and thrive in the academy as a woman: Gianna Katsiamboura, Helen Drenoyianni, Bessie Mitsikopoulou, and Eleni Skourtou have always been friends and allies, and I have enjoyed our thought-provoking

ACKNOWLEDGMENTS

conversations. I have learned a great deal from Bessie Dendrinos thanks to her integrity, power, solid research agenda and true commitment to the field.

This book would have not been possible had it not been for the important and substantive collaboration with my research 'dream team,' the amazing doctoral students in the Applied Linguistics Department at the University of Massachusetts Boston: Nasiba Norova, Vanessa Quintana Sarria, Minh Nghia Nguyen, Rachel LaRusso and Iuliia Fakhrutdinova have all been involved in different degrees with the manuscript. I am deeply grateful to all of them for their commitment, professionalism, solidarity, support, and most of all, their ongoing encouragement for and enthusiasm about the project.

Evy Kamouzis and Apostolos Koutropoulos at UMass Boston have been assisting me with my administrative obligations as Department Chair since 2015. They are treasures to work with and I have been incredibly lucky to have them. They have always helped me to carve out time to do my research without drowning in administrative tasks.

Corinne Etienne has been a friend, an ally, and my sounding board for so many years; we have been through hell and heaven together, and we can still laugh about some really painful experiences in academia. Ismael's margaritas and sound advice have helped as much. David Terkla, my late Dean at the College of Liberal Arts has been a force of good, I wish he was around to see this—I know he would be proud of me.

My Sisters, Yianna and Ioanna, I love you more than you know—thank you for the ride all these years! Deep appreciation goes to my Boston family—the Kamouzis family, for their support, warmth, and love since I immigrated to the United States.

I have tested many ideas in this book with graduate students in APLING 643 Foundations of Critical Pedagogy and I am grateful to them for the feedback. Thanks also goes to Jeremiah Morelock for giving me space the last few years to revive my passion for Critical Theory through his invitations to publish in his edited volumes. The two anonymous reviewers have provided important and constructive feedback that only made this manuscript better, and I am indebted to them for their meaningful suggestions.

Finally, I am deeply grateful to Bill Reynolds for believing in my book project from the beginning. His support came at a time when I was second-guessing myself and my ideas, and his enthusiasm and positivity were instrumental in pushing me forward. Evelien van der Veer and Alessandra Giliberto at Brill have been patiently supportive and understanding in the various stages of the manuscript preparation.

This book wouldn't have even existed had it not been for Panos, my partner 'in love and in crime,' my biggest fan and most serious, sincere, and tough critic. He and I have engaged in myriads of discussions, and I have tested my ideas with him over and over, while he patiently listened and gave me honest and substantive feedback. He has been the one lifting me up during my self-doubt moments, and I have been enjoying every second of our life together, especially our talks during long beach walks on the sunny days of year 2020.

This book is nothing more than a snapshot of the author and thinker I am right here, right now, and I am fully responsible for its content.

Figures

1.1   Triangle of far-right authoritarian populism.   31

3.1   Iron March website landing page (Internet Archive, n.d.).   74

3.2   The fight/battle metaphor (Trump's speech in Ellipse).   84

3.3   The fight/battle metaphor (Parler).   84

3.4   'Us' vs 'them' (Iron March).   87

3.5   'Us' vs 'them' (Parler/Telegram).   88

3.6   Iron March race 'War Central' (Internet Archive, n.d.).   89

3.7   Iron March users' attitudes towards Trump.   91

Introduction

On January 6th, 2021 at exactly 2:11 pm a mob of pro-Trump rioters comprised of die-hard supporters, white supremacists and nationalists, conspiracy theorists, paramilitaries and others, storms the Capitol building in Washington D.C. while a joint session takes place in the House of Representatives to count Electoral College votes for the 2020 Election. Rioters waving Trump flags, confederate flags, donning MAGA hats and carrying other racist and hateful white supremacist symbols such as hung nooses, face off and start clashing with the police on Capitol steps, breach police lines, break the Capitol windows and find their way into the building's chambers. There are reports of pipe bombs outside the Capitol and in multiple locations around DC, while people working inside the building hear what sound like multiple gunshots. An armed standoff takes place at the House of Representatives' front door, and members of the U.S. Congress are asked to shelter in place and later are evacuated in escape hood gear, a special suit that can provide up to thirty minutes of protection from carbon monoxide, chemical, biological, radiological, and nuclear contaminants. The joint session is suspended, and the U.S. Vice President and lawmakers are moved to a safe undisclosed location. Teargas is fired inside the Capitol chambers and scenes of chaos ensue.

This could have easily been the scenario of a political thriller movie. Or, it could have happened in any country around the world, usually with the support of the United States. But it was the first attempted coup in the country that has, historically, supported coups around the world—a few prominent examples come to mind such as Iran 1953, Guatemala 1954, Congo 1960, Brazil 1964, Greece 1967, Chile 1972, among others, as well as the more recent attempts in Bolivia in 2019 and Venezuela in 2020.

Almost every moment, every minute of the January 6th Capitol violence has been documented visually. In addition to journalists reporting on the spot, rioters walked around, live-streaming the scene on social media, carrying selfie-sticks, and taking their own pictures, or posing for their picture and video to be taken. Thousands of videos were shared on different social media platforms, giving the event a performative yet carnivalesque character. In its severity, the entire scene had something risible and ridiculous, resembling a dark circus performance with extras improvising without a script. In the videos and pictures shared while the events were still unfolding, a largely white crowd, mostly male, can be seen, some in tactical gear, with many of them armed with bats, shields and chemical spray—others, with real guns. There are people wearing furs and horned hats, their faces painted with the American flag, covered in

© KONINKLIJKE BRILL NV, LEIDEN, 2022 | DOI: 10.1163/9789004510470_001

2 INTRODUCTION

tattoos, wearing t-shirts and gear bearing different symbols (such as QAnon, camp Auschwitz, and many others), carrying signs which read 'stop the steal,' 'treason' and 'Save the Children' (alluding to the supposed election fraud, and the QAnon conspiracy that there is a pedophile ring), alongside members from the far-right hate group Proud Boys, Chris Hood and members of his neo-Nazi National Socialist Club, the Boogaloo club, and the far-right, anti-government militia armed group Three Percenters, most wearing helmets and Kevlar vests adorned with the group's symbol, a Roman numeral three. There's a group flying a green and black banner known as the Kekistan flag, a symbol used by far-right white nationalist groups that was modeled after a German Nazi war flag. A man is spotted wearing a 'Camp Auschwitz' sweatshirt in reference to the Nazi Germany-operated concentration camp where more than 1 million Jews were killed during the Holocaust, and others wearing t-shirts bearing the anti-Semitic slogan 6MWE that means '6 Million Wasn't Enough'—referring to the 6 million Jewish people murdered during the Holocaust. There are Trump supporters flashing the once-innocuous 'OK' hand signal, now adopted as a white power symbol and often used by pro-Trump and Alt-right figures to troll the media.

In the scenes of chaos that follow, a protester is seen sitting with his feet on a desk in House Speaker Nancy Pelosi's office that is vandalized, his American flag resting to the left on a file cabinet. Another individual carries Pelosi's lectern from the House of Representatives chamber. A pro-Trump rioter poses for a photo with the vandalized statue of former President Gerald Ford holding a Trump 2020 flag. A markedly heterogeneous group is united under the ideological confusion that Trumpism, as a far-right authoritarian populist movement has been generating for over four years.

The outcome: Five people dead, over 570 arrested and 638 people charged as of this writing, extensive damage, stolen property, and a host of questions in need of answers.

There is nothing surprising in this surreal historical development for those who have been paying attention to the Trump administration. The violence and ensuing chaos at the Capitol have been the culmination of four years of emboldening extremist hate groups and fomenting racism, hate, division, and polarization. The events of January 6th in the U.S. Capitol are the lowest point of four years of far-right governance, right-wing populism, authoritarianism, the resurrection of American fascism, coupled with the strengthening of white supremacism, racism, and patriarchy. They come to further complicate a question that has been on many people's minds and, often, publicly debated in media, public opinion, and scholarly work: *have we, in fact, been living through a fascist historical moment?* And, if that is the case, what are its features in

INTRODUCTION

the given sociohistorical moment? How do these features manifest in the discourse? How are they embodied in language? Has mediatization amplified their proliferation and power and normalized their ideologies? How do social media (the users actually) produce and promote far-right discourses? Finally, if we look at this historical moment as a pedagogical moment, as an instance of public pedagogy, where what is happening in the public realm shapes and impacts our knowledge about the word, what kinds of knowledge, agency, identities, values, and ideologies has it been reflecting and producing? And how might these give rise to a revisionist version of history that whitewashes racism, oppression, and unequal distribution of wealth and resources? These are some of the core questions that guide the discussion and analysis in this book. My proposal is that we need to understand this new phenomenon both historically but also in the here and now. We need to explore the ways it has gained so much appeal in the 21st century, using different language and different tactics from the 1930's and 1940's.

Trump himself might have left office but he is still a major force in the Republican party. Trumpism, as a far-right populist movement, with its 74 million votes in the 2020 U.S. Election, its deliberate ideological confusion, extremist rhetoric, anti-blackness, anti-immigration, misogyny, nationalism, and white supremacism, is here to stay and stain our human societies. For scholars and researchers in different fields, Trumpism is an important phenomenon, too important to be ignored as simply the antics of a pathological narcissist. Similarly, Trumpist discourse should not be reduced to "frivolity of form, pose and style" or "void of serious content" (Pells 2012, cited in Wodak & Krzyżanowski, 2017, p. 6). On the contrary, it is crucial in analyzing and understanding far-right authoritarianism to acknowledge that the "specific propaganda—realized in many genres and across various social fields—always combines and integrates form and content, targets specific audiences and adapts to specific contexts" (Wodak & Krzyżanowski, 2017, p. 6). The new far-right populist authoritarianism has been rewriting public discourse, politics, governance, ways of thinking and ways of being, and even history itself.

The book starts with a camera click in front of the U.S. Capitol wrapped in a cloud of smoke with crowds yelling and shouting. The shot is the crack, the fissure on the surface that prompts us to uncover the processes beneath, to peel multiple layers to understand the whole picture by delving deep into a sociohistorical analysis of far-right politics and authoritarian populism. It is not surprising that articles in mainstream publications and investigative journalism on the topic of far-right extremists, neo-Nazis and their respective platforms in the United States, have peaked since Trump took office. There is something to be noted about the way Trumpist politics and discourse have revitalized these dark forces that have been lurking around for a long time giving newfound legitimacy to neo-Nazi groups, extremist militia, and Alt-right proponents.

The themes of this book turn the spotlight to a discussion that is now more relevant than ever. It reveals, among other things, the role of social media and the ways they have been used by reactionaries; the fundamental role that authoritarian and far-right populist discourses have played in the public debate; and the real material consequences that these discourses along with their policies might have had. This is a broader and larger-than-Trump discussion. Words matter. Language matters. Discourses matter. As the relevant literature points out, the affordances of mediatization of right-wing populist authoritarian discourses are among the main reasons behind the rise, success and stubbornness of far-right populism that also ensure its longevity (Morelock & Narita, 2021; Wodak & Krzyżanowski, 2017). As Wodak and Krzyżanowski stress, "the manifold patterns of mediated communication and the ubiquitous appropriation of dominant media agenda and frames by right-wing populism cannot be dismissed as a mere coincidence" (2017, p. 4). As a linguist, I am particularly fascinated by discourses as embodiments of social practices and I look at how ideological aspects of late capitalism are articulated through language, that is, through the use of particular discursive formations; and, more specifically, through far-right authoritarian discourses. How is one-dimensional language of far-right authoritarianism taking over public discourse? The shift in language use is not natural or neutral, but it reflects, refracts, and shapes a deeper shift in its framing and therefore, in policies and politics. Those institutions that have the power to produce politics and ideologies, have also the power to produce a 'strong discourse' and, thus, have hegemony over that discourse. In analyzing social media, I have been enthralled by the uses of language in their inescapable textual form.

1 Far-Right Populist Authoritarianism

1.1 *Authoritarianism*
The discussion in this book is built around the concept of authoritarianism. Authoritarianism here is understood neither as a specific regime, nor as a psychological trait but, rather, as a set of properties found in 'one-dimensional' capitalist societies that amass specific core characteristics: obedience and consent, repressive control, concentration of power, hierarchical structures that enforce law and order, and lack of pluralism coupled with the implementation of far-right populist politics. Authoritarianism can be seen as the "attempt at

INTRODUCTION

imposing unity in heterogeneous societies" through coercion and arises amidst relationships "between power and resistance [and] domination and freedom" (Morelock & Narita, 2021, p. 88). In our modern capitalist societies, coercion does not need to be necessarily physical and/or material. It can be symbolic or discursive as well, borrowing the features of Antonio Gramsci's concept of *hegemony*. Hannah Arendt notes that

> authority can be vested in persons or in offices. Its hallmark is unquestioning recognition by those who are asked to obey; neither coercion, nor persuasion is needed. To remain in authority requires respect for the person or the office. The greatest enemy of authority, therefore, is contempt and the surest way to undermine it is laughter. (Arendt, 1970, p. 45)

Features of authoritarianism are embodied in different realms of human life, from politics to interpersonal and family relationships, school curricula, modes of governance, labor, media and so on. These features are further embodied in the respective discourses produced in authoritarian societies. More importantly, these features are not the distinctive element of so-called repressive regimes. They flourish and thrive in liberal democracies. In his *Thoughts on Working Through the Past* (2005), Theodor Adorno has argued that the survival of National Socialism *within* democracy for him was "potentially more menacing than the survival of fascist tendencies *against* democracy. Infiltration indicates something objective; ambiguous figures make their comeback and occupy positions of power for the sole reason that conditions favor them" (p. 90).

In this book, I am using interchangeably authoritarian populism, far-right (or right-wing) populist authoritarianism and far-right authoritarianism. Populism is a core element of far-right authoritarianism. And while populism can be Left or Right, I adhere by Gandesha's (2018) differentiation that Right populism "conflates 'the people' with an embattled nation confronting its external enemies: Islamic terrorism, refugees, the European Commission, the International Jewish conspiracy" while Left populism "defines 'the people' in relation to the social structures [...] that thwart its aspirations for self-determination." For right-wing authoritarian populism, the enemy is personalized, while left-wing populism tends "to define the enemy in terms of bearers of socio-economic structures and rarely as particular groups" (Gandesha, 2018, p. 63).

In examining authoritarianism in the Trumpist context, one could identify what might come across as a paradox. In Trumpism, we find a strong anti-authoritarian element, as illustrated for example in the discourse of 'freedom' from masks and resistance to a vaccine mandate, or to lockdowns during the

6 INTRODUCTION

pandemic; or the freedom from what Trumpists perceive as Left hegemony. Any mandate on the part of the government is seen as authoritarian and oppressive, infringing on individual liberties. However, since extreme-right authoritarianism thrives in the capitalist context, it should not be surprising that the neoliberal discourse around freedom has found its way into authoritarian far-right discourses and claims. The projected Trumpist anti-authoritarianism is on one hand selective, in that freedom (from masks, to use guns, to choose, etc.) does not apply, for example, to a woman's option to choose whether to have an abortion or not, as was the case with the far-right inspired and supported 2021 law in Texas that bans abortions. On the other hand, this contradiction—the anti-authoritarianism of authoritarianism, further contributes to ideological ambiguity and confusion. In a sense, this paradox is a useful element in helping sustain and promote authoritarianism.

1.2 *Far-Right Populism*

Far-right populism can be defined as "hybrid political ideology that rejects the hegemonic post-war political consensus and usually, though not always, combines laissez-faire liberalism and anti-elitism or other, often profoundly different and contradictory ideologies" (Wodak & Krzyżanowski, 2017, p. 5). It is meant to appeal to the People as a homogeneous group unified by ethnic identity and nativism. Since authoritarianism demands blind obedience, populism functions as the linking mechanism that shapes People's consent. The populist element in the authoritarian mix is crucial because it further obscures "conflict where it originates" (Wodak & Krzyżanowski, 2017, p. 5), as part of a normalization campaign. 'The stated is the evident,' as illustrated, for instance, in counselor to former President Trump, Kellyanne Conway's epic phrase 'alternative facts.' Morelock and Narita discuss a "constellation of elements" comprising authoritarian populism and call for "the expansion of the mainstream definition of populism [...] in order to grasp the nuances and contradictory moments underlying the construction of 'the people' vis- à- vis the non-people, outsiders and so on" (2021, p. 93). This view further supports Wodak and Krzyzanowki's assessment that right-wing populism is, in fact, an elusive phenomenon, better understood as hybrid, that is, situated at the "intersection of a range of both traditional and new forms and formats of political action and political behavior" (2017, p. 4).

Far-right populism is built on a powerful binary, an ideological and political dichotomy between two constructed homogeneous antagonistic groups. The in-group, the Pure People and the out-group, the non-people, the outsiders, the scapegoats: the People "operate as non-elites when contrasted with elites, and as insiders when contrasted with outsiders" (Morelock & Narita, 2021,

INTRODUCTION

p. 88). The two groups are kept in antagonism through nativism, the illusion of sharing common values and culture, law and order, and conservativism. Far-right populism detracts rather than focuses on the real problems that capitalism and its neoliberal manifestations are producing, offering a great service to the privileged classes. Finally, far-right authoritarian populist agendas have become increasingly mediatized and, thereby, normalized and mainstreamed using social media as their necessary implement.

1.2.1 What's Trumpism Got to Do with Education? Teaching in the Age of Trump

The discussion on right-wing populism and authoritarianism is deeply pedagogical; Pedagogy here is not a method of teaching or simply the theory and practice of education. It is, rather, the struggle over meaning and knowledge production, and over what kinds of knowledge matter and to whom. Given the vagueness, ideological confusion and hybridity embedded, and the ingenious ways language is used to produce and disseminate these ideologies, it is not an exaggeration to talk about an idiosyncratic discourse with its ensuing construction of meaning and knowledge that includes producers, interpreters, and an actual process of coding and decoding. Earlier in this chapter, I asked whether the Trump administration could be characterized as fascist. The answer to this overarching question has important ramifications for different realms of human life and institutions. It certainly has important ramifications for education. The question, itself, articulates a deeply pedagogical project at hand, in understanding fascism in the current sociohistorical juncture. With the rise of the far-right populism and the increasing authoritarianism worldwide, what is the role of schools and education in this context? How is Trumpism with its racism, sexism, historical distortions and conspiracy theories and other dangerous ideologies affecting school, knowledge, and curricula? And what does it mean to teach in a far-right authoritarian political landscape?

Two additional elements of right-wing authoritarian populism also add a significant pedagogical layer: historical revisionism and the distortion of reality, alternative facts, and fake news. The normalization of far-right authoritarian populism begs the articulation of a pedagogical project that stands as the antithesis of ideological distortions, conspiracy theories, fake news propaganda and historical revisionism. A key question is under what conditions are people moved to embrace irrational theories and believe fake news that border on metaphysics in their explanations of social reality. What are the ideological, political, cognitive, psychological, and discursive mechanisms that make this possible? The answer is also pedagogical. It further connects with the ways schools and other consciousness-shaping, knowledge-producing institutions and mechanisms work. As I discuss in Chapter 5, historical thinking as a pedagogical project can support people in developing the kind of critical awareness needed to understand and deconstruct far-right populist discourses and eradicate their inhumane practices.

Trump's presidency has been an important teachable moment (Timsit, 2019) with two dimensions to it. The first has to do with the strand of scholarship that has developed to document what has been termed the 'Trump effect' on education, that is, the impact of a right-wing populist governance model on schools, students, and their communities. It documents how Trumpism has affected day-to-day schooling, classroom discussions, teacher attitudes, and student interaction inside and outside of the classroom (Gounari, 2020; Verma & Apple, 2020). The second dimension articulates a pedagogical project around identifying and understanding authoritarianism and fascism through historical thinking, especially as they manifest in different pedagogical sites outside school, like social media. It attempts to grasp the paradox of human societies on one hand, celebrating the International Holocaust Remembrance Day on January 27th when the last death camp of Auschwitz-Birkenau is liberated, while at the same time witnessing people marching in the extremist right Charlottesville Rally shouting 'Jew will not replace us!' It strives to understand historical remembrance and forgetting, screams and silences, the past, the present, and the future as deeply pedagogical. It sets out to make the critical historical and the historical critical.

'Teaching in the age of Trump' is now a research direction in educational studies that already counts numerous publications. The impact of the 45th presidency on schools calls for careful study and in-depth analysis. Since the 2016 election, multiple incidents have been recorded in the news involving teachers, schools, and students, many of those taking place 'in the name of President Trump.' Incidents started emerging while Donald Trump was still a presidential candidate on the campaign trail, as evidenced for example in the many comments from educators across the United States left in the National Educational Association website, reporting on his inflammatory rhetoric and behavior (Perez, 2016).

A number of studies have documented the *Trump effect on school climate* (Costello, 2016; Dunn et al., 2019; Gewertz, 2019; Hamann & Morgenson, 2017; Huang & Cornell, 2019; McNeela, 2017; Rogers et al., 2017; Rogers et al., 2019; Sondel et al., 2018) and their findings are alarming. In many schools in America, a regular school day after the election included verbal harassment, the use of slurs and derogatory language directed at students of color, Muslims, immigrants and people based on their gender or sexual orientation; disturbing incidents involving graffiti with swastikas, Nazi salutes and Confederate

INTRODUCTION

flags; assaults on students and teachers, property damage, fights and threats of violence; and incidents of bigotry and harassment that can be directly traced to election rhetoric (Costello, 2016; Rogers et al., 2017; Rogers et al., 2019). Educators and other stakeholders have been reporting "a drastic increase in post-election hate speech" in schools (Rogers et al., 2017, 2019; Wallace & Lamotte, 2016, as cited in Au, 2017). At the same time, there have been cases of educators who have felt emboldened to express their discriminatory views and perpetuate a rhetoric of hate. After a divisive campaign and four years of presidency filled with racially charged rhetoric, fake news, and the degrading of public discourse and debate, schools are unique sites that both reflect and reproduce what is going on in the broader society. They are also production sites for alternative practices and discourses.

While educational researchers have been mostly reluctant to establish an explicit and clear correlation between the increased hostility and violence in the schools and the former President's rhetoric of hate, the findings from the large studies cited here make this correlation evident: the former U.S. President has legitimized and incited hate and violence. Discourses, such as those embodied in the presidential rhetoric, have social effects (Fairclough, 2003) that are realized in actual material practices that, in turn, affect in equally real ways the lives of people. In this equation the importance of representational media cannot be overemphasized in our attempt to understand how different societies value and use different modes of representation. Gunther Kress's work has been instrumental around the construction of a social individual in response to available 'representational resources' (1989). Along these lines, Kress thought about the "content of educational curricula in terms of representational resources and their use by individuals in their constant transformation of their subjectivities, the process usually called 'learning'" (Wodak, 2001, p. 6). In the case of this book, 'representational resources' largely consist of social media. Social media are not a new entry in the pedagogical discussion. In my analysis, I view social media as sites of public pedagogy, that is, as educational activity that takes place in extra-institutional places and discourses (Sandlin et al., 2010). Public pedagogy occurs beyond formal schooling and involves learning in sites traditionally not associated with education. I view social media as a major site of public pedagogy, rivaling formal education in power and influence.

1.2.2   Trumpism, Authoritarianism, Historical Thinking, and Public
         Pedagogy

Another teachable moment of the Trump presidency has to do with a renewed pedagogical project of historical thinking as part of developing critical consciousness. In trying to make the critical historical and the historical critical, in the context of re-writing human history to legitimize politics of hate, the project of providing students the learning conditions to think historically, and therefore, dialectically must be at the core of the educational agenda, particularly the agenda of Critical Pedagogy. What role can a critical public pedagogy of praxis (theory and practices) play in the current explosive authoritarian sociopolitical landscape? And in what ways can an understanding of discourses produced in social media shape this pedagogy?

In Thesis VI, in *On the Concept of History* written in 1940, Walter Benjamin notes that "to articulate what is past does not mean to recognize 'how it really was.' It means to take control of a memory, as it flashes in a moment of danger." The return of fascism is a moment of danger, and we need Benjamin's history flash to grasp it and fight it. Benjamin goes on to say that the only thing that can spark hope in writing history is to understand that if the enemy (fascism) is victorious "not even the dead will be safe" adding that "this enemy has not ceased to be victorious." Apprehending discourses historically, attempts to situate critical public pedagogy in the current capitalist/authoritarian sociopolitical context and make it relevant by identifying its strengths and limitations, as well as paths for new research. It opens a space to rethink critical public pedagogy at the current historical and sociopolitical juncture. Anchored in social critique, this project addresses some core issues that connect social reality with education and vice versa. Against this background, this work seeks to re-invent those aspects, theoretical constructs, and practices of critical pedagogy that can serve as tools for developing and shaping consciousness and agency. Understanding social issues historically, such as the rebirth of fascist ideologies, generates knowledge, and produces identities, and subjectivities. Furthermore, understanding them through the critical analysis of the discourses they use as vehicles, is educational at its core, as it challenges existing values, beliefs and assumptions and produces meaning and knowledge about the current social order. This awareness can potentially awake a type of critical consciousness.

One can argue that the five chapters here could work as standalone and autonomous. While they can be read separately, they, nevertheless, articulate a different story when read as parts of one uniform project. They unfold, holding together a common thread that twists around the threat of far-right populist authoritarianism and the return of fascism materially, symbolically, and discursively. I look at this threat from a *historical, sociopolitical, discursive,* and *pedagogical* lens, as it manifests in the United States. These four lenses are dialectically interconnected as their respective embodiments (social media, discourses, educational practices) are analyzed.

Chapter 1 sets the thread in motion at Capitol Hill and articulates a necessary historical and theoretical framework where far-right populist authoritarianism, and Trumpism as its embodiment, can be situated and understood. Chapter 2 draws on the work of the Frankfurt School for Social Research to build a theoretical framework to understand right-wing authoritarian populist discourses in general, and their contemporary mediatized iteration in social media. Chapter 3 puts to work the framework presented in Chapter 2 to read and critically analyze a corpus of texts produced and disseminated through the neo-Nazi platform Iron March, conservative social media platforms Parler and Telegram, as well as the more mainstream digital platform Twitter, on the days leading to the Capitol events and a few days afterwards. The second part of this chapter employs the Discourse Historical Approach and may appeal more to discourse analysts and linguists as it presents the linguistic building blocks of Trumpist discourse. Chapter 4 moves the discussion to the pedagogical plane. Authoritarianism in education functions on different levels, including the organization and standardization of curricula and the control of forms and content of knowledge, as well as the physical control and discipline, the ritualistic organization of school routines and the regulation of student bodies; in all these aspects, authoritarianism registers overtly and covertly as a main driving force. With the rise of the far right and the increasing authoritarianism worldwide, what is the role of schools in this context? After critically revisiting the historical roots and theoretical perspectives of Critical Pedagogy, I am articulating a research agenda for the future of this intellectual tradition that includes the struggle against authoritarianism through multiple channels. The final chapter (Chapter 5) attempts to bring together all the themes weaved through the book under the light of history and the process of historicization, that is, situating social phenomena in their historical dimension. The discussion challenges the dangerous notion of historical revisionism and the efforts on the part of the far-right to rewrite history, using as an example the current debate over Critical Race Theory and the implementation of the Trumpist Patriotic Education.

At the end of the day, the core issue for readers to wrestle with is the gradual fascistization of human societies, the celebration of the banality of evil, and the increasing tolerance, if not apotheosis of authoritarianism in our human societies worldwide; it is the new concentration camps for refugees; the border violence against immigrants; racial violence; it is the authoritarian patriarchal violence against women; the day-to-day authoritarian ritual performances for school kids; and many more. The appeal of neo-fascist ideas keeps reaching new highs among many strata of the population. After all, fascism was not an accident of history, and *it has not yet ceased to be victorious.*

Refernces

Adorno, T. W. (2005). *Critical models: Interventions and catchwords.* Columbia University Press.

Arendt, H. (1970). *On violence.* Harcourt, Brace and Company.

Au, W. (2017). When multicultural education is not enough. *Multicultural Perspectives, 19*(3), 147–150. https://doi.org/10.1080/15210960.2017.1331741

Benjamin, W. (1974). *On the concept of history* (D. Redmond, Trans.). Suhrkamp Verlag.

Costello, M. B. (2016). *The Trump effect: The impact of the 2016 presidential election on our nation's schools.* Southern Poverty Law Center. https://www.splcenter.org/sites/default/files/the_trump_effect.pdf

Dunn, A. H., Sondel, B., & Baggett, H. C. (2019). "I don't want to come off as pushing an agenda": How contexts shaped teachers' pedagogy in the days after the 2016 U.S. presidential election. *American Educational Research Journal, 56*(2), 444–476. https://doi.org/10.3102%2F0002831218794892

Forchtner, B., Krzyżanowski, M., & Wodak, R. (2013). Mediatization, right-wing populism and political campaigning: The case of the Austrian Freedom Party (FP). In A. Tolson & M. Ekstrom (Eds.), *Media talk and political elections in Europe and America* (pp. 205–228). Palgrave Macmillan. doi:10.1057/9781137273321_10

Gandesha, S. (2018). Understanding right and left populism. In J. Morelock (Ed.), *Critical theory and authoritarian populism* (pp. 49–70). University of Westminster Press.

Gewertz, K. (2019, March 13). Principals dealing with hostility and division in the age of Trump, survey shows. *Education Week.* https://www.edweek.org/leadership/principals-dealing-with-hostility-and-division-in-the-age-of-trump-survey-shows/2019/03

Gounari, P. (2020). 'Hail Trump, hail our people, hail victory!' Teaching in authoritarian times. In R. Verma & M. Apple (Eds.), *Disrupting hate: Teacher activists, democracy and pedagogies of disruption* (pp. 39–55). Routledge.

Hamann, E. T., & Morgenson, C. (2017). Dispatches from flyover country: Four appraisals of impacts of Trump's immigration policy on families, schools, and communities. *Anthropology & Education Quarterly, 48*(4), 393–402. https://doi.org/10.1111/aeq.12214

Huang, F. L., & Cornell, D. G. (2019). School teasing and bullying after the presidential election. *Educational Researcher, 48*(2), 69–83. https://doi.org/10.3102/0013189X18820291

Kress, G. (1989). History and language: Towards a social account of linguistic change. *Journal of Pragmatics, 13*(3), 445–466.

Mazzoleni, G. (2008). Populism and the media. In D. Albertazzi & D. McDonnell (Eds.), *Twenty-first century populism* (pp. 49–64). Springer. doi:10.1057/9780230592100_4

McNeela, C. (2017). Creating space for student voice after the election. *Perspectives and Provocations, 6*(2). https://www.earlychildhoodeducationassembly.com/uploads/1/6/6/2/16621498/2.creatingspaceforstudentvoice_.pdf

Morelock, J., & Narita, F. (2021). A dialectical constellation of authoritarian populism un the United States and Brazil. In J. Morelock (Ed.), *How to critique authoritarian populism: Methodologies of the Frankfurt School* (pp. 85–107). Brill.

Morelock, J., & Sullivan, D. (2021). Introduction: Frankfurt School methodologies. In J. Morelock (Ed.), *How to critique authoritarian populism: methodologies of the Frankfurt School* (pp. 1–45). Brill.

Perez, F. (2016). *Educators shine light on the effect of Donald Trump's bullying on students.* National Educational Association. https://educationvotes.nea.org/2016/10/03/educators-trace-surge-student-bullying-donald-trump/

Rogers, J., Franke, M., Yun, J. E., Ishimoto, M., Diera, C., Geller, R. C., Berryman, A., & Brenes, T. (2017). *Teaching and learning in the age of Trump: Increasing stress and hostility in America's high schools.* UCLA's Institute for Democracy, Education, and Access. https://idea.gseis.ucla.edu/publications/teaching-and-learning-in-age-of-trump

Rogers, J., Ishimoto, M., Kwako, A., Berryman, A., & Diera, C. (2019). *School and society in the age of Trump.* UCLA's Institute for Democracy, Education, and Access. https://idea.gseis.ucla.edu/publications/school-and-society-in-age-of-trump/

Sondel, B., Baggett, H. C., & Dunn, A. H. (2018). "For millions of people, this is real trauma": A pedagogy of political trauma in the wake of the 2016 U.S. presidential election. *Teaching and Teacher Education, 70,* 175–185. https://doi.org/10.1016/j.tate.2017.11.017

Timsit, A. (2019, January 13). American educators are treating Trump's presidency as the ultimate teachable moment. *Quartz.* https://qz.com/1519239/american-educators-are-treating-trumps-presidency-as-the-ultimate-teachable-moment/

Verma, R., & Apple, M. (Eds.). (2020). *Disrupting hate: Teacher activists, democracy and pedagogies of disruption.* Routledge.

Wodak, R. (2001). What is CDA about. In R. Wodak & M. Meyer (Eds.), *Methods of critical discourse analysis* (pp. 1–33). Sage.

Wodak, R., & Krzyżanowski, M. (2017). Right-wing populism in Europe & USA: Contesting politics & discourse beyond "Orbanism" and "Trumpism." *Journal of Language and Politics, 16*(4), 1–14. https://doi.org/10.1075/jlp.17042.krz

CHAPTER 1

Far-Right Authoritarian Populism, Fascism, New Fascism, Trumpism

> How can anyone tell the truth about Fascism, unless he is willing to speak out against capitalism, which brings it forth?
> BRECHT (*Galileo*, 1966)

∙∙∙

> He who does not wish to discuss imperialism should stay silent on the subject of fascism
> POULANTZAS (*Fascism and Dictatorship*, 1974)

∙∙

1 Introduction

In 1967, twenty-two years after the fall of the Reichstag, Herbert Marcuse, a prominent member of the Frankfurt-based Institute for Social Research (*Institut für Sozialforschung*) made an important prediction about what he termed the 'new fascism.' He noted that it be very different from the old fascism, coming not as a repetition of the old, but rather as a new iteration, embodied in massive consent to legislation by authoritarians who will gain enough power to legislate the curtailment of civil and political liberties, gagging dissent and promoting authoritarian politics. Referring to America, Marcuse claimed that all this would happen in the context of a 'democracy': "the mass basis does not have to consist of masses of people going out into the streets and beating people up, it can also mean that the masses support increasingly actively a tendency that confines whatever scope still exists in democracy, thus increasingly weakening the opposition" (Marcuse, 1967, para. 22). Massive consent is central here, because "authoritarian political systems continue to make obedience the human cornerstone of their existence" (Fromm, 1981, p. 22). Marcuse claimed that in the 'new fascism' context, there may be no need for physical violence (use of military, police as repressive apparatuses), as was the case

© KONINKLIJKE BRILL NV, LEIDEN, 2022 | DOI: 10.1163/9789004510470_002

with classical forms of fascism. In late capitalism, the goal is "to remodel the populace into a combat-ready collective for civil and military purposes, so that it will function in the hands of the newly formed ruling class" (Horkheimer, 1939, para. 8). This would be done through massive obedience and consent. The mob that attacked the United States Capitol appears to have obeyed the President's call to 'fight hard' and became a 'combat-ready' collective for civil purposes. When interviewed, many of the protesters claimed that they raided the Capitol because the President told them so.

Marcuse knew something about fascism. The early 1920s, when the Institute was first established at Goethe University in Frankfurt, Germany, was a crucial time period for the history of Germany and the entire world, considering that Nazis assumed power just a few years later, on January 30th, 1933. Critical Theory coming out of the Institute was applied to the most pressing problem of the time: the rise of European fascism. Members of the Institute had an early interest in studying problems of authority and set on a series of empirical research projects and theoretical hypotheses about the emergence and shape of authoritarian politics in that era (Brown et al., 2018), even before their forced migration fleeing Nazism (Fuchs, 2018; Gordon, 2019). From the vantage point of 1964, with experience from the Weimar Republic, Herbert Marcuse had already identified a kind of authoritarianism deeply ingrained in advanced capitalist societies (Gounari, 2021). Notwithstanding the very real differences between the fascist movements of the mid- twentieth century and the antidemocratic movements of our own time, critical theory remains of urgent relevance today, when many of the same phenomena that first aroused the critical attention of the Frankfurt School seem to have resurfaced in a new guise (Brown et al., 2018; Morelock, 2019, 2021).

After the end of World War II, the Nazi atrocities, violence, and the sentiments of aversion these provoked in the mainstream collective imaginary, seemed to have been enough to relegate fascism in the trashcan of history. But, alas, that famous trashcan must have been for recyclables. And as Marx had warned in the *18th Brumaire of Louis Napoleon*, history always repeats itself, "first as tragedy, then as farce" (1972, p. 10). The return of the (new) fascism is not a simple phenomenon to explain as a number of factors intertwine to bring it to the fore. Among them we can identify the rise and subsequent dominance of neoliberal market ideologies as a result of the global economic collapse of the 1970s; the deterioration of working-class people's lives and the gradual eradication of the welfare state amplified by the elites' and global financial institutions' attacks; and the war on workers' organizations, including trade unions, culminating in the second global financial collapse of 2007–2008 (Mullen & Vials, 2020). At the same time, the widespread Islamophobia that resulted from 9/11 and the War on Terror, coupled with massive movements of population precipitated by the United States' imperial wars, has fueled more xenophobia and racism. The new fascism is both a product of the global capitalist financial crisis and a political plan to manage its jarring contradictions. Therefore, the new fascism, seen in the context of an ongoing rise of far-right authoritarian populism and authoritarian politics, should not be disconnected from the ways capitalism, in its neoliberal manifestations, has failed humanity on multiple levels. Political developments in the authoritarian direction need to be connected to "the structural crisis of monopoly-finance capital—that is, to the regime of concentrated, financialized, and globalized capitalism" (Foster, 2017, para. 4). Fascism should be understood as a recurrent feature of capitalism in that it

> thrives on bitterness and alienation, both of which capitalism nourishes with regular doses of unemployment and crisis. This fuels despair, which further stimulates fascism to grow. Fascism lives off racism, sexism and elitism, while capitalism promotes its own prejudices, guised as common-sense beliefs, which seem to fit people's experiences, while effectively holding them back from challenging the system. Capitalism generates the myths of racism and elitism, which fascists use for themselves. (Renton, 1999, p. 16)

In many traditionally democratic and capitalist Western states, these events have worked in tandem

> to erode lateral affiliations necessary for left-democratic politics and helped actuate a political third space, beyond conservatism and social democracy, a predominantly white, racist, nationalist, middle-class 'backlash' that finds expression in a politics of resentment, victimhood, xenophobia and anti-leftism traditionally associated with classical fascism. (Mullen & Vials, 2020, pp. 16–17)

It is deeply painful and uncomfortable to revisit the dark pages of human history and yet, human history is one of darkness and gloom. Human history is the history of violence. Fascism has returned in the public debate "as an animating political idea and an aspirant mode of political rule" (Mullen & Vials, 2020, p. 16) but are we using the term too lightly? How are present sociopolitical structures creating a continuity between the past and the present, what Enzo Traverso (2017) has called a 'transhistorical' character, that is, the ways "collective memory establishes a link between a concept and its public use, which usually exceeds its purely historiographical dimension" (p. 14). In this sense, fascism can be seen as transcending "the age that engendered it" (Traverso, 2017, p. 14).

FAR-RIGHT AUTHORITARIAN POPULISM, FASCISM, NEW FASCISM, TRUMPISM   17

Similarly, Donald Trump's ascent to power in 2016 and the explosion of Trumpism, evidenced first in his election to office and, subsequently, in the 74 million votes he received in the 2020 election he ended up losing, are the outcome of a centuries-long settler colonialism, militarization and racialization that would have otherwise made American fascism unthinkable (Mullen & Vials, 2020).

2   A New Fascism?

What is fascism? There is not one perfect definition of the term, and a lot depends on the lens one is looking through. From the vantage point of historiography, the only two fascisms that are typically legitimized are the classic Hitler in Germany and Mussolini in Italy and there are many scholars who embrace this restricted definition. However, I want to make the case that this is a limiting understanding of fascism that dangerously masks fascist manifestations in the present. The contemporary brand of fascism, the *post-fascism* (Traverso, 2017), *new fascism* (Marcuse, 1967), *neofascism* (Kellner, 2018), *proto-fascism* (Giroux, 2008) or *authoritarian capitalism* (Fuchs, 2018), share some common characteristics with classical historical fascism; this is exactly the reason why it must be explored and studied in depth. Dylan Riley suggests an understanding of fascism as an authoritarian democracy, where democracy means a "principle of legitimacy or sovereignty" in the sense that "fascist political elites claimed a form of democratic legitimacy even as they ruled through authoritarian means" (Riley, 2019, p. 40).

Some scholars find the analogy exaggerated and caution against using fascism to talk for present-day U.S. politics (or European and South American, for that matter), simply because the conditions of interwar Europe that permitted fascism's existence in the first place, no longer exist (Matthews, 2020). For instance, Riley has questioned the historical analogizing of Trump and other new-right leaders (i.e., Bolsonaro) with the experience of the 1930s. Riley insists that these "analogies are rarely placed in a properly comparative and historical perspective" (2018, p. 6). "Instead," he claims, "they treat the past as a storehouse of disconnected examples to be pulled out so that we can construct morality tales for the present or construct yardsticks against which the contemporary moment should be measured" (p. 6). He correctly questions the lack of historical context that, in turn, creates "a false immediacy in which the past appears as a reservoir of 'lessons'" (p. 6). Historical analogizing can be a double-edged sword (Feldman, 2019) and it is, therefore, important to talk about the context of the present-day new fascism. Fascism in contemporary politics has no meaning unless it is situated and "inscribed into a precise time and space" (Mondon, as cited in Renton, 2019, p. 14).

In his attempt to answer the same question, Michael Cole (2019) notes that fascism has not defined Trump's presidency, even though "a number of its features resonate with Trump" (p. 14). Among them, he identifies a "deep and populist commitment to an integral nation"; low tolerance of ethnic or cultural diversity; Trump's own obsession with power and his authoritarianism; his war on the working class as he undermines trade union rights; his islamophobia and racism; and his demagogy and tolerance of armed fascists and white supremacists (pp. 14–16).

On the other hand, Doug Kellner (2018) asserts that Trump does fit the authoritarian character model, acting like classical fascist leaders but insists that "Trump is not Hitler and his followers are not technically fascists" (Kellner, 2018, p. 68) even though his rallies are reminiscent of fascist parades and Trump himself has been compared to Benito Mussolini (Kellner, 2018; Traverso, 2017). According to Kellner, the Trump phenomenon could be better labeled as "authoritarian populism or neofascism" (2018, p. 72).

From Critical Discourse Studies, Ruth Wodak (2015) believes that "the terms 'extreme right' or even 'fascist right' should be reserved for parties that explicitly and openly endorse fascist and Nazi ideologies and physically violent traditions" (p. 30). At the same time, she cautions that

> it must be acknowledged that boundaries between right-wing populism and the extreme/fascist right are sometimes blurred and that some extreme right parties have also succeeded in winning seats at democratic parliamentary elections while simultaneously maintaining and supporting violent paramilitary troops [...] and masking their violent agenda. (p. 30)

Along the same lines, Christian Fuchs also talks about right-wing authoritarianism, referring to Trump's governance, but he also cautions on what he terms the "dynamic historical adaptability of the concept of fascism" (2018, p. 24) that breaks out of its classical historical definition to inhabit other societies in different historical times. While we claim that history repeats itself, there are no carbon copies as there are no watertight definitions and variations in types of fascism (Paxton, 2004; Riley, 2019). Therefore, in this book the term 'fascism' will be treated as a transhistorical, dynamic concept that will allow us to capture a moment of our contemporary history in a way that lays bare its contradictions, similarities, characteristics, and trajectories, traces its roots, and cautions about its consequences. Using the term 'fascism,' as I will discuss later,

FAR-RIGHT AUTHORITARIAN POPULISM, FASCISM, NEW FASCISM, TRUMPISM

has also a pedagogical value, where pedagogy is a contested space of agency and possibility. Because, unfortunately, "it remains true that fascism, which was a small, unpopular and isolated tradition [...] has been reborn" (Renton, 1999, p. 16) and there are lessons to be learned here. Paxton (2004), very much along the lines of Marcuse's opening quote in this chapter, claims that

> a fascism of the future—an emergency response to some still unimagined crisis—need not resemble classical fascism perfectly in its outward signs and symbols. Some future movement that would 'give up free institutions' in order to perform the same functions of mass mobilization for the reunification, purification, and regeneration of some troubled group would undoubtedly call itself something else and draw on fresh symbols. That would not make it any less dangerous. (p. 174)

Working as the ancillary to, or backup of capitalism, fascist and right-wing populist ideologies need to be taken seriously, as they are implicitly and explicitly embodied in political parties that are part of our political landscape in liberal democracies. As Critical Theory scholars have stressed "fascism does not mark a radical break from mass democracy but rather emerges as an intensification of its inner pathologies" (Brown et al., 2018, p. 4). Capitalist systems of production and consumption "do not leave intact the 'real' interests of democratic citizens who imagine that the mechanisms of representative democracy permit them to express their preferences through the procedure of elections" (Brown et al., 2018, p. 4).

These contemporary iterations of fascism, while not bearing structural commonalities with the classic historical fascism of Hitler's Germany and Mussolini's Italy, must be studied and understood. That is, we must grasp the contemporary historical conditions, characteristics, and qualities of the new faces of fascism, and its relationship to capital, dominant elites, the deep state, democracy, and, ultimately, the class interests it serves and those it claims to serve. The analogy of contemporary authoritarian regimes around the world with fascism, despite some theoretical objections and debates, is, nevertheless, an important and powerful pedagogical and political tool for awareness, awakening and intervention; it brings to the fore a cautionary tale about what Hannah Arendt has called 'the banality of evil' (1972) especially in the context of a so-called democracy. 'Evil' can be born and nurtured in the context of an illiberal democracy, and evil can unravel in human life. We do not need a military coup d'état and a mass movement to recognize the traits of authoritarianism, democratic regression, and right-wing extremism that Trumpism has revived.

20   CHAPTER 1

2.1 *Latin America and Authoritarian Politics*

Earlier I noted that the January 6th, 2021 Capitol insurrection was the first attempted coup in the United States, a country that has historically aided insurrection and establishment of dictatorships (euphemistically called 'regime change') across the world.

Pulling out recyclables from the trashcan of history and trying to see the connection with other authoritarian historical moments, on September 11th, 1973, democratically elected Chilean President Salvador Allende was overthrown by a CIA-backed coup d'état led by General Augusto Pinochet. This is a case where as Renton (1999) notes,

> Pinochet's greatest support came from within the army, and his regime was not strictly fascist, in that it emerged within the structures of the existing state, but there were fascist elements involved, and the victory of the coup gave a clear boost to the extreme right, internationally. (p. 6)

The military aggression and subsequent violence that erupted in Chile with torture, assassinations, and absolute immiseration of the Chilean people lasted close to 17 years. It was one of the first well-documented neoliberal experiments that would test the ideas of the 'Chicago Boys' under the leadership of Milton Friedman—what we now know as the 'economic shock treatment.' Building on the ideas of the 'Chicago boys,' all social movements and political organizations of the left were violently repressed, all forms of political organization dismantled, while in the economic realm, nationalizations were reversed and public assets privatized, natural resources handed over to private companies, social security was privatized, and foreign direct investment was facilitated guaranteeing the right to foreign companies to repatriate profits from their Chilean operations. Meanwhile, the price of food skyrocketed, wages had been frozen to ensure economic stability and fend off inflationary pressures. In a short span of time, an entire country had been precipitated into abysmal poverty; 85% of the Chilean population had been driven below the poverty line (Harvey, 2005). For his economic contribution, that is, the creation of an economy of wretchedness, Milton Friedman, the architect of this economic and sociopolitical crime, was awarded the Nobel Prize in Economics, just three years after the coup. Because the system knows how to reward its loyal servants. The establishment of free-market rule, neoliberalism, as an economic and political doctrine is still testing the limits of humanity worldwide today.

Therefore, while we are looking at an authoritarian ruler in the United States, we also need to not lose sight of the United States' interventions in Latin America with the goal of establishing authoritarian governments/dictatorships through coups, as is the case with Argentina, Bolivia, Brazil, Chile, Cuba, El Salvador, Grenada, Guatemala, Haiti, Honduras, Nicaragua, Panama, and so forth (Coatsworth, 2005). Also, let us not forget here that former Nazis that evaded prosecution found safe heavens in Latin America, particularly in Brazil, Argentina, Colombia, Chile, Peru, Paraguay, Uruguay, Mexico, Guatemala, Ecuador, Bolivia, as well as the United States through what came to be known as 'ratlines'—Nazi escape routes.

2.2   Right-Wing Populism and the Far Right in Europe

U.S. neofascism embodied in Trumpism is interesting because it attempts to legitimize and make fascism relevant (if not fashionable) again, albeit in new conditions of violent capitalism and in the context of a so-called liberal democracy. Donald Trump's rhetoric, while in office, created a spectacle of symbolic and material violence, fueling political divisions and hate crimes and stoking fear (Stewart, 2018) in, possibly, one of the most polarized times in American history (Pew Research Center, 2017, 2018; Vandermaas-Peeler et al., 2018).

Trumpism cannot be understood outside a global trend that makes up the stark reality of the rise of right-wing populism, extremism, and neofascist parties in Europe and other places around the world. This phenomenon has its roots in the 1990s' surge of nationalism in the Balkans and Eastern Europe, after the fall of 'real socialism' and the subsequent ethnic cleansing that took place. Extremist right-wing parties emerged across Europe, violently opposing the influx of immigrants from Eastern Europe (after the fall of the Soviet Bloc), and, later, those immigrants from 'developing' countries where the financial crisis was pushing people out, in search of a better life. While there is not one uniform explanation for the popularity of right-wing populist extremist ideologies, some common patterns can be identified and summarized under the umbrella of *fear*: the influx of immigrants and refugees and the different governments' inability to manage this influx in a sustainable way; calls for national sovereignty; fear of globalization with the disappearance of manufacturing jobs; corruption of ruling elites; and increasing income inequality. More recently, far right populist parties' targets have been refugee populations moving due to the financial crisis of 2018 and the massive displacement of people from the Middle East (Syria, Lebanon, etc.) due to imperialist wars. The new face of the enemy for fascism is not the Jewish or the Romani people anymore; it's the newcomer immigrants, refugees, the wretched of the earth who are trying to escape their violent reality, only to be (un)welcomed by right-wing extremists. The massive movement of populations from the periphery, the poor south, to the north has created an explosive situation as the autochthonous populations of some of the 'receiving' countries have at the same time, been living through the consequences of forty years of neoliberal policies, austerity, and financial insecurity with increasing job precarity, unemployment and poverty.

The 1990s signaled the new beginnings of the fascist extreme right in Europe: First, in Italy the neo-fascist party National Alliance (*Alleanza Nationale*) participated in the Berlusconi government in 1994, followed by the participation of Georg Haider's *Freedom Party* of Austria (FPO) in the Austrian government in 2000, and Jean Marie Le Pen's *Front National* second place in the first round of the 2002 French election. The right-wing extremist and neo-Nazi parties quickly spread across European parliaments. According to a 2017 Bloomberg analysis of decades of election results in 22 European countries,

> support for populist radical-right parties [has been] higher than it's been at any time over the past 30 years. These parties won 16 percent of the overall vote on average in the most recent parliamentary election in each country, up from 11 percent a decade earlier and 5 percent in 1997. (Tartar, 2017, para. 2)

In 2019, at least 21 countries in Europe had one influential right-wing populist party, while in 2018 "the governments of eight countries of the European Union (Austria, Belgium, Denmark, Finland, Italy, Poland, Hungary, and Slovakia) were led by far-right, nationalist, and xenophobic parties" making this "one of the most remarkable features of our current historical moment." A similar growth of the radical right has not been experienced in the world "since the 1930s, a development which inevitably awakens the memory of fascism" (Traverso, 2017, p. 13).

With the meteoric rise of all the right-wing populist or extremist parties in Europe, the political discourse has also shifted (Krzyżanowski & Wodak, 2009a; Wodak, 2015, 2019; Wodak & Krzyżanowski, 2017; Wodak et al., 2013; Wodak & Pelinka, 2002). Some of these parties were direct descendants of fascist parties or drawing on their respective countries' fascist history (such as in Austria, Italy, France, and Hungary). Others have been mostly packaged as right-wing populist parties with Nazi imagery and semantics occasionally serving as the shock factor, therefore creating different political imaginaries (Wodak, 2015). Right-wing populist leaders have long marked the political life in Europe after the 1990s, with Berlusconi, Jean-Marie Lepen, Georg Haider, etc. It was about time that the United States claimed its own. As Feldman notes (2019), the success of the far-right parties was due to an 'ideological trade-off':

> far right movements reframed their political message for the mainstream, from ethno-centrism and biological racism to one of nativism and cultural

identity. Another trend is the emergence of [...] the 'near right,' straddling traditional conservatives and the more familiar far right. This 'illiberal democracy,' or 'right-wing populism,' has gained enormous force across the continent of late, bridging the gap between the center ground and far right. (p. 23)

In what follows, I will discuss the Trump administration as an authoritarian capitalist model of far-right populist governance that flourishes in the current global geopolitical landscape. By linking capitalism with authoritarianism and, in turn, with Marcuse's 'new fascism' (1967), I am making the case for a type of fascism that is, in turn, embodied in different realms of public life and discourse. I believe that the use of 'right-wing populism' (RWP) over 'neofascist' possibly misses the opportunity to name not just the ideology behind these political formations, but also the material conditions and consequences, that is, the ways far-right populist ideologies function as a superstructure vehicle for a fascist regime to strengthen the capitalist classes. Fascism has historically done this, as accurately captured by Foster (2017) who claims that "right-wing populism is a euphemism introduced into the European discussion in the last few decades to refer to movements in the 'fascist genus' (fascism/neofascism/post-fascism)." These movements are characterized "by virulently xenophobic, ultra-nationalist tendencies, rooted primarily in the lower-middle class and relatively privileged sections of the working class, in alliance with monopolistic capital. [...] The same basic phenomenon has now triumphed in the United States, in the form of Trump's rise to chief executive" (Foster, 2017, paras. 2–3).

3   Fascism, Neofascism, Far Right and Trumpism

These dark forces had been building for years, waiting for the right kind of figure—charismatic, rich, fearlessly bombastic—to come along and put them into play. (Neiwert, 2017, p. 22)

Authoritarian politics has been casting a heavy shadow over different realms of public life across the world. From the rise of right-wing populism and far-right extremism in Europe (Hungary's Viktor Orbán, Austria's Heinz Christian Strache and Norbert Hofer, France's Marine Lepen, Netherlands' Geert Wilders and the UK's Nigel Farage) to Brazil's Bolsonaro, India's Narendra Modi, Philippines' Rodrigo Duterte, Turkey's Tayyip Erdogan, to Donald Trump's 'fantasy of nationalist revival' (Uetricht, 2019, para. 8) there is growing support for these types of authoritarian populist leaders and their movements. The rebirth of fascism and its growing support also resulted from the game played by the Right. Right-wing parties realized early on that there should be a balance when it comes to using the fascist or extreme right wing to do politics in the context of a liberal democracy (Renton, 2019). Therefore, these parties have tolerated neo-Nazis when it was convenient and beneficial to do so. Going through multiple waves of purging itself from extremism, the Right has managed to whitewash its own extremist and violent history while keeping their far-right base intact. A case in point is the Greek neo-Nazi party Golden Dawn and its gradual normalization in mainstream politics and the public debate, through a deliberate whitewashing political and media campaign, and the legitimization of its ideologies and practices by right-wing politicians. When this kind of extremism was not needed anymore, their friendly right-wing parties marginalized them and eventually destroyed them using the judicial system of a liberal democracy. Later, a large number of people from their base was absorbed in the extreme-right wing of the mainstream conservative Right party. Feldman calls this phenomenon a 'revolutionary right-wing neo-fascism masquerading as a vision of reform':

> It is white paint over asbestos. Yet, in place of far-right parties that at one time were firmly beyond the cordon sanitaire, this is the new fringe, trying to find meme-friendly ways to advance biological racism back into the mainstream. From CasaPound in Italy to the transnational British Blood and Honor music scene, these would-be fashionable white supremacists are, of course, not the only neo-fascist game in town (Fielitz & Laloire, 2016; Feldman & Jackson, 2014). Yet what the alt-right and overt fascists share is the attempt to force neo-fascism back onto the public agenda. No doubt, this attempted rebranding owes much to the political space vacated by a far right that is moving towards the mainstream. (Feldman, 2019, p. 41)

3.1 Radical Right, U.S.-Style

In the United States, under the Trump administration we have witnessed the legitimation and proliferation of white supremacy, sexism, corporatism, casino capitalism and militarization, and an aversion to labor and the working class, reminiscent of fascist ideologies and practices. In a perfect capitalist dystopia, the Trump administration's war on the United States working class was manifested in a tax bill "that tilts the tax system further against workers" (Cole, 2019, p. 85) as well as in the radical changes in the workplace in terms of rights, equal opportunity, and workers' protection (Cole, 2019; Madland et al., 2018). For instance, the Supreme Court's Janus decision in June 2018, an attack on workers and their right to organize, overturned forty years of precedent, ending compelled union dues for public employees.

The Trump administration's discourse and policies have been openly legitimizing a backlash on immigration (the Wall on the Mexico border, the travel bans, ICE raids, deportations and family separations); a renewed nationalism and trade protectionism (America first, import restrictions, trade war with China); an attack on social welfare (distribution of wealth upward, slashing social programs and dismantling social safety nets); a form of social Darwinism, and the most reactionary and violent policies in healthcare, education, and labor, that have adversely affected the lives and existence of ordinary people (Gounari, 2018). Clearly the loss of jobs and job precarity, financial insecurity, and fear of social downfall translated into blaming immigrants and political enemies and reclaiming the 'grandeur' of the country, while uniting behind a homogenized notion of The People as the nation. In this class-devoid soup, national identity, birthrights, and biology have been the uniting and driving force together with fear of the 'other.'

Fascist ideologies in the United States are not exactly new. Trump's appeal to the nativist and racist sentiments of a large segment of the population did not happen overnight. The racist far right has been re-emerging in recent years with its explosive mix of material, symbolic, and discursive repression, and violence, coupled with racism and xenophobia. As soon as Trump took center stage, so did "an array of white nationalists and supremacists, conspiracy theorists and xenophobes, even Klansmen and skinheads and other violent radicals, who for decades had been relegated to the fringe of right-wing politics" (Neiwert, 2017, p. 14).

Before the emergence of the Alt-right in the 2010s in the United States, there existed a right-wing landscape consisting of "Holocaust revisionists of the Liberty Lobby and the Institute of Historical Research," as well as" home-grown racists of the Ku Klux Klan, the biological racists of the Mankind Quarterly, the conspiracy theorists that make up the dominant figures within the militia movement and the unadulterated Nazis of the Aryan Nations" (Renton, 1999, p. 9).

Furthermore, extremism is not new to Republicans. Loretta Ross (2021) discusses the 'nazification' of the Republican Party noting that it is not entitled to exist as a legitimate political party because

> this authoritarian backlash has been building since new Civil Rights laws were passed in 1964 and 1965 in response to white racist violence captured on TV that required the National Guard to quell. Then-President Lyndon Johnson predicted that most white people would flee the Democratic

26   CHAPTER 1

> Party to join the pro-segregationist, anti-feminist, and anti-gay revan-
> chist political movement of George Wallace, Richard Nixon, and Ronald
> Reagan. Every undemocratically selected Republican president since the
> 1960s (by an electoral college designed to be disenfranchising) has failed
> to repudiate this neo-fascist wing of their party. (para. 9)

Who can forget former leading Klansman, Grand Wizard David Duke's 1991 campaign to become Governor of Louisiana? Duke not only was nominated as the
official Republican Party candidate, but he also came awfully close to winning
a majority vote in the election, despite his well-documented Nazi background,
and his continuing racism. This is the same Republican Party that elected and
nominated Donald Trump as the Republican presidential candidate in 2016.

3.2   *You Can Get Trumpism out of Trump, But You Can't Get Trump out of Trumpism*

'Hail Trump, hail our people, hail victory!' That's how Richard B. Spencer
saluted more than 200 attendees at the annual conference of the National Policy Institute in Washington, DC in November 2016, after Trump had won the
election. His pronouncement was met with cheers and Nazi salutes from the
crowd. He later went on to say that "America was until this past generation
a white country designed for ourselves and our posterity," and that "it is our
creation, it is our inheritance, and it belongs to us." Richard Spencer, a well-
known American neo-Nazi, white supremacist and Alt-right activist, urged his
supporters after Donald Trump's election to "party like it's 1933" (Woodrow,
2016), the year Hitler came to power in Germany. After the ultra-nationalist,
white supremacist *Unite the Right* Rally in Charlottesville, Virginia in August
2017 that resulted in the killing of activist Heather Hayer and left 19 wounded,
Spencer proudly gave credit to Trump, reiterating that the rally would not have
happened without Trump occupying the top post in the country. As Graham et
al. have noted, Trump's campaign created the potential for "a nationalist candidate who was resonating with the public in a very intense way. The alt-right
found something in Trump. He changed the paradigm and made this kind of
public presence of the alt-right possible" (Graham et al., 2019, para. 80).

Spencer is not alone in his vision for a rebirth of the race wars that would
establish the United States as a 'white country.' White supremacy is part of
Trumpism's explosive mix of hate politics and discourses. Among the seventy-three million Americans who voted for Donald Trump, we can safely assume
that there is a sizable percentage of people who share parts of this vision.

I doubt that Trump has ever read Hitler's *Mein Kampf.* Or that he has
watched Leni Riefenstahl's *Triumph of the Will,* the German Nazi propaganda

FAR-RIGHT AUTHORITARIAN POPULISM, FASCISM, NEW FASCISM, TRUMPISM   27

film of 1935 showcasing military parades and other Nazi imagery. And yet he has embodied the type of authoritarian personality: the 'charismatic' leader, an "uncontrollable and unpredictable loose cannon" (Traverso, 2019, p. 28). He is a politician without politics or a leader without a party. He rose to prominence not as a staunch Republican, or through a mass movement, but rather as a reality TV persona, famous for his arrogance, cynicism, and narcissism. He checks all the boxes for Adorno et al.'s *Authoritarian Personality* (2019), the landmark book that explores the origins of fascism "as the manifestation of dispositions that lie at the very core of the modern psyche" (Gordon, 2019, p. XXIII). He is the digital demagogue (Fuchs, 2018), someone who seems to only have a personal agenda, and that is to increase his wealth and promote his brand through the presidency. He is the "celebrity 'un-politician'" (Vials, 2020, para. 19), a "postfascist leader without fascism" (Traverso, 2019, p. 23). He does have the support of different militia groups, as evidenced in the Capitol insurrection, and plays friend with any extremist group that is willing to bow to him. His utter contempt for the law and the Constitution was witnessed at different moments during his presidency, including his denial to condemn the members of Wolverine Watchmen Militia who were arrested in October 2020 for conspiring and planning to kidnap, put to trial, and potentially execute for treason Michigan Governor Gretchen Whitmer. The epitome of Trump's contempt for the Constitution was undoubtedly his incitement of the Capitol insurrection on January 6th, 2021. Law and order applied only to repress activist groups such as Black Lives Matter or anti-fascist movements, while far-right extremists have had a carte blanche to do as they please.

Trump's personality is relevant to the degree that it helps us understand (a) why his specific personality traits are not only acceptable, but even desirable in a leader, ultimately making him popular and electable; (b) how his personality serves as a political plan to represent the interests of a dominant part of the American capital of state mechanisms in conditions of decadence and decline for American imperialism; (c) how the far-right populist politics that carry his name (Trumpism), and that he has shaped, will continue to impact the United States and the world.

3.3   *Trumpism*

What he said was always the same, expressed in the same words. The longer one listened to him, the more obvious it became that his inability to speak was closely connected with an inability to think, namely, to think from the standpoint of somebody else. No communication was possible with him, not because he lied but because he was surrounded by the most reliable of all safeguards against the words and the presence of others, and hence against reality as such. (Arendt, 1994)

After the 2020 U.S. election, it is safe to say that while Trump lost, Trumpism won, with seventy-three million Americans renewing their trust in his leadership and politics. Biden's victory represents largely the resentment to Trump's persona and to the vulgarization and fascistization of discourse and society that can be summed up in Trump's support of bogus conspiracy theories (QAnon and others); his terrible management of the COVID-19 pandemic on the basis of rejecting science, resulting in millions of new cases and deaths; his encouragement of extreme-right and racist groups (Proud Boys, Charlottesville extremists and others); and his daily parade of sexism, racism, right-wing populism and pure stupidity, evidenced in his non-stop Tweets. Trump spent his first (and final) term distracting the public debate from important issues while the Republican agenda was in full development and implementation.

However, in the 2020 election as in 2016, the main issue on the ballot seemed to be the economy. Trump appealed to the fear and insecurity of those strata mostly hit by the neoliberal policies of the last forty years, Republican and Democrat alike. He promised economic development, law and order. He blamed financial recession on the 'left-wing extremist' democrats and on globalization, as well as on immigrants 'invading' the United States, stealing 'our jobs' and taking advantage of 'our system' to enrich themselves. In full alignment with a typical right-wing authoritarian populist agenda, he further promised trade protectionism, implementing more national introversion, and he invited the 'real Americans' to align with his vision to make America great again, return to its old glory and regain its hegemony in the world stage—now seriously threatened by China. To materialize his plan, he also appealed to the most reactionary segments of the population. Trump amassed support from the ultra-conservative Tea Party, "the living embodiment of right-wing populism" (Neiwert, 2016, para. 9) with its nativist, anti-immigrant sentiments; Second Amendment enthusiasts and militia; white supremacists and white nationalists like Richard Spencer, and former grand Klan Wizard David Duke and Rocky Suhayda, chair of the American Nazi Party. These reactionary forces have thrived and remained active on social media and in the dark web working up on their moment. In order to get a good grasp at the situation, we would have to look not simply at Trump's persona, but also explore the conditions that nurtured Trump and Trumpism, as well as the reasons behind the massive popular support. Part of his success has been due to the unwillingness of the Democratic party to acknowledge and express the living and working conditions of a large percentage of U.S. population hit by austerity and neoliberal policies—also promoted by both the Clinton and Obama administrations. Not only has the Democratic party turned its back to the needs, fears and desires of a population that has suffered the consequences of casino capitalism. Democrats vehemently resisted the emergence of a more progressive political agenda within the party, expressed by Bernie Sanders and embodied in the massive support he has enjoyed. Once more, the Democratic party failed to live up to the expectations and needs of everyday Americans because, let's face it, capitalism can be red and blue alike.

Trump's increased electoral percentages in the 2020 election and the loyalty of his base further raise questions not just about populist leaders like Trump but also about their supporters and their openness to authoritarian ideas. Trump's passage from U.S. politics may have been brief in historical terms (as a one-term president and twice impeached) but his meteoric rise in the national and global political scene and the imprint of his governance will be long lasting. Exit polls from the 2020 U.S. Election have shown that Trump received 82% of the vote centering on the economy, despite the pandemic, a 14% unemployment rate, and the fact that the economy has not bounced back to its pre-pandemic levels notwithstanding a relative rebound in the third trimester of 2020. As Fuchs (2018) notes, "Trump's voting base is comparable to one of the European far-right parties" (p. 42). In 2016 he managed to flip the vote in deindustrialized Rust Belt states from Democratic to Republican. He won in areas with high concentrations of manufacturing, agriculture, and mining and oil and gas extraction. According to Revelli (2019),

> Trump's America is the rural America of scattered houses and farms lost amidst the prairies; the America of half-depopulated villages and small provincial centers ever more disconnected from their respective capitals; the America of the peripheries, of all the isolated peripheries forgotten by the centers. (p. 62)

Trump's America is also the America of the ruling classes, the capital and the elites who all saw in his persona and politics a pre-emptive solution to the growing immiseration and dissatisfaction of some large segments of the population, coupled with the radicalization of other segments (as is, for instance, the case with the Black Lives Matter movement) that was breeding social unrest—capitalism's most threatening enemy.

We cannot claim that Trump's base is a coherently organized movement. But that does not mean that it cannot become one. Trump had no well-articulated party apparatus, nor the full-blown ideology of the Nazis, he lacked a mass party organization in a fascist sense (Fuchs, 2018; Riley, 2019). He does, however, have a spontaneous popular movement made up by diverse groups. Vials (2020) cautions that while Trump "never built a coherent neofascist movement [...] we should be very vigilant lest those atomized militias congeal into something unified, and with a clear relationship to the Republican Party" (para. 10).

Finally, Trump did not face a mass socialist political party (Riley, 2019), neither a powerful organized labor movement. In his case, labor and other progressive movements were revitalized *after* his ascent to power as a response to his reactionary and anti-labor politics. While in 1930s, Germany there was a highly politicized civil society and a highly organized middle class, as well as a highly organized international working class, this is not the case in the United States.

3.3.1 Characteristics of Trumpism

Devoid of a movement but fueled by the "failed reformism of the Obama years" (Riley, 2019, p. 34) Trumpism entered our lives as an extreme-right populist authoritarian manifestation of capitalism. It solidified the vote of dissatisfaction that should have been capitalized by the Left. The label 'Trumpism' resonates with other similar far-right populist movements such as Orbanism in Hungary (Wodak & Krzyżanowski, 2017). Populism, as an ideology that is constituted of discursive and material practices functions as the instrument of representation and governance. Through excessive exposure in the media, far-right populism functions as a 'right-wing perpetuum mobile' prompting "intentional and excessive provocation of scandals and the subsequent recurrent dynamic of victimization, launching of conspiracy theories, frequent denials and lies, and finally to ambivalent apologies" (Wodak & Krzyżanowski, 2017, p. 5).

At the core of Trumpism, in line with other far-right and right-wing populist movements lies, according to Revelli (2019), the political, discursive and performative dichotomy between two poles, a 'vertical distinction' created by intentional, deliberate ideological confusion.

On the one side, we have The People, or 'true people' (Wodak, 2019), that includes an "uncontaminated original purity." On the other side stands a) the enemy *from above* "a usurping elite, a privileged gang, a hidden power," the 'swamp;' and on the other, b) the enemy *from below*—immigrants, foreigners, travelers, refugees. This political, imaginary, ideological and social divide works top/down and cuts across Left and Right ideologies. Between the two groups stands the 'idea of betrayal' where honest citizens, the pure people are cheated by "some abuse, some undue misappropriation, some conspiracy" (Revelli, 2019, p. 20). The charismatic leader stands on the top of this triangle claiming to represent the interests, hopes, fears and aspirations of the pure

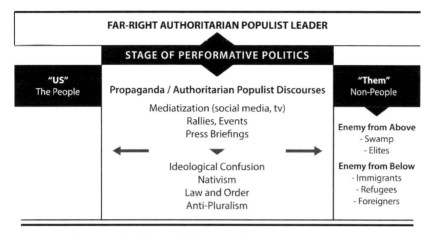

FIGURE 1.1   Triangle of far-right authoritarian populism

people (Figure 1.1). One inherent contradiction of right-wing populism lies in the fact that, while it proposes governance in the name of the People, claiming to represent them, it is deeply centered around one and only person and cashes in on his 'charismatic' character.

The triangle functions through and using the mechanisms as shown in Figure 1.1.

3.4   *The Creation of Purposeful Ideological Confusion*

Trumpism embodies a political style that meshes various ideologies and brings together "lower-middle class insecurities, while allying with core elements of the ruling class" (Foster, 2017, para. 35). This is a *thin ideology* "because it does not constitute a coherent structure of beliefs but assembles contradictory ideologemes in an eclectic fashion" (Wodak, 2019, p. 26).

Trump needed both the support of the elite political circles and the corporate media. Renton makes the case that "Trumpism crosses class; it speaks to the abandoned worker, the scared petit bourgeois, and enjoys the support of a certain part of what we call the one percent" (as cited in Jacobs, 2020, para. 5). The base for alliance between the different groups supporting Trump is not homogeneous and Trumpism allies radically different groups, because there is something for everybody in this ideological mix, as an all-purpose populist political commodity. Trumpism brings together people who embrace any of the following: racism, white supremacy, misogynism, sexism, militarism, free markets, conspiracy theories, aversion for the system, republican values, anti-abortion, faith, different versions of Christianity, and so forth. According to Vials (2020) in 2016, many Trump voters were "'whites without college degrees' who, at the same time, had incomes above the national average. The

Trumpian base, much like the base of fascist movements across the twentieth century, is strongest in what is sometimes called 'the old middle class'" (para. 24). Occupationally, it is less often white-collar professionals or office workers ('the new middle class') and more often small business owners, independent contractors, and skilled workers" (Vials, 2020, para. 24). Trumpist ideology is a strange amalgam that unites different groups of people. Trumpism does not convey a coherent narrative and ideology but rather proposes a mixed, often contradictory array of beliefs, stereotypes, attitudes, and related programs that aim to address and mobilize a range of equally contradictory segments of the electorate. This is the reason why, for example, despite Trump's misogyny and sexism, he gets support from women (mostly White) and despite his racism, xenophobia, and anti-immigration rhetoric, there is a base of Latino Trump supporters and other people of color; and, in spite of his wealth and social class, he has also appealed to the impoverished strata of the United States population. This ideological confusion is embodied in the far-right populist leader's discourse and deliberately cultivated in different modes of communication.

3.5 Stage of Performative Politics

The leader employs "front stage performance techniques that are linked to popular celebrity culture" (Wodak, 2015, p. 21) to communicate thoughts and ideas. This performative way, illustrated in the many Trump rallies or COVID-related press conferences at the White House during 2020 are an "act—something between a tragic recital and a clownish pantomime" (Lowenthal & Guterman, 1949, p. 4). For instance, in his return to the White House, from Walter Reed Medical Center where he was treated for COVID, Trump made a grand entrance reminiscent of Nazi propaganda films. After disembarking from Marine One, he walked up the staircase to the South Portico entrance of the White House, he stood on the balcony, turned to face the cameras, removed his mask, and gave his signature two thumbs up as a sign of strength and invincibility.

The authoritarian leader relies on the politics of the personal as an individual brand, what Ruth Wodak calls "personalization and commodification of current politics and politicians" (2015, p. 21). Trump's brand embodies many characteristics of Adorno et al. Authoritarian Personality: *power and toughness* are promoted as virtues while the binaries *dominance-submission, strong-weak, leader-follower* are central to his persona and discourse. There is an overemphasis on the conventionalized attributes of the ego and an exaggerated assertion of strength and toughness. Despite the leader's material and symbolic power, he still uses a narrative of victimhood for himself (as is, for instance, the case with Trump's treatment of the press). Finally, he demonstrates "destructiveness and cynicism" manifested as generalized hostility and vilification of humans (Adorno et al., 2019).

3.6 The Digital Propaganda Machine

The digital propaganda machine distorts reality and historical facts, produces fake news stories, and is at war with intellectualism and scientific knowledge, what Wodak terms the "arrogance of ignorance" (2015, p. 2). The propaganda machine includes Twitter (Blommaert, 2019; Ott & Dickinson, 2019) as well as the emergence of a network of media that have supported Trump and legitimized his existence, discourse, and policies. Trump, like a typical far-right populist leader has been at war with mainstream media, often gagging stories that negatively affect him. Finally, in addition to some mainstream media (like Fox), in Trump's case many alternative digital platforms friendly to Alt-right, white supremacism and conspiracy theories have provided space to Trumpism. These include Parler, Telegram, 4Chan, Gab and others. Trumpism's digital spin machine is particularly interesting because he has been doing the spinning himself. He has been the spinner-in chief, using unapologetic bluntness, and political incorrectness. Media did not need to spin what the leader said because the leader is his own spinning machine. In a reversal of roles, we have often seen Trump himself spinning news stories through his social media accounts. If he says something, it is true by default because he is the monarch, and his mere institutional role legitimizes information and knowledge. He is the source of the ultimate truth and information. Trump's Twitter platform has played an important role as an integral part of his administration's propaganda machine. According to a report by the Washington Post, Trump, during his term as president, made 30,573 false statements (Kessler, 2021). Therefore, after his Twitter went silent on January 7th, 2021, it seems as if he ceased to exist in the mainstream discourse. The systematic manipulation and control achieved through the propaganda machine aims to reconcile the individual with the mode of existence which his society imposes on him (Marcuse, 1964).

4 Conclusion

In this chapter, I have provided a socio historical, theoretical, and conceptual framework as the grounds for understanding the rise of authoritarian far-right populist politics, ideologies, and discourses as a realization of 'new fascism' in the United States. I explored Trumpism as a far-right, authoritarian, populist movement, in line with other similar movements in Europe, and presented its characteristics, and main mechanisms of survival, reproduction, and dissemination. The activation of theoretical and historical knowledge about authoritarianism and the new fascism serves as a foundation and a lens for my analyses and discussion throughout the book, especially in the ways they shape authoritarian far-right discourse through social media.

References

Adorno, T., Frenkel-Brunswik, E., Levinson, D., & Sanford, N. (2019). *The authoritarian personality*. Verso.

Arendt, H. (1972). *Crises of the republic: Lying in politics; Civil disobedience; On violence; Thoughts on politics and revolution*. Harcourt Brace Jovanovich.

Arendt, H. (1994). *Eichmann in Jerusalem: A report on the banality of evil*. Penguin Books.

Au, W. (2017). When multicultural education is not enough. *Multicultural Perspectives, 19*(3), 147–150. https://doi.org/10.1080/15210960.2017.1331741

Benjamin, W. (1940). *On the concept of history*. Marxists.org. https://www.marxists.org/reference/archive/benjamin/1940/history.htm

Bevelander, P., & Wodak, R. (Eds.). (2019). *Europe at the crossroads. Confronting populist, nationalist and global challenges*. Nordicum Press.

Blommaert, J. (2019). Political discourse in post-digital societies. *Trabalhos em Linguística Aplicada, 59*(1), 390–404.

Brecht, B. (1966). *Galileo*. Grove Press.

Brown, W., Gordon, P., & Pensky, M. (2018). Introduction: Critical theory in an authoritarian age. In W. Brown, P. Gordon, & M. Pensky (Eds.), *Authoritarianism* (pp. 1–6). University of Chicago Press. https://doi.org/10.7208/9780226597300-001

Coatsworth, J. H. (2005, May). United States interventions. What for? *ReVista* (Spring/Summer), 5–9. https://archive.revista.drclas.harvard.edu/book/united-states-interventions

Cole, M. (2019). *Trump, the alt-right and public pedagogies of hate and for fascism*. Routledge.

Costello, M. B. (2016). *The Trump effect: The impact of the 2016 presidential election on our nation's schools*. Southern Poverty Law Center. https://www.splcenter.org/sites/default/files/the_trump_effect.pdf

Dunn, A. H., Sondel, B., & Baggett, H. C. (2019). "I don't want to come off as pushing an agenda": How contexts shaped teachers' pedagogy in the days after the 2016 U.S. presidential election. *American Educational Research Journal, 56*(2), 444–476. https://doi.org/10.3102%2F0002831218794892

Fairclough, N. (2003). *Analyzing discourse: Textual analysis for social research*. Routledge.

Feldman, M. (2019, September 6). Seductive fascist style. *Verso*. https://www.versobooks.com/blogs/4430-seductive-fascist-style

Foster, J. B. (2017). This is not populism. *Monthly Review, 69*(2), 1–24. https://monthlyreview.org/2017/06/01/this-is-not-populism/

Fromm, E. (1981). *On disobedience*. Harper Perennial.

Fuchs, C. (2018). Authoritarian capitalism, authoritarian movements and authoritarian communication. *Media, Culture and Society, 40*(5), 779–791. https://doi.org/10.1177/0163443718772147

Gewertz, C. (2019, March 13). Principals dealing with hostility and division in the age of Trump, survey says. *Education Week*. https://www.edweek.org/leadership/principals-dealing-with-hostility-and-division-in-the-age-of-trump-survey-shows/2019/03

Giroux, H. (2008). *Against the terror of neoliberalism politics beyond the age of greed*. Paradigm Publishers.

Gordon, P. (2019). Introduction. In T. Adorno, E. Frenkel-Brunswik, D. Levinson, & N. Sanford (Eds.), *The authoritarian personality* (pp. xxxiii–xxlv). Verso.

Gounari, P. (2018). Authoritarianism, discourse and social media: Trump as the 'American agitator.' In J. Morelock (Ed.), *Critical theory and authoritarian populism* (pp. 207–228). University of Westminster Press.

Gounari, P. (2020). 'Hail Trump, hail our people, hail victory!' Teaching in authoritarian times. In R. Verma & M. Apple (Eds.), *Disrupting hate: Teacher activists, democracy and pedagogies of disruption* (pp. 39–55). Routledge.

Gounari, P. (2021). One dimensional social media: The authoritarianism of discourse and the discourse of authoritarianism. In J. Morelock (Ed.), *How to critique authoritarian populism: Methodologies of the Frankfurt school* (pp. 431–454). Brill.

Graham, D., Green, A., Murphy, C., & Richards, P. (2019, June). An oral history of Trump's bigotry. *The Atlantic*. https://www.theatlantic.com/magazine/archive/2019/06/trump-racism-comments/588067

Hamann, E. T., & Morgenson, C. (2017). Dispatches from flyover country: Four appraisals of impacts of Trump's immigration policy on families, schools, and communities. *Anthropology & Education Quarterly, 48*(4), 393–402. https://doi.org/10.1111/aeq.12214

Harvey, D. (2005). *A brief history of neoliberalism*. Oxford University Press.

Horkheimer, M. (1939, December). *The Jews and Europe*. The Charnel-House. https://thecharnelhouse.org/2015/03/20/the-jews-and-europe/

Huang, F. L., & Cornell, D. G. (2019). School teasing and bullying after the presidential election. *Educational Researcher, 48*(2), 69–83. https://doi.org/10.3102/0013189X18820291

Jacobs, R. (2020, November 12). Fascism, Trumpism and future. *Counterpunch*. https://www.counterpunch.org/2020/11/12/fascism-trumpism-and-the-future/

Kellner, D. (2018). Donald Trump as authoritarian populist: A Frommian analysis. In J. Morelock (Ed.), *Critical theory and authoritarian populism* (pp. 71–82). University of Westminster Press.

Kessler, G. (2021, January 23). Trump made 30,573 false or misleading claims as president. Nearly half came in his final year. *The Washington Post*. https://www.washingtonpost.com/politics/how-fact-checker-tracked-trump-claims/2021/01/23/ad04b69a-5c1d-11eb-a976-bad6431e03e2_story.html

Krzyżanowski, M., & Wodak, R. (2009). *The politics of exclusion: Debating migration in Austria*. Transaction.

Lowenthal, L., & Guterman, N. (1949). *Prophets of deceit: A study of the techniques of the American agitator.* Harper & Brothers.

Madland, D., Walter, K., Rowell, A., Willingham, Z., & Wall, M. (2018). *President Trump's policies are hurting American workers.* Center for American Progress. https://www.americanprogress.org/issues/ext/2018/01/26/445822/president-trumps-policies-hurting-american-workers/

Marcuse, H. (1964). *One-dimensional man.* Beacon Press.

Marcuse, H. (1967). *The problem of violence: Questions and answers.* Herbert Marcuse Archive. https://www.marxists.org/reference/archive/marcuse/works/1967/questions-answers.htm

Marx, K. (1972). *The eighteenth Brumaire of Louis Bonaparte.* Progress Publishers.

Matthews, D. (2020, October 23). *Is Trump a fascist? 8 experts weigh in.* Vox. https://www.vox.com/policy-and-politics/21521958/what-is-fascism-signs-donald-trump

McNeela, C. (2017). Creating space for student voice after the election. *Perspectives and Provocations, 6*(2), 1–2.

Morelock, J. (2019). Resuscitating sociological theory: Nietzsche and Adorno on error and speculation. In C. A. Payne & M. J. Roberts (Eds.), *Nietzsche and critical social theory* (pp. 340–360). Brill.

Morelock, J. (Ed.). (2021). *How to critique authoritarian populism: Methodologies of the Frankfurt school.* Brill.

Mullen, B., & Vials, C. (Eds.). (2020). *The U.S. anti-racism reader.* Verso.

Neiwert, D. (2016, June 21). *Trump and right-wing populism.* Political Research Associates. https://www.politicalresearch.org/2016/06/21/trump-and-right-wing-populism-a-long-time-coming.

Neiwert, D. (2017). *Alt-America: The rise of the radical right in the age of Trump.* Verso.

Ott, B., & Dickinson, G. (2019). *The twitter presidency: Donald J. Trump and the politics of white rage.* Routledge.

Paxton, R. O. (2004). *The anatomy of fascism.* Cambridge University Press.

Perez, F. (2016). *Educators shine light on the effect of Donald Trump's bullying on students.* National Educational Association. https://educationvotes.nea.org/2016/10/03/educators-trace-surge-student-bullying-donald-trump/

Pew Research Center. (2017). *The partisan divide on political values grows even wider.* https://www.pewresearch.org/politics/2017/10/05/the-partisan-divide-on-political-values-grows-even-wider/

Pew Research Center. (2018). *Why do people belong to a party? Negative views of opposing party are a major factor.* https://www.pewresearch.org/fact-tank/2018/03/29/why-do-people-belong-to-a-party-negative-views-of-the-opposing-party-are-a-major-factor/

Poulantzas, N. (1974). *Fascism and dictatorship.* New Left Books.

Renton, D. (1999). *Fascism: Theory and practice.* Pluto.

Renton, D. (2019). *The new authoritarians: Convergence on the right*. Pluto.

Revelli, M. (2019). *The new populism: Democracy stares into the abyss*. Verso.

Riley, D. (2018). What is Trump? *New Left Review, 114*, 5–31.

Riley, D. (2019). *The civic foundations of fascism in Europe*. Verso.

Rogers, J., Franke, M., Yun, J. E., Ishimoto, M., Diera, C., Geller, R. C., Berryman, A., & Brenes, T. (2017). *Teaching and learning in the age of Trump: Increasing stress and hostility in America's high schools*. UCLA's Institute for Democracy, Education, and Access. https://idea.gseis.ucla.edu/publications/teaching-and-learning-in-age-of-trump

Rogers, J., Ishimoto, M., Kwako, A., Berryman, A., & Diera, C. (2019). *School and society in the age of Trump*. UCLA's Institute for Democracy, Education, and Access. https://idea.gseis.ucla.edu/publications/school-and-society-in-age-of-trump/

Ross, L. (2021, January 20). The nazification of the republican party. *Counterpunch*. https://www.counterpunch.org/2021/01/20/the-nazification-of-the-republican-party/

Sondel, B., Baggett, H. C., & Dunn, A. H. (2018). "For millions of people, this is real trauma": A pedagogy of political trauma in the wake of the 2016 U.S. presidential election. *Teaching and Teacher Education, 70*, 175–185. https://doi.org/10.1016/j.tate.2017.11.017

Stewart, E. (2018, October 28). *Republicans don't want to acknowledge that Trump's rhetoric is fueling political divisions*. Vox. https://www.vox.com/policy-and-politics/2018/10/28/18034922/trump-synagogue-pence-paul-ryan-pipe-bomb

Tartar, A. (2017, December 11). *How the populist right is redrawing the map of Europe*. Bloomberg. https://www.bloomberg.com/graphics/2017-europe-populist-right/

Timsit, A. (2019, January 13). *American educators are treating Trump's presidency as the ultimate teachable moment*. Quartz. https://qz.com/1519239/american-educators-are-treating-trumps-presidency-as-the-ultimate-teachable-moment/

Traverso, E. (2017). *Left-wing melancholia: Marxism, history, and memory*. Columbia University Press.

Traverso, E. (2019). *The new faces of fascism: Populism and the far right*. Verso.

Trump, D. (2021, January 6). *Save America* [Rally speech transcript]. Rev.com. https://www.rev.com/blog/transcripts/donald-trump-speech-save-america-rally-transcript-january-6

Uetricht, M. (2019, January). The beginning of the end of capitalist realism. *JACOBIN*. https://www.jacobinmag.com/2019/01/capitalist-realism-mark-fisher-k-punk-depression

Vandermaas-Peeler, A., Cox, D., Najle, M., Fisch-Friedman, M., Griffin, R., & Jones, R. P. (2018). *Partisan polarization dominates Trump era: Findings from the 2018 American values survey*. Public Religion Research Institute. https://www.prri.org/research/partisan-polarization-dominates-trump-era-findings-from-the-2018-american-values-survey/

Vials, C. (2020, November 15). Here's what we learned about the far right from Donald Trump's presidency. *JACOBIN*. https://jacobinmag.com/2020/11/donald-trump-presidency-far-right-fascism-nationalism

Wodak, R. (2015). *The politics of fear: What right-wing populist discourses mean*. Sage.

Wodak, R. (2019). The trajectory of far-right populism–a discourse-analytical perspective. In B. Forchtner (Ed.), *The far right and the environment: Politics, discourse and communication* (pp. 21–37). Routledge. https://doi.org/10.4324/9781351104043-2

Wodak, R., KhosraviNik, M., & Mral, B. (Eds.). (2013). *Right-wing populism in Europe: Politics and discourse*. A&C Black.

Wodak, R., & Krzyżanowski, M. (2017). Right-wing populism in Europe & USA: Contesting politics & discourse beyond "Orbanism" and "Trumpism. *Journal of Language and Politics, 16*(4), 1–14. https://doi.org/10.1075/jlp.17042.krz

Wodak, R., & Pelinka, A. (2002). *The Haider phenomenon in Austria*. Transaction Publishers.

Woodrow, C. J. (2016, November 22). 'Let's party like it's 1933': Inside the alt-right world of Richard Spencer. *The Washington Post*. https://www.washingtonpost.com/local/lets-party-like-its-1933-inside-the-disturbing-alt-right-world-of-richard-spencer/2016/11/22/cf81dc74-aff7-11e6-840f-e3ebab6bcdd3_story.html

CHAPTER 2

One-Dimensional Discourse, Authoritarianism and Social Media

A Theoretical Framework

1 Introduction[1]

"These machines won't kill fascism"[2] claim Nantina Vgontzas and Meredith Whittaker in a 2021 article in *The Nation*. By 'machines' they mean Big Tech companies running digital media and controlling algorithms. Often, when we think of digital networks and social media, we have this abstract image of an immaterial, almost metaphysical space, a 'cloud' that exists somewhere 'out there.' Referring to Big Tech as a 'machine,' I believe, goes to the core of the matter, that is, to the actual existence of companies with material infrastructure (buildings, equipment), leadership (CEOs, consultants, lawyers, and accountants) that utilize labor made up by the underclass in the gig economy, and are fully integrated in and making profits off the capitalist system they thrive in. Clearly, reframed this way, the Big Tech machine will not kill fascism because let's admit it, Big Tech does not care about fascism. Big Tech cares about business. If fascism is good for business, then so be it. Vgontzas and Whittaker (2021) make the case that "the modern fascist movement relies on Big Tech to reproduce," noting how the far right has been using social media (like YouTube, Facebook, Twitter, as well as far-right-friendly platforms such as Parler, Gab or Telegraph) "to radicalize people who follow algorithmic recommendations to hate speech and misinformation" (para. 6) while at the same time, they undercut attempts to uncover fake news, and to deplatform hate groups and their hateful discourses. Through the use of algorithmic targeting and social media, far-right extremists have been building a powerful propaganda shadow network "that bypasses more responsible media" (para. 31). For instance, a lot has been written already in mainstream media about the role that social media played in coordinating the 2021 U.S. Capitol insurrection. The insurrection can be seen as a culminating moment of social media fomenting a far-right populist agenda during the four years of Trump's administration and providing a friendly platform to the fascist agenda, illustrating "Big Tech's historical permissiveness and perverse business incentives" (Vgontzas & Whittaker, 2021, para. 31).

© KONINKLIJKE BRILL NV, LEIDEN, 2022 | DOI: 10.1163/9789004510470_003

Social media have been occupying an increasingly larger space in our daily lives. The COVID-19 pandemic that erupted in 2020 and the ensuing lockdowns and public safety crisis worldwide abruptly moved even more human activity online, further digitizing our lives. As physical spaces of work, schooling, commerce, services, and leisure shut down, online 'presence' for a large majority of people became the new normal. In the United States, in June 2020, 42% of the U.S. labor force was working from home full-time. Having said that, 33% of people were not working at all. In many lines of work, workers were laid off, putting unemployment at 20.5 million Americans in May 2020. Finally, a significant 26% of the labor force—those deemed 'essential service workers'—still woke up every morning to go to work, to factories, grocery stores, farms, public transportation, hospitals, and other physical labor sites, often with minimal to no protection. According to national surveys from the Stanford Institute for Economic Policy (SIERP), "only 51 percent of respondents—mostly managers, professionals and financial workers who can carry out their jobs on computers—reported being able to work from home at an efficiency rate of 80 percent or more" (Bloom, 2020, p. 2). The remaining (nearly) half could not work remotely. Those were mostly workers in "retail, healthcare, transport and business services, and needed to see customers or work with products or equipment" (Bloom, 2020, p. 3). According to the same survey, of those Americans working from home, 35% have unreliable internet connection that makes teleconferencing very difficult, and they usually work from shared rooms or their bedrooms.

With the onset of the pandemic, social media further became central points of reference for public health information, school and work announcements, and for state and federal government COVID-19 updates. We resorted to these 'familiar' digital places to read news, to talk with our friends, family, and networks, attend panel discussions and conferences, plan protests, engage in debate, play games, watch concerts and theater. And with the digitization of our lives, "all the problems of civil society are now problems for Facebook" (Hern, 2020, para. 14) including racism, sexism, bullying, sexual abuse, political polarization, and conspiracy theorists. Granted, all these existed long before Facebook and Twitter, but "all took on new contours as they moved online" (Hern, 2020, para. 14). It is not just that life moved to social media, merging the private and the social; the digital environment seems to have intensified those social problems, contributing to more misinformation, superstition, and perpetuation of fake stories and news. This intensification often came through the proliferation of authoritarian discourses that in turn, brought more violence, aggression, and authoritarianism, making up a new dark age: a digital new dark age.

In this chapter, I am drawing on the work of the Institute of Social Research (*Institut für Sozialforschung*) also known as the Frankfurt School, and particularly on Herbert Marcuse's 1964 seminal book *One-Dimensional Man* to build a theoretical framework to understand right-wing authoritarian discourses in general, and particularly their contemporary iteration in social media. Marcuse's work related to discourse offers theoretical, conceptual, and analytical tools that can support and enrich inquiry into far-right authoritarian discourses, as they manifest in social media. In order to do this, I read Marcuse's theoretical work from a linguistic/discursive perspective, to structure a frame of reference where authoritarian discourse, as one-dimensional discourse, can be analyzed and understood as it manifests in different realms of human life. In this framework, I identify six features of authoritarian discourse: (1) *dehistoricization*, (2) *instrumentalism/operationalism*, (3) *digital aggressiveness*, (4) *discourse as commodity*, (5) *self as a brand*, and the (6) *discourse of amusement*.

I provide this framework hoping that it will address current needs for those scholars who work on authoritarianism in social media. I, further, discuss social media and (social)mediatization as an extension of mediatization and I present the ways in which this framework is most appropriate for social media as a site of authoritarian discourses. I illustrate this further in Chapter 3, where I explore social media discourse on Twitter and on three different conservative far-right friendly and neo-Nazi platforms: Iron March, Parler, and Telegraph.

My aim is not to provide a closed 'grand theory,' as this would be antithetical to the core of Critical Theory that held an aversion to all closed systems (Jay, 1996). I am, rather, revisiting work that was borne out of a historical moment of authoritarian triumph (as embodied in German fascism at the time) and later transposed to the United States of the 1950s "where ideological conformity and the introjection of domination in the form of false needs were 'advanced' over anything" (Agger, 1988, p. 324) in order to cast some light to contemporary far-right authoritarian populism and neofascism in the current aggressive capitalist context. I appreciate Morelock and Narita's concept of *dialectical constellation* (2021) as the "development of conceptual moments (a process) that composes a larger view of objects instead of imposing unity [...]. Constellations afford us the opportunity to name and explore a proposed class of phenomena—an abstract object—without confining ourselves to narrow, limiting designations" (p. 86).

2 What Is One-Dimensional Discourse?

> The ritual-authoritarian language spreads over the contemporary world, through democratic and non-democratic, capitalist and non-capitalist countries. (Marcuse, 1964, p. 102)

One-Dimensional Man is eerily relevant and timely today, as is most of Marcuse's work, at a time of global capitalist crises, increased authoritarianism, right-wing populism and the explosion of social media—an embodiment of technological rationality. As Andrew Robinson (2010) has astutely observed, *One-Dimensional Man* (written in 1964) reads as if it could have been written today:

> the flattening of discourse, the pervasive repression behind a veil of 'consensus,' the lack of recognition for perspectives and alternatives beyond the dominant frame, the closure of the dominant universe of meaning, the corrosion of established liberties and lines of escape, total mobilization against a permanent Enemy built into the system as a basis for conformity and effort... It was product of a previous period of downturn and decomposition, similar in many ways to our own. (para. 1)

Much in the way that Marcuse identified new forms of social administration that closed off possibilities for radical change and dispelled the myth of freedom in advanced capitalist consumer societies, similarly, he and his Frankfurt School colleagues saw language and power to be organized "around economic and political structures of domination" with the relationship between meaning and power taking "the form of ideological domination" (Chouliaraki, 2008, p. 680). Even though scholars in the Institute were not linguists, language was part of their theoretical preoccupations in terms of its function within authoritarian advanced capitalist societies, often referred to as 'affluent' or 'sick' societies. They engaged with the role of language in social life offering important contributions "to the study of mass popular culture and the emergence of consumer and media culture in capitalist modernity" (Chouliaraki, 2008, p. 680). In *One-Dimensional Man*, Marcuse is preoccupied, among other things, with discourses in advanced capitalist industrialized societies, as well as with answering more philosophical questions about language and critiquing the empiricism of linguistic analysis (see for example chapter 7, "The Triumph of Positive Thinking: One Dimensional Philosophy").

"The Closing of the Universe of Discourse" is appropriately positioned under the "One-Dimensional Society" section of the book that immediately establishes the connection between social issues and discourses. The one-dimensional society is an affluent, yet unfree society with citizens deprived of the critical functions who passively accept the prevailing order; they are, however, not aware of their unfreedom. On the contrary, they are convinced of their unlimited freedom. One-dimensional society expects blind acceptance of its principles and institutions and, in exchange, fulfills people's false needs and lulls them into the glam of consumerism and commodification, as well as the technological advances that colonize the human experience in the name of progress. This also resonates with Gramsci's notion of hegemony (Gramsci, 1971). One-dimensionality produces one-dimensional thought and behavior and is carried by and embodied in one-dimensional discourse.

Marcuse identifies discourse as a fundamental element of analysis and presents a compelling account of the role of language in a totalitarian industrial capitalist society that has been commodified, and where human beings have been losing their freedom, autonomy, and their basic critical function. This state of affairs, he claims, is mostly unknown to them, since the one-dimensional society survives and proliferates exactly because people do not recognize the totalitarian character of the system. In this one dimension, not only are humans complicit in their unfreedom, but also they actively participate in their subjugation, maintaining the illusion that this is in fact a choice that liberates them. "Totalitarian," for Marcuse (1964), is "not only a terroristic political coordination of society, but also a non-terroristic economic technical coordination which operates through the manipulation of needs by vested interests" (p. 3). 'Totalitarian' is an economy and culture that effectively controls people's thinking, needs and desires; a feature deeply ingrained in the fabric of advanced industrial capitalist societies, embodied in positivism, instrumental reason, and one-dimensional thought and discourse. Accordingly,

> the new reality of domination, rooted in the instinctual structure of individuals, is more difficult to dispel than was previous economic exploitation; domination covers exploitation in the illusions of false harmony and material abundance, but it does not eliminate it. (Agger, 1988, p. 315)

In this dystopian reality, the prevailing forms of social control are also technological, and by technological, I also include here the digital world, as the "very embodiment of Reason for the benefit of all social groups and interests" (Marcuse, 1964, p. 9). All this is operationalized and embodied in the *Language of Total Administration*: a 'rational' language, permeated by magical, authoritarian and ritual elements, deprived of mediations, a functionalized language that has fully integrated conformism, unfreedom, even opposition; a language that "militates against a development of meaning" where concepts are absorbed by the word: "the thing is identified by its function"; and where "transgression of the discourse beyond the closed analytical structure is incorrect or propaganda" (Marcuse, 1964, p. 88). In this language, the prevailing mode of freedom is servitude, equality is superimposed inequality, war is peace. The closed universe of discourse unifies the opposites in perfect harmony: The Constitution is unconstitutional, breaking the law is legal, democracy is oligarchy, science is unscientific, humans are non-human, the truth is untrue. Marcuse (1968) claims that,

> the loaded language proceeds according to the Orwellian recipe of the identity of opposites: in the mouth of the enemy, peace means war, and defense is attack, while on the righteous side, escalation is restraint, and saturation bombing prepares for peace. Organized in this discriminatory fashion, language designates a priori technological aggression and satisfaction. (p. 196)

3   Features of One-Dimensional Discourse

> The noun governs the sentence in an authoritarian and totalitarian fashion, and the sentence becomes a declaration to be accepted. (Marcuse, 1964, p. 87)

Authoritarianism is broadly understood as a political regime or system, a form of government that concentrates and exercises power arbitrarily, with little to no regard to the rule of law or the Constitution. It entails seeking "social homogeneity though coercion" (Morelock, 2018, p. XIV) material or symbolic. A leader (or a small group) is usually the central authority in charge and holds no accountability for their actions as there are no checks and balances in power. The leader is a 'savior' and he is "worshipped, alternating between the roles of Robin Hood (protecting the welfare state, supporting the 'simple folk') and the 'strict father'" (Lakoff, 2004). Such charismatic leaders require a hierarchically structured party and authoritarian structures to guarantee 'law and order' and 'security'" (Wodak, 2019, p. 198). Governance is conducted through secrecy, propaganda, and misinformation, with the goal of maintaining the authoritarian regime. Repressive control and blind obedience lie at its core and are imposed through the curtailment of individual freedoms and increased surveillance. Juan Linz (1964) discussing Spain's Franco era has provided an influential definition suggesting that authoritarian regimes are

> political systems with limited, not responsible, political pluralism: without elaborate and guiding ideology (but with distinctive mentalities); without intensive, nor extensive political mobilization (except at some points of their development), and in which a leader (or occasionally a small group) exercises power within formally ill-defined limits but actually quite predictable ones. (p. 297)

Other characteristics of authoritarianism include limited or total lack of political pluralism, manipulation of public opinion through media and propaganda machines; and "the identification of the regime as a necessary evil to combat 'easily recognizable societal problems' such as underdevelopment or insurgency" (Linz, 1964, p. 297). Since authoritarianism, as a mode of governance, often emerges in the context of liberal democracies, it can be implemented with varying degrees of opaqueness.

For my purposes here, I will refrain from a rigid definition of authority as "it would be empty, like all conceptual definitions which attempt to define single moments of social life in a way which encompasses all of history" (Horkheimer, 1952, as cited in Jay, 1996, p. 118). However, as I keep grounding my discussion in Frankfurt School's Critical Theory, I want to stress that there is a social, political, and psychological dimension to authoritarianism. The latter is presented as the desire for fascism and the development of what Adorno et al. have labeled *The Authoritarian Personality* (2019). This book is now a classic in understanding authoritarian and fascistic tendencies and what makes people susceptible to such ideologies. In my discussion, I look at authoritarianism neither as a specific regime, nor as a psychological trait but, rather, as a set of properties found in one-dimensional capitalist societies that aggregate the core characteristics described above: concentration of power, repressive control, obedience, ideological confusion, and lack of pluralism. These properties are embodied in different realms of human life, from politics to interpersonal and family relationships, school curricula, modes of governance, labor, and so forth. More importantly, these properties are not the unique characteristic of so-called repressive regimes—they often flourish and thrive in liberal capitalist democracies.

Drawing on Marcuse's work on one-dimensional thought and discourse, I propose to explore the discursive features of the *language of total administration* as an embodiment of authoritarianism and conformity, and to draw parallels with the discourse of social media. Concerns around surveillance, privacy, the role of bots and trolls and algorithms, and the degree to which social media monitor and control user information make it a *par excellence* control device; a closed universe that is tightly monitored and controlled— and it does so under the veil of freedom, when in fact it is, by and large, an example of 'democratic unfreedom.' Here, I do not want to make a totalitalizing claim that social media only produce and reproduce one-dimensional discourse, or that they are the absolute medium of control and domination. As Strath and Wodak (2009) note "the media neither completely dominate our views globally top-down, nor do they influence decision-making in politics in a unidirectional, simple and causal way" (p. 15). Along these lines, I, rather, want to suggest that because of their commodity character, and their functioning in conditions of violent capitalism, social media are important sites for the production of authoritarian discourse and have powerful potential for total control. They are also important sites of public pedagogy in that they produce massive amounts of 'knowledge' and information that shape human identities and understandings. Social media platforms are not owned by 'the people' as I explained at the beginning of this chapter. Digital advertising has seen a meteoric rise particularly during the Coronavirus pandemic "a development that has concentrated ad spending with several tech giants at the expense of other platforms, including newspapers, local television and magazines" (Vranica, 2020, para. 2). Facebook reported a total revenue of over $86 billion dollars in 2020, thanks to its ability to monetize content that users willfully shared. Three companies tower above all others in counts of combined monthly active users of the social media platforms they own. Facebook also owns WhatsApp, Facebook Messenger and Instagram, Google owns YouTube, and Tencent owns QQ, WeChat and QZone (Internet Health Report, 2018).

Social media, as tools for producing and consuming different kinds of texts in the context of *communicative capitalism* (Dean, 2009) are fertile sites for the production of *one-dimensional discourse* as the "materialization of ideals of inclusion and participation in information, entertainment, and communication technologies in ways that capture resistance and intensify global capitalism" (Dean, 2009, p. 2). In my analysis, authoritarian discourses are one-dimensional, and one-dimensional discourses are authoritarian. As I have argued elsewhere (Gounari, 2018), we can distinguish six specific features of one-dimensional authoritarian discourse. These, as we will see, can be applied to the critical analysis of social media discourse in the context of authoritarian capitalist societies.

3.1   *Dehistoricization*

A core feature of authoritarian discourses is the erasure of historical thinking and the apotheosis of the present—the 'here-and-now.' One-dimensionality works as a celebration of the present, rendering the historical dimension invisible or, worse, irrelevant. Marcuse notes that in the context of the loss of critical function, also lost are the other dimensions of an event, a social structure, as way of thinking. A-historical thinking shapes and is shaped by the flattening of discourse. A sentence is simply a declaration to be accepted. In the social media realm, while there is around-the-clock exposure, constant access, and immediacy (all content is immediately available for reading and commenting), the message is often decontextualized and largely depends on the 'reading' of it by different audiences and individuals. The context is always that of-the-moment, limiting broader interpretations, connections, and exploration of ramifications. There is a planned obsolescence in social media, as the next tweet, the next post, the next photo, or the next story will now draw even more attention, commentary, visibility, and currency; and possibly even cancel out the previous one. A news story just breaking will often only draw from a limited temporary understanding and coverage since what matters is speed and not the quality, validity, or truthfulness of information; there is no time to dig in, verify sources and investigate the background.

The lack of historical dimension can further be attested in the multiple distorted versions of 'history' that circulate in social media and their selective use to legitimize politics of fear and hatred. The revival and legitimation of neo-Nazi and authoritarian politics also owes its popularity to social media and the networks created therein, as the story on the Iron March data dump presented in the next section shows. More importantly, this constructed capitalist universe of social media discourse closes itself against any discourse not in its own terms, blocks intertextuality (the way texts are linked to other texts synchronically and diachronically[3]) and literally serves as the antithesis of historical thinking.

Technological rationality as embodied in the new digital technologies becomes the great vehicle for better domination, creating a truly totalitarian universe. In this universe, meanings are contained, fragmented and dehistoricized, and language serves as an ahistorical social bond that connects people based on who their enemy is. This is antithetical to Critical Theory's refusal to eternalize the present (Jay, 1996). Dehistoricized discourses suppress the development of critical consciousness and historical thinking about the social world. A historical-discourse analysis of social media with its focus on the historical dimension can uncover the multiple layers of synchronic and diachronic histories that shape discourses and discursive practices.

3.2   Operationalism/Instrumentalism

Marcuse (1964) makes the case for the *language of total administration,* a ritual, authoritarian language that serves as an instrument of control. It is fragmented and decontextualized and it "tends to express and promote the immediate identification of reason and fact, truth and established truth, essence and existence, the thing and its function" (p. 85). Names are indicative of their function and concepts are absorbed by the actual word. Everything that is ideologically contrary is fake news. Think, for instance, Donald Trump's famous statement that he is a very smart person, because he knows the 'best words.' What are 'best words' and how do they align with intelligence? As van Leeuwen notes, "Meaning loses its bearings and becomes fragmented and heterogeneous.

48   CHAPTER 2

Social action becomes increasingly regimented, homogenized, and proceduralized. This is what Zijderveld (1979) called the 'supersedure of meaning
by function in modernity'" (2008, p. 3). This is a central characteristic of the
closing of the universe of discourse where language, neutralized and purged of
its historical meanings and significations, is operationalized in the service of
capitalist significations. The content authored on social media promotes this
development of meaning as 'natural' and 'neutral.'

In the current authoritarian revival, operationalist language is used in official political discourse. Operationalist language expresses a very high degree of
familiarity (so close to everyday language and yet so far from everyday people's
issues), a familiarity that resonates with Fairclough's (2010) *conversationalization* of public life or with what Montgomery (2017) terms *vernacular folksiness*.
Repetition as a rhetorical device is another characteristic of operationalism. This
device has been very often used by Trump in speeches, rallies, and tweets. Repetition asserts self-righteousness, imposes conviction, closes down discussion,
and is frequently combined with appeals to authority (Wodak, 2015). Repetition
is also attributed as a characteristic to "publicity and information practiced by
the mass media" (Marcuse, 1968, p. 201). Permanent repetition means

> the same commercial with the same text or picture broadcast or televised
> again and again; the same phrases and clichés poured out by the pur-
> veyors and makers of information again and again; the same programs
> and platforms professed by the politicians again and again [...] Hit-
> ler knew well the extreme function of repetition: the biggest lie, often
> enough repeated, will be acted upon and accepted as truth. Even in its
> less extreme use, constant repetition, imposed upon more or less captive
> audiences, may be destructive: destroying mental autonomy, freedom of
> thought, responsibility and conducive to inertia, submission, rejection of
> change. The established society, the master of repetition, becomes the
> great womb for its citizens. (Marcuse, 1968, p. 12)

3.3   *The Language of Digital Aggressiveness*

In his 1968 essay on aggressiveness in advanced industrial societies, Marcuse
makes the case for the *language of aggressiveness* and for the ways the impact
of great technological advances initiates "new modes of work and of leisure and
thereby affect all social relationships and bring about a thorough transvalua-
tion of values" (p. 192). Marcuse talks about the "brutalization of language and
image" to refer to the ways media present violence as commonsensical, factual
and even humorous, reducing it "to the level of natural events and contingen-
cies of daily life": "a specific vocabulary of hate, resentment, and defamation

is reserved for opposition to the aggressive policies and for the enemy. The pattern constantly repeats itself" (p. 195). The examples here abound: Trump's Twitter account during his presidency has been notorious for not only degrading his opponents, but also openly inciting violence against them. One need simply to look at Trump's treatment of the media, immigrants and Democrats, and the nouns he has been using to characterize them; or his posting of a video with graphic violent footage targeting Democratic Representative Ilhan Omar. These have been reposted and shared by thousands of users in Trump's base of supporters. Beyond official discourses, a wandering around far-right platforms or neo-Nazi sites can readily produce examples of celebrating violence, death, the apotheosis of militarization, gun culture and so forth. Kellner (1991) claims that the destructiveness unleashed in advanced industrialized societies is more lethal and it

> finds a mass base of approval in those who have been conditioned to approve of aggression. Aggressive behavior thus provides a social bond, unifying those who gain in power and self-esteem through identifying with forms of aggression against shared objects of hate. (pp. XXXVIII–XXXIX)

Aggression (both discursive and material) as the social glue that holds together groups is very much an element of far-right populist regimes (e.g., of Trump, Bolsonaro, etc.) that thrive on hatred, dehumanization of the other and the creation of a *permanent enemy* (Marcuse, 1964) and "shared objects of hate" (Kellner, 1991). Trump's rallies have been vivid examples of discursive aggression: his followers seem unified against a common enemy, and through his discourse and discursive strategies he has legitimized and promoted aggression. Aggression also serves as political glue that holds together very different people with different individual and collective experiences, ideologies, values, and diverse relations to the means of production. What's more disturbing though is that the digital aggression further prompts real physical aggression, as will be illustrated in the next chapter.

3.4   *Discourse as Commodity*

Cultural commodities consist of signs—they are semiotic (Chouliaraki & Fairclough, 1999); they are the communicative aspect/layer of material commodities; they embody the material object, its production, decoding and consumption. The vast majority of social media content are cultural commodities branded, sold and consumed (fashion, law, history, public opinion). Central themes include beauty, leisure, travel, pets, etc. Politics are glossy and gossipy. Social media, as products of the capitalist culture industry and illustrations of technological progress, "are deeply embedded in capitalism's commodity logic and therefore reflect individual private property, individualism and structures of exploitation and domination" (Fuchs, 2016, p. 114). Digital media, as tools of the capitalist imaginary, "are modes of reification and therefore expressions of instrumental/technological rationality" in that they "reduce humans to the status of consumers of advertisements and commodities" while as cultural commodities they are "produced by cultural wage-workers that are bought by consumers and audience commodities that the media consumers become themselves by being sold as an audience to capitalist media's advertising clients" (Fuchs, 2016, p. 132). In this sense, politics also becomes a highly valued commodity in social media. Authoritarianism permeates and shapes all layers of the culture industry, and this includes discourse. Social media even produce fascism as a commodity, to be consumed by particular groups of people. Fascism online uses specific language and other semiotic signs coming across communicatively as 'friendly fascism' (Gross, 1980). Discourse as commodity operates in an 'affluent' society, a 'totalitarian' society where economy and culture control and shape people's thoughts, needs and desires. In this 'affluent' society the individual self has also become a commodity.

3.5 The Self as a Brand

"We are possessed by our images, suffer our own images" (Marcuse, 1964, p. 250). One of the most valued commodities on social media, as it emerges in capitalist societies, is now the *self*. The self is a human construction that is constantly reflected in the mirror of others. How people look, what they wear, what they think is constantly reflected and refracted through digital interaction. The trend of influencers on Instagram—the photo-sharing application, and other social media are the most glorious examples. As of June 2018, Instagram had reached one billion monthly users with 500 million daily active users and with over 50 billion pictures shared to date (Clement, 2019; Tankovska, 2021). In 2018, there were approximately 3.7 million sponsored influencer posts on the platform. Influencer culture is inextricably connected to consumerism and the rise of social media. The term is "shorthand for someone (or something) with the power to affect the buying habits or quantifiable actions of others by uploading some form of original—often sponsored—content to social media platforms like Instagram, YouTube, Snapchat, or, god forbid, LinkedIn" (Martineau, 2019, para. 3). The financial stakes are high. Influencers with smaller followings (also known as 'nanoinfluencers') can make between $30,000 and $60,000 a year; micro-influencers can make anywhere from $40,000 to $100,000 while for celebrities the figures can be astronomical (Lieber, 2018).

Self-branding takes place in multiple semiotic ways and most importantly, it can be monetized. Even users who create content without being associated with a brand or paid to advertise, are still deeply engaged in creating a certain profile for themselves, as reflected in their semiosis. In addition to this type of brand, different people also brand themselves symbolically and semiotically in the way they decide to present and represent themselves on Facebook, Twitter, and other platforms. An image of the political activist, the reactionary, the 'devil's advocate,' the 'revolutionary,' the 'life goes on,' and other types create their own self-branding. A study coming out of Brigham Young University has identified four categories of Facebook users: relationship builders, town criers, selfies, and window shoppers. While people may identify to some degree with more than one category, according to the researchers most people have at least some 'selfie' tendencies, concluding that social media is so ingrained in everything we do right now (Robinson et al., 2017). The politics of the self are illustrative of a *promotional culture* (Fairclough, 2010). They are further embodied in far-right authoritarian populism. Wodak (2015) succinctly notes that one of the salient elements of right-wing populist politicians' success is their well-crafted strategic frontstage performance in traditional and new media including social media, in election rallies, press conferences and speeches, always oriented towards a specific audience.

Frontstage performance, a strategy often employed in branding populist right-wing leaders, is also widely used by individuals in social media. In the case of right-wing populism, the populist leader (as a brand) develops his own discourse and discursive strategies, always finds the right register to speak to his voters, articulating a specific authoritarian discourse. His branding includes marketing, marking, and indexing his recognizable political stance and identity for all listeners and viewers that might identify (Wodak, 2015). The populist leader's discourse is characterized by the use of simple, impoverished language, the kind that Umberto Eco notes can be found in Nazi or fascist schoolbooks: "an impoverished vocabulary, and an elementary syntax, in order to limit the instruments for complex and critical reasoning" (Eco, 1995, p. 8). According to KhosraviNik (2018),

> the appeal of affective political engagement and the rise of Social Media personality politics are, on the one hand, predicated on internalization of the equation: *visibility/popularity is legitimacy* (derived from accumulated symbolic power, i.e., power is legitimacy) and, on the other hand, works as a revolt against the perceived monolithic nature of traditional mass media/politics. (p. 428)

3.6 *Discourse of Amusement*

Marcuse's (1964) *happy consciousness* sums up his idea of what an unfree, authoritarian society does to consciousness. In the state of happy consciousness individuals are happy in their ignorance because they have lost their autonomy, critical capacity, and ability to understand. For Marcuse, however, there is "euphoria in unhappiness" (1964, p. 5). Marcuse introduces the idea of true and false needs and their implications for human life. Human needs are always developed in a historical and social context. Human beings have true biological needs (food, shelter, clothing) and false needs; the latter are "superimposed upon the individual by particular social interests in his repression: the needs which perpetuate toil, aggressiveness, misery and injustice" (Marcuse, 1964, p. 5). For example, "to relax, to have fun, to behave and consume in accordance with the advertisements, to love and hate what others love and hate" (Marcuse, 1964, p. 5) are also false needs. This way people recognize themselves in their commodities and they become euphoric.

This kind of euphoria is produced in social media as part of the culture industry, since social media are marketed as entertainment—an entertainment that is accessible 24/7. The ideology behind this type of 'amusement' is hardly new. Facebook, Twitter and other sites serve as "the prolongation of work" that is "sought after as an escape from the mechanized work process, and to recruit strength in order to be able to cope with it again" (Horkheimer & Adorno, 1994, p. 137). Social media are now the new prolongation of work relegating people to a hypnotic state, "an effective aggression against the mind in its socially disturbing, critical functions" (Marcuse, 1968, p. 202). Marcuse notes that this inertia may well reduce the stress of intelligence, the pain and tension which accompany autonomous mental activity—thus it may be an effective aggression against the mind in its socially disturbing, critical functions (Marcuse, 1968).

"Effective aggression against the mind" is achieved through the fetishization of technology where "autonomous mental activity" is severely inhibited (Marcuse, 1968, p. 202). Doing politics on social media is essentially creating content to be consumed. This content ends up being "mere contributions to the circulation of images, opinion, and information, to the billions of nuggets of information and affect trying to catch and hold attention, to push or sway opinion, taste, and trends in one direction rather than another" (Dean, 2009, p. 24). This content is often funny and created as amusement—think political memes, for example. However, as Salehi (2017) notes: "No amount of memes can ever really unify the fragmented corners of our personalities. The enormous breadth of community and information online will always carry the risk of letting young, frustrated people retreat into subcultures that divert their energy" (para. 49).

4 (Social) Media

At a time of post-truth, fake news, alternative facts, conspiracy theories, online trolls, and the infamous 'Twitter presidency,' it is challenging to redefine 'media' and to identify exactly who produces content, on behalf of whom and for whom. Besides, it is now hard to think about media outside social media, especially since more Americans are, in fact, getting their news from social media (mostly Facebook and Twitter), according to a 2020 Pew Research Center report. Fifty-five percent of U.S. adults get their news from social media either 'often' or 'sometimes'—an 8% increase from last year. About three-in-ten (28%) said they get their news 'often,' up from 20% in 2018. The report notes that those adults who rely mostly on social media to get political news "tend to be less likely than other news consumers to closely follow major news stories, such as the coronavirus outbreak and the 2020 presidential election [...] this group also tends to be less knowledgeable about these topics" (Mitchell et al., 2020, para. 3) and more prone to gravitate towards unproven and fake claims. Demographically, U.S. adults who rely most on social media for news tend to have lower levels of education than those who mainly use several other platforms (Mitchell et al., 2020).

Social media here are understood as a "new communicative paradigm" that includes "electronically mediated communication across any platforms, spaces, sites, and technologies" (KhosraviNik, 2017, p. 582). In these semiotic spaces users may "(a) work together in producing and compiling content; (b) perform interpersonal communication and mass communication simultaneously or separately—sometimes mass performance of interpersonal communication and; (c) have access to see and respond to institutionally (e.g., newspaper articles) and user-generated content/texts" (KhosraviNik, 2017, p. 582). KhosraviNik (2020) notes a new communicative dynamic embodied in media and stresses in the context of CDS-SM (Social Media) that it is important to "unpack the nature of contemporary digital discourses by considering digital practice as a unique and relevant dynamic" (p. 2), as opposed to simply conducting critical discourse analysis to materials found online.

Social media are interactive platforms that constantly produce content in the form of 'text.' Text here is multimodal. Sociologist Erving Goffman in his 1959 seminal book *The Presentation of Self in Everyday Life* defined interaction (in a digital-network-unsuspecting time) as

> the reciprocal influence of individuals upon one another's actions when in one another's immediate physical presence. An interaction may be defined as all the interaction which occurs throughout any one occasion

when a given set of individuals are in one another's continuous presence; the term 'an encounter' would do as well. A 'performance' may be defined as all the activity of a given participant on a given occasion which serves to influence in any way any of the other participants. (Goffman, 1959, pp. 15–16)

Social media now maintain the interaction ad infinitum, without the need for physical presence, creating a permanent encounter without beginning, middle and end, composed of ongoing performances. The permanence of presence and of performance can be best illustrated in the typing dots in all the unfinished discussions on different messaging platforms. While there is no verbal communication, the intent manifests in a performative way.

Social media are 'social' because they enable these interactions and are "means of sharing, communication, community and collaboration" (Fuchs, 2016, p. 113). However, just because they are 'social' and 'shared' one cannot ignore the fact that they still function in the context of what Jodi Dean (2009) terms *communicative capitalism*: "The proliferation, distribution, acceleration, and intensification of communicative access and opportunity [that] result in a deadlocked democracy incapable of serving as a form for political change" (p. 22). In the context of this democracy, social media are "deeply embedded in capitalism's commodity logic, and therefore reflect individual private property, individualism and structures of exploitation and domination" (Fuchs, 2016, pp. 113–114). This point is often lost in the hype of social media as the great equalizer, a participatory platform or as bottom-up organizing tools and as alternative open spaces for oppositional voices, not to mention as an indicator of massive political involvement. As KhosraviNik astutely notes, "the design values and processes at work in Social Media technologies, their political economic model, their starting assumption of post-ideological status of contemporary societies and obsoleteness of critical structural politics are constitutively aligned with promoting an affective-driven, anti-establishment, anti-elite/expert, everyday/banal politics" (2018, p. 428). What is missed in understanding the commodity character of social media is the fact that they are the product and services of massive corporations who have total control over content, audience, and market. Seymour (2019) makes the case that:

> while some platforms are about enabling industry to make its work processes more legible, more transparent and thus more manageable, data platforms like Google, Twitter and Facebook turn their attention to consumer markets. They intensify surveillance, rendering abruptly visible huge substrata of behavior and wishes that had been occulted, and

making price signals and market research look rather quaint by comparison. Google accumulates data by reading our emails, monitoring our searches, collecting images of our homes and towns on Street View and recording our locations on Google Maps. And, thanks to an agreement with Twitter, it also checks our tweets. (p. 22)

It would be useful to situate the role and function of social media in the context of what Marcuse (1968) has called *affluent society*. Some of its characteristics include: (1) an abundant industrial and technological capacity which is sold as improving people's lives but, in reality, it contributes to the production and distribution of 'unproductive goods and services': luxury goods, tech gadgets, and digital tools, waste, planned obsolescence, and military equipment; (2) a high degree of concentration of economic and political power, combined with a high degree of organization and government intervention in the economy, albeit to benefit the big corporations, but implementing deregulation when it comes to the protection of the welfare state; (3) "scientific and pseudoscientific investigation, control, and manipulation of private and group behavior, both at work and at leisure (including the behavior of the psyche, the soul, the unconscious, and the subconscious) for commercial and political purposes"; the creation of fake news, the proliferation of conspiracy theories and alternate truths (Marcuse, 1968, p. 187).

In what follows, I am discussing *(social)mediatization* as a process emerging in the affluent society from the increasing reliance on and use of social media to go about our daily human activities. As humans are constantly producing 'texts' through 'mediation with social media, this process goes beyond electronically "mediated communication" (KhosraviNik, 2017, p. 582) to significantly impact human life. Texts produced on social media articulate social practices on one hand, while they are produced through specific discourses, and in turn, articulate a wide array of discourses.

5   From Mediatization to (Social) Mediatization

The most relevant place to look for ideology in the world of culture is online. (Salehi, 2017, para. 5)

Media scholars have long made the case that we live in an era of mediatization. Mediatization has existed since the time of black and white TV and print newspapers. Today it is a major force in the profit-making industry with Big Tech emerging as a core player in shaping politics, public opinion, commerce and every realm of human life. This extreme mediatization aligns with Marcuse's (1964) argument that, in advanced capitalist societies, technological rationality colonizes everyday life, imposing rules for thinking and living that prevent individuals from exercising their critical capacity. He also makes the point that the role of the media is essentially to "mediate between the masters and their dependents" (Marcuse, 1964, p. 85).

The term 'mediatization' has gained traction in the bibliography (Couldry & Hepp, 2013; Mazzoleni, 2008, 2017; Mazzoleni & Schulz, 1999) identifying the essential role, and increasing and extended use of media in all spheres of society, public life, and politics, making the case for the interrelated and inevitable relationship between media, politics, and society (Mazzoleni, 2008). Mediatization has "broad consequences for everyday life and practical organization (social, political, cultural, economic) of media" (Couldry & Hepp, 2013, p. 191). The term has been adopted in the media studies literature in a wide domain of uses ranging from the mediatization of culture, of war, of fashion, of the artist, of disaster, to the mediatization of everyday life, of music, of childhood and education, diplomacy, companies, memory, and health (Mazzoleni, 2017) making it inevitable to talk about the mediatization of human life as we know it.

Our lives are now lived between the material and digital, an "online-offline nexus" where the two "can no longer be separated and must be seen as fused into a bewildering range of new online-offline practices of social interaction, knowledge exchange, learning, community formation and identity work" (Blommaert, 2019, p. 1). This digitization of humanity may have appeared to broaden the terrain we inhabit physically with unlimited space in the digital realm. It appeared to give human beings space and opportunity to interact in an otherwise socially inert world. In reality, this digitization has increasingly been shrinking the terrain.

In the realm of politics, 'media' *are* political engagement, as opposed to dictating the rules of political engagement. They are embodied in different sites, genres, discourses, communication tactics, modes of delivery and content creation. Media exercise "growing authority over the organizing principles of our everyday lives" (Higgins, 2017, p. 384) as they further shape and impose rules on how politics should be conducted, and not the opposite (Corner & Pels, 2003; Flew, 2017; Higgins, 2017; Mazzoleni & Schultz, 1999). John Corner (2018) differentiates between *politicized media,* as an imbalance in the direction of a circumscribed media system, and *mediatized politics,* as a situation where politics has "become colonized by media logics and imperatives" (p. 4).

I want to build on this line of thinking to offer a theoretical framework wherein *(social)mediatization* now replaces mediatization. Contemporary 'media' cannot be understood *outside of* and are dominated *by* social media.

Social media serve as the new technological rationality and tool of control, domination, and exploitation in an authoritarian capitalist context (Fuchs, 2016). Social media, embodied in contemporary mediatization, are reconfiguring language use and discourse in ways that still need to be explored. In this direction, Social Media-Critical Discourse Studies (SM-CDS) has dealt with what has been termed Social Media Communication (SMC) urging researchers to deal "with how the participatory web may have changed the politics of discursive dynamics, the quality of the very content and the overall structure of discursive participation" (p. 2). KhosraviNik urges facing "these changes and their impact on conceptualization regarding Discourse Studies and acknowledge the fact that critical analysis of digital meaning-making is not complete without effective consideration of the impact of the new mediation paradigm" (2020, p. 2).

Aggression and control are digitized, and this digitization also crosses through language and other semiotic signs. Mediatization often erases mediation, an important "stage in the cognitive process that does not exist anymore" because "language tends to express and promote the immediate identification of reason and fact" (Marcuse, 1964, p. 85). The closed language does not demonstrate and explain—it communicates decision, dictum, command. It is, according to Barthes, a language proper to all authoritarian regimes. Language not only reflects the controls set by the system. It becomes itself an instrument of control, "even where it does not transmit orders but information; where it demands not obedience but choice, not submission but freedom" (Marcuse, 1964, p. 103). But what exactly is this closed language?

5.1 Critical Discourse Studies, Mediatization and Digital Extremism

There is a well-established connection in the Critical Discourse Analysis/Studies[4] literature between the rise of right-wing populist parties, authoritarianism, Alt-right groups and mediatization (Bartlett, 2014; Chilton, 2017; Enli, 2017; Enli & Rosenberg, 2018; Forchtner, et al., 2013; Gounari, 2018; Kreis, 2017; Montgomery, 2017; Ott, 2016; Reisigl, 2013; Wodak, 2017; Wodak & Krzyżanowski, 2017). Kreis (2017) notes that "Right-wing populist politicians seem to have been particularly successful in adopting social media for campaign purposes and have used them as a strategic communication tool and as an instrument of power politics" (p. 2) while Wodak and Krzyżanowski (2017) insist that the mediatized and individualized model of right-wing populism is best exemplified by 'Trumpism' (p. 474). With the explosion of social media, in addition to the more traditional political communication genres (such as speeches, press conferences/interviews, rallies and print/online political material), political parties and candidates have been turning to digital media (Forchtner et al., 2013), online communication, and online communities, and use novel tools for political influence, including memes, trolling subcultures, etc. (Seymour, 2019). Social Media Critical Discourse Studies (SM-CDS) have emerged as an approach drawing on the dynamic discursive power of social media (KhosraviNik, 2017) together with literature that "foregrounds discursive practice as the central focus of discourse analysis in Social Media" drawing on Scollon's (2001) work on mediated discourse (as cited in KhosraviNik, 2017, p. 584).

As I have argued earlier, the rise of right-wing authoritarian populism is strongly connected to mediatization and social media (Blommaert, 2019; Forchtner et al., 2013). Social media power is so pervasive that it even led some researchers to claim Donald Trump would not be (and remain) the U.S. President had it not been for Twitter (Ross & Caldwell, 2019). To that point, Blommaert (2020) adds that Trump has moved from a 'Twitter presidency' to 'Twitter governance': "Twitter here is no longer simply the vehicle for communicating the president's political message: - it has become an instrument for formal bureaucratic procedures regulating the communication between the president and other branches of government" (para. 5).

Extremist ideologies and far- and Alt-right politics have found fertile ground and free space to develop and flourish in online fora under the anonymity of digital technology. There is a wealth of online communities that have been attracting far-right, neo-Nazi users and these include the more innocuous Facebook and Twitter, but also more 'specialized' sites such as Gab, a censorship-free alternative to Twitter, Parler, Telegram and the neo-Nazi discussion board Iron March. Thanks to a massive data dump leaking in 2019, the infamous violent white supremacist site Iron March was fully uncovered. As Lewis and Hughes note, "while most domestic extremists are typically described as lone actors, online platforms serve as non-stop, virtual white supremacist rallies where coordination can happen in real-time, regardless of location" (Lewis & Hughes, 2020, p. 7).

In a study by the *Data and Society Research Institute*, Lewis (2018) analyzed a network of 65 political influencers appearing on 81 YouTube channels who cross-promote seemingly differing ideologies, but which all impart a 'reactionary' stance toward social justice and progressive politics. This network, referred to as the Alternative Influence Network (AIN), comprises "individuals from academic and media institutions and reactionary or extremist movements" (p. 43) who capitalize on their internet popularity to validate and propagate views popular among white supremacists. Serving as a 'coherent' interdiscursive public platform, YouTube enables individual content creators to position their channels as an alternative media source broadcasting far-right ideological content in the form of news, political commentary, and entertainment using pseudo-scientific information and academic jargon, meanwhile building shared audiences through guest appearances, collaborative experiences, and referencing others in videos.

J.M. Berger (2018), who analyzed 30,00 Twitter accounts that self-identified as Alt-right or followed someone who did, powerfully argues that Trump is the glue that binds the far right. Alt-right signs have effortlessly penetrated mainstream imagery, as is the case of the appropriation of trolling icon 'Pepe the Frog.' Pepe has long been a 'react' meme on 4chan message boards but was more recently adopted by the Alt-right, "associating it with white-supremacist ideology" (Seymour, 2019, p. 33). Pepe was subsequently depicted as Adolf Hitler, as a member of the Ku Klux Klan, and as Donald Trump. Trump is notorious for using memes (including Alt-right inspired ones), and presidential candidate Mike Bloomberg paid social media influencers to post memes and other messages that make him look "cool" (Derysh, 2020).

In our highly mediated communications environments, social media now embody the new technological rationality in that they produce authoritarian, one-dimensional thinking and discourse. Under the pretense of unlimited freedom, mass participation, access, participatory practices and democratic processes, mediatization builds the new unfreedom of our times: "We believe in the potential of people when they can come together" claims the Facebook motto.[5] 'When they come together to do what? one might ask. Who brings them together and for what purposes? What is to be said about privacy concerns, sharing personal information and online activity with third parties?

There has never been a time in human history where people have voluntarily provided so much personal and private information to the market. There has never been a time in human history where so many knew so much about so many others. Zygmunt Bauman in a discussion of the Foucauldian panopticon/synopticon had argued back in 1999 that the 'panopticon' (the few watching the many) has been replaced by the 'synopticon' (the many watching the few). The synopticon, he claimed, reflects the "disappearing act of the public, the invasion of the public sphere by the private; its conquest, occupation and piecemeal but relentless colonization" (Bauman, 1999, pp. 70–71). With the (social)mediatization of human life, while the few (Big Tech Corporations) watch the many, it is now the many (users) who watch the many (other users), a type of 'omniopticon' where the private is public and the public is privately owned. Watching is voyeuristic and hedonistic, it has nothing to do with looking over or caring for someone and their troubles. In a new global trend, people are investing their lives in playing a voyeuristic role in the private affairs of others. There is no realm of public or private life that has not been broadcasted in social media. These broadcasts test the limits of our humanity while they largely promote individualism, human disposability, exclusion and eradication of any spirit of community. As Bauman (2002) so poignantly argued, "what is tested now are the limits of deregulated, privatized and individualized spontaneity; the inner tendency of a thoroughly privatized world" (pp. 67–68). The content produced in this 'watching' act is monetized to the last cent.

6   Conclusion

In this chapter I have attempted to provide a theoretical framework for discussing and analyzing one-dimensional, authoritarian discourse as it manifests in social media. In the context of (social)mediatization of human life and building on Herbert Marcuse's work, I identified six features of this discourse that can enhance our understanding and analysis of the far right and its presence online. In the next chapter, I put these features to test, as I analyze the discourse produced in the neo-Nazi platform *Iron March* and on conservative social media *Parler* and *Telegram*.

Notes

1   This chapter draws on Gounari, P. (2021). One Dimensional Social Media: The Discourse of Authoritarianism and the Authoritarianism of Discourse. In J. Morelock, (Ed.), *How to Critique Authoritarian Populism: Methodologies of the Frankfurt School*. Brill.
2   Paraphrasing singer-songwriter Woody Guthrie's motto placed on his guitar in the 1940s that read "This machine will kill fascists."
3   Synchronic and diachronic views (Saussure, 1916) are two ways to conduct linguistic analysis. A synchronic view considers language at a particular moment, a given point in time, while a diachronic view considers language historically in its development through time.
4   There has been a shift in the literature from Critical Discourse Analysis (CDA) to Critical Discourse Studies (CDS). Not all scholars agree on the shift or use the new term, so I will be using CDS as a broader term to include all CDA work and studies here. I will also be using the abbreviation CDA/S.
5   See https://about.fb.com

References

Adorno, T., Frenkel-Brunswik, E., Levinson, D., & Sanford, N. (2019). *The authoritarian personality*. Verso.

Agger, B. (1988). Review essay: Marcuse's one-dimensionality: Socio-historical and ideological context. *Dialectical Anthropology, 13*(4), 315–29. https://www.jstor.org/stable/29790288?seq=1

Bartlett, J. (2014). Populism, social media and democratic strain. In C. Sanelind (Ed.), *European populism and winning the immigration debate* (pp. 99–116). Fores.

Barton, D., & Lee, C. (2013). *Language online: Investigating digital texts and practices*. Routledge.

Bauman, Z. (1999). *In search of politics*. Stanford University Press.

Bauman, Z. (2002). *Society under siege*. Polity.

Berger, J. M. (2018, October 29). Trump is the glue that binds the far right. *The Atlantic*. https://www.theatlantic.com/ideas/archive/2018/10/trump-alt-right-twitter/574219/

Blommaert, J. (2019). Political discourse in post-digital societies. *Trabalhos em Linguística Aplicada, 59*(1), 390–404.

Blommaert, J. (2020, January 14). Twitter politics: The next stage. *Diggit Magazine*. https://www.diggitmagazine.com/column/twitter-politics-next-stage

Bloom, N. (2020, June 2020). *How working from home works out*. Stanford PolicyBrief. https://siepr.stanford.edu/sites/default/files/publications/PolicyBrief-June2020.pdf

Chilton, P. (2017). "The people" in populist discourse. *Journal of Language and Politics, 16*(4), 582–594. https://doi.org/10.1075/jlp.17031.chi

Chouliaraki, L. (2008). Discourse analysis. In T. Bennett & J. Frow (Eds.), *Sage handbook of cultural analysis* (pp. 674–698). Sage.

Chouliaraki, L., & Fairclough, N. (1999). *Discourse in late modernity: Rethinking critical discourse analysis*. Edinburgh University Press.

Clement, J. (2019). *Number of daily Instagram stories users from October 2016 to January 2019*. Statista. https://www.statista.com/statistics/730315/instagram-stories-dau/

Corner, J. (2018). *Mediatization: Media theory's word of the decade*. Media Theory. http://mediatheoryjournal.org/john-corner-mediatization/

Corner, J., & Pels, D. (2003). *Media and the restyling of politics*. Sage.

Couldry, N., & Hepp, A. (2013). Conceptualizing mediatization: Contexts, traditions, arguments. *Communication Theory, 23*(3), 191–202.

Dean, J. (2009). *Democracy and other neoliberal fantasies: Communicative capitalism and left politics*. Duke University Press.

Derysh, I. (2020, February 14). *Mike Bloomberg is paying social media influencers to post fake messages to make him look "cool."* Salon. https://www.salon.com/2020/02/14/mike-bloomberg-is-paying-social-media-influencers-to-post-fake-messages-to-make-him-look-cool/

Eco, U. (1995, June 22). Ur-fascism. *The New York Review*. http://www.nybooks.com/articles/1995/06/22/ur-fascism/

Enli, G. (2017). Twitter as arena for the authentic outsider: Exploring the social media campaigns of Trump and Clinton in the 2016 presidential election. *European Journal of Communication, 32*(1), 50–61. https://doi.org/10.1177/0267323116682802

Enli, G., & Rosenberg, L. (2018). Trust in the age of social media: Populist politicians seem more authentic. *Social Media + Society, 4*(1), 1–18. https://doi.org/10.1177/2056305118764430

Fairclough, N. (2010). Discourse, change and hegemony. In N. Fairclough (Ed.), *Critical discourse analysis: The critical study of language* (pp. 126–145). Longman.

Fairclough, N. (2014). *Language and power.* Routledge.

Feldman, M. (2019, September 6). *Seductive fascist style.* Verso. https://www.versobooks.com/blogs/4430-seductive-fascist-style

Flew, T. (2017). The "Theory" in media theory. *Media Theory, 1*(1), 43–56.

Forchtner, B., Krzyżanowski, M., & Wodak, R. (2013). Mediatization, right-wing populism and political campaigning: The case of the Austrian Freedom party. In M. Ekström & A. Tolson (Eds.), *Media talk and political elections in Europe and America* (pp. 205–228). Palgrave Macmillan.

Fuchs, C. (2016). *Critical theory of communication: New readings of Lukács, Adorno, Marcuse, Honneth and Habermas in the age of the internet.* University of Westminster Press.

Goffman, E. (1959). *The presentation of self in everyday life.* Doubleday.

Gordon, P. (2019). Introduction. In T. Adorno, E. Frenkel-Brunswik, D. Levinson, & N. Sanford (Eds.), *The authoritarian personality* (pp. xxxiii–lxxv). Verso.

Gounari, P. (2018). Authoritarianism, discourse and social media: Trump as the 'American agitator.' In J. Morelock (Ed.), *Critical theory and authoritarian populism* (pp. 207–228). University of Westminster Press.

Gramsci, A. (1971). *Selections from the prison notebooks* (Q. Hoare & G. Nowell-Smith, Eds. & Trans.). International Publishers. (Original work published 1971)

Gross, B. (1980). *Friendly fascism.* South End Press.

Hern, A. (2020, November 11). Facebook, QAnon and the world's slackening grip on reality. *The Guardian.* https://www.theguardian.com/technology/2020/nov/11/how-2020-transformed-big-tech-the-story-of-facebook-qanon-and-the-worlds-slackening-grip-on-reality

Higgins, M. (2017). Mediatization and political language. In R. Wodak & B. Forchtner (Eds.), *The Routledge handbook of language and politics* (pp. 383–397). Routledge.

Horkheimer, M., & Adorno, T. (1994). *Dialectic of the enlightenment.* Continuum.

Internet Health Report. (2018). *Social media giants Facebook, Tencent, Google reign.* https://internethealthreport.org/2018/social-media-giants-facebook-tencent-google-reign/

Jay, M. (1996). *The dialectical imagination.* University of California Press.

Jones, R. H., Chik, A., & Hafner, C. (Eds.). (2015). *Discourse and digital practices: Doing discourse analysis in the digital age.* Routledge.

Kellner, D. (1991). Introduction to the second edition. In H. Marcuse (Ed.), *One-dimensional man* (pp. xi–xxxix). Beacon Press.

KhosraviNik M. (2017). Social Media Critical Discourse Studies (SM-CDS). In J. Flowerdew & J. Richardson (Eds.), *Handbook of critical discourse analysis* (pp. 582–596). Routledge.

KhosraviNik, M. (2018). Social media techno-discursive design, affective communication and contemporary politics. *Fudan Journal of the Humanities and Social Sciences, 11*(4), 427–442.

KhosraviNik, M. (2020). Digital meaning-making across content and practice in social media critical discourse studies. *Critical Discourse Studies.* https://doi.10.1080/17405904.2020.1835683

KhosraviNik, M., & Unger, J. (2016). Critical discourse studies and social media. Power, resistance and critique in changing media ecologies. In R. Wodak & M. Meyer (Eds.), *Methods of critical discourse analysis* (pp. 205–234). Sage.

Kreis, R. (2017). The 'Tweet politics' of President Trump. *Journal of Language and Politics, 16*(4), 1–12. https://doi.org/10.1075/jlp.17032.kre

Lewis, J., & Hughes, S. (2020). *White supremacist Terror: Modernizing our approach to today's threat.* George Washington Program on Extremism. https://extremism.gwu.edu/sites/g/files/zaxdzs2191/f/White%20Supremacist%20Terror%20final.pdf

Lewis, R. (2018). *Alternative influences: Broadcasting the reactionary right on YouTube.* Data & Society Research Institute. https://datasociety.net/library/alternative-influence/

Lieber, C. (2018, November 28). *How and why do influencers make so much money?* Vox. https://www.vox.com/the-goods/2018/11/28/18116875/influencer-marketing-social-media-engagement-instagram-youtube

Linz, J. (1964). An authoritarian regime: Spain. In E. Allardt & Y. Littunen (Eds.), *Cleavages, ideologies and party systems: Contributions to comparative political sociology, transactions of the Westermarck society* (pp. 291–341). Academic Bookstore.

Marcuse, H. (1964). *One-dimensional man.* Beacon Press.

Marcuse, H. (1968). *Negations: Essays in critical theory.* Beacon Press.

Martineau, P. (2019, December 6). *The WIRED guide to influencers.* Wired. https://www.wired.com/story/what-is-an-influencer/

Mazzoleni, G. (2008). Mediatization of society. In W. Donsbach (Ed.), *The International encyclopedia of communication* (pp. 3052–3055). Blackwell.

Mazzoleni, G. (2017). Changes in contemporary communication ecosystems ask for a "new look" at the concept of mediatization. *Javnost – The Public, 24,* 136–145. https://www.tandfonline.com/doi/abs/10.1080/13183222.2017.1290743

Mazzoleni, G., & Schulz, W. (1999). Mediatization of politics: A challenge for democracy? *Political Communication, 16*(3), 247–261.

Mitchell, A., Jurkowitz, M., Oliphant, J. B., & Shearer, E. (2020). *Americans who mainly get their news on social media are less engaged, less knowledgeable.* Pew Research

Center. https://www.journalism.org/2020/07/30/americans-who-mainly-get-their-news-on-social-media-are-less-engaged-less-knowledgeable/

Montgomery, M. (2017). Post-truth politics? Authenticity, populism and the electoral discourses of Donald Trump. *Journal of Language and Politics, 16*(4), 619–639. https://doi.org/10.1075/jlp.17023.mon

Morelock, J. (2018). Introduction: The Frankfurt School and authoritarian populism – A historical outline. In J. Morelock (Ed.), *Critical theory and authoritarian populism* (pp. xiii–xxxviii). University of Westminster Press.

Norris, S., & Jones, R. H. (2005). *Discourse in action: Introducing mediated discourse analysis.* Routledge.

Ott, B. (2016). The age of Twitter: Donald J. Trump and the politics of debasement. *Critical Studies in Media Communication, 34*(1), 59–68.

Pew Research Center. (2018). *Why do people belong to a party? Negative views of opposing party are a major factor.* https://www.pewresearch.org/fact-tank/2018/03/29/why-do-people-belong-to-a-party-negative-views-of-the-opposing-party-are-a-major-factor/

Reisigl, M. (2013). Critical discourse analysis. In R. Bayley, R. Cameron, & C. Lucas (Eds.), *The Oxford handbook of sociolinguistics* (pp. 67–90). Oxford University Press.

Robinson, A. (2010, October 22). In theory- Herbert Marcuse: One dimensional man? *Ceasefire.* https://ceasefiremagazine.co.uk/in-theory-6-marcuse/

Robinson, T., Callahan, C., Boyle, K., Rivera, E., & Cho, J. (2017). I ♥ FB: A Q-methodology analysis of why people 'like' Facebook. *International Journal of Virtual Communities and Social Networking, 9*(2), 46–61.

Ross, A., & Caldwell, D. (2019). Going negative: An APPRAISAL analysis of the rhetoric of Donald Trump on Twitter. *Language & Communication, 70,* 13–27. https://doi.org/10.1016/j.langcom.2019.09.003

Salehi, K. (2017, October 2). *What would Frankfurt School think of social media?* Verso. https://www.versobooks.com/blogs/3417-what-would-the-frankfurt-school-think-of-social-media

Saussure, F. (1916). *Leçons de linguistique générale.* Payot.

Scollon, R. (2001). *Mediated discourse: The nexus of practice.* Routledge.

Seymour, R. (2019). *The twittering machine.* The Indigo Press.

Strath, B., & Wodak, R. (2009). Europe-discourse-politics-media-history: Constructing 'crises'? In A. Triandafyllidou, R. Wodak, & M. Krzyżanowski (Eds.), *The European public sphere and the media: Europe in crisis* (pp. 15–33). Palgrave Macmillan.

Tankovska, H. (2021, January 27). *Number of monthly active Instagram users 2013–2018.* Statista. https://www.statista.com/statistics/253577/number-of-monthly-active-instagram-users/

van Leeuwen, T. (2008). *Discourse and practice: New tools for critical discourse analysis.* Oxford University Press.

Vgontzas, N., & Whittaker, M. (2021, January 29). *These machines won't kill fascism: Toward a militant progressive vision for Tech.* The Nation. https://www.thenation.com/article/society/tech-labor-progressive/

Vranica, S. (2020). Google, Facebook and Amazon gain as coronavirus reshapes ad spending. *The Wall Street Journal.* https://www.wsj.com/articles/google-facebook-and-amazon-gain-as-coronavirus-reshapes-ad-spending-11606831201

Wodak, R. (2015). *The politics of fear.* Sage.

Wodak, R. (2017). Discourses about nationalism. In J. Richardson & J. Flowerdew (Eds.), *Handbook of critical discourse analysis* (pp. 403–421). Routledge.

Wodak, R. (2019). The trajectory of far-right populism – A discourse-analytical perspective. In B. Forchtner (Ed.), *The far right and the environment: Politics, discourse and communication* (pp. 21–37). Routledge.

Wodak, R., KhosraviNik, M., & Mral, B. (Eds.). (2013). *Right-wing populism in Europe: Politics and discourse.* Bloomsbury.

Wodak, R., & Krzyżanowski, M. (2017). Right-wing populism in Europe & USA: Contesting politics & discourse beyond "Orbanism" and "Trumpism." *Journal of Language and Politics, 16*(4), 1–14. https://doi.org/10.1075/jlp.17042.krz

Wong, M. (2020, June 29). Stanford research provides a snapshot of a new working-from-home economy. *Stanford News.* https://news.stanford.edu/2020/06/29/snapshot-new-working-home-economy/

CHAPTER 3

From Twitter to Capitol Hill

One-Dimensional Discursive Extremism and the Language of Digital Aggressiveness

1 Introduction

On January 8th, 2021, just two days after the Capitol insurrection, former President Trump's Twitter account was permanently suspended. The decision was made after "close review of recent Tweets from @realDonaldTrump account and the context around them" deemed to present "risk of further incitement of violence" (Twitter Inc., 2021, para. 1). The decision came as a response to two tweets Trump made after twelve hours of initial ban on January 8th, 2021 that, according to Twitter, violated the 'Glorification of Violence' policy. It is worth noting that in Twitter's announcement, the context of the tweets was discussed at length and a mini discourse analysis and interpretation was provided about how these tweets might be read by different audiences (see Appendix A). Twitter's announcement concluded that "the two Tweets [...] are likely to inspire others to replicate the violent acts that took place on January 6, 2021, and that there are multiple indicators that they are being received and understood as encouragement to do so" (Twitter Inc., 2021, para. 17). Twitter, essentially, claimed that tweets (texts of 280 characters max) may push people to do things/to act (see Appendix B).

Facebook, Instagram, and Snapchat followed with similar suspensions. The first social media presidency was now, officially, over. For those familiar with the ex-president's online activity, this move went beyond the actual suspension of a social media account to mark the eradication of Trump's core governing instrument: the tool he has been using to communicate with his followers and the world, the outlet for his ideas and (unfiltered) thoughts, the platform for foreign and national policy, his PR front, and human resources department (Secretary of State Rex Tillerson, National Security Advisor Michael Bolton, Cybersecurity and Infrastructure Security Agency Christopher Krebs, Defense secretary Mark Esper, all were fired through a tweet). It is, therefore, not an exaggeration to, once again, talk about a "Twitter presidency" (Blommaert, 2019; Ott & Dickinson, 2019). Trump hasn't simply used the Twitter platform to serve his communicative purposes for four years. With over 25,000 tweets during his presidency, he has redefined the rules of engagement, launching

© KONINKLIJKE BRILL NV, LEIDEN, 2022 | DOI: 10.1163/9789004510470_004

FROM TWITTER TO CAPITOL HILL

what was, admittedly, a unique communication style for a head of state that, in turn, has generated a great amount of scholarly work in Linguistics (Blommaert, 2019; Chilton, 2017; Enli, 2017; Enli & Rosenberg, 2018; Fuchs, 2018; Gounari, 2018, 2021; Kreis, 2017; Krzyżanowski & Tucker, 2018; Lakoff, 2016; McIntosh & Mendoza-Denton, 2020; Montgomery, 2017; Ott, 2016; Ott & Dickinson, 2019; Ross & Caldwell, 2019; Sclafani, 2017; Wignell et al., 2020; Wodak & Krzyżanowski, 2017).

Twitter, Trump's preferred digital platform as a site of mediatized politics or political mediatization, has been highly visible and impactful and, using his personal brand, he has put it to work producing, reproducing and disseminating a hegemonic discourse that has become very popular. Trump's use of social media is important, as a characteristic embodiment of far-right authoritarian populism, witnessed in many countries around the world and documented in the Critical Discourse Studies literature (Gounari, 2018; KhosraviNik, 2018, 2020; Wodak & Krzyżanowski, 2017). As I have discussed in detail in Chapter 2, Trump's social media discourse amasses all the characteristics of *one-dimensional authoritarian populist discourse:* it is *dehistoricized,* erasing historical thinking and promoting a warped version of history, disseminating fake news, using distorted videos and images and producing a revisionist type of history; it is *instrumentalist,* expressing thoughts in soundbites and exhibiting a false familiarity through short sentences, slogans, fragmented and decontextualized language; it embodies and promotes *digital aggressiveness,* cultivating and inciting symbolic and material violence; it functions as a commodity, to the degree that Trump has been selling his own 'presidential' brand in order to accumulate more personal wealth; and finally, it has embodied the *discourse of amusement,* both in its blunt political incorrectness and by promoting a misleading *happy consciousness* that manifests in the arrogance of ignorance of Trump himself and his supporters. All these characteristics are ripped from the far-right authoritarian populist manual that Trumpism draws from.

In this chapter, I am drawing on Critical Discourse Studies and the one-dimensional authoritarian discourse framework presented in Chapter 2, to read and critically analyze a corpus of texts produced and disseminated through the neo-Nazi platform Iron March, conservative social media platforms Parler and Telegram, as well as the more mainstream digital platform Twitter, on the days leading to the Capitol events and a few days afterwards. I am seeking to explore in what ways the characteristics and features of authoritarianism and authoritarian populist discourse discussed in Chapters 1 and 2 are realized linguistically and discursively. In order to bring a more textured discussion and to establish intertextuality and interdiscursivity (that is, the ways texts and discourses dialogue and/or interact with each other synchronically and diachronically), I read those texts and discourses in conjunction with the former President's final speech at the Ellipse on January 6th, 2021 for the 'Save America Rally.' I look at the discourses produced in all these sites as far-right authoritarian populist discourses, emerging in digital platforms, in an attempt both, to illustrate their characteristics, as a way of signifying a particular domain of social practice from a particular perspective (Fairclough, 1995) but also to connect them with material consequences (actual practices, actions and events).

We know that texts have social effects and, as elements of social events, they also have causal effects (Fairclough, 2003). Even though exploring this kind of causality may be a far-reaching and intricate endeavor, it is useful and interesting to examine how discourses may 'do' things. Fairclough cautions for clarity in establishing causality between texts and social practices noting that "we cannot [...] claim that particular features of texts automatically bring about particular changes in people's knowledge or behavior or particular social or political effects" (p. 9). He stresses that,

> we may textually construe (represent, imagine, etc.) the social world in particular ways, but whether our representations or construals have the effect of changing its construction depends upon various contextual factors—including the way social reality already is, who is construing it, and so forth. (p. 9)

It is, therefore, essential, to explore and establish the mitigating and/or intensifying contextual factors involved.

2 Critical Discourse Analysis/Studies (CDA/S) and the Discourse-Historical Approach (DHA)

Discourses are linguistic and other semiotic acts that are always embodied cognitively and socially. And I use 'embodied' here purposely, to stress their realization, interpretation, and expression in human beings as both cognitive and social beings, as agents immersed in societies, and in complex social relations, structures, institutions, and situations. This 'embodiment' thus, generates a dialectical relationship in that "discourses as linguistic social practices can be seen as constituting non-discursive and discursive social practices and, at the same time, as being constituted by them" (Wodak, 2001, p. 66). As Wodak notes, discourse can be understood as "a complex bundle of simultaneous and sequential interrelated linguistic acts, which manifest themselves within and across the social fields of action as thematically interrelated semiotic, oral or written tokens, very often as 'texts,' that belong to specific semiotic types, that is genres" (p. 66).

Critical Discourse Analysis/Studies (CDA/S) is a problem-oriented inter-disciplinary research program (Wodak & Meyer, 2009) that studies "language and other semiotic systems in use and subsume 'a variety of approaches, each with different theoretical models, research methods and agenda'" (Fair-clough et al., 2011, as cited in Catalano & Waugh, 2020, p. 1). CDA/S's aim is "to advance our understanding of how discourse figures in social processes, social figures, and social change" (Flowerdew & Richardson, 2018, p. 1). CDA/S sees language as a social practice (Fairclough & Wodak, 1997) always embedded in a social and historical context. It explores how discourses are both embodied in diverse social practices and how, in turn, these social practices generate, shape, inform, structure and/or distort discourses. CDA/S examines language in use to identify, uncover, analyze, problematize, and challenge power and ideology nested in discourses, as well as the ideological effects of texts, through the investigation of semiotic data (written, spoken or visual). CDA/S is inter-ested in "studying social phenomena which are necessarily complex" (Wodak & Meyer, 2009, p. 2) and, therefore, calls for a multidisciplinary, multi-theoret-ical, and multi-methodical critical and self-reflective approach (Wodak, 2001; Wodak & Meyer, 2009). Critical Discourse Analysis has always had a political project since its inception: "broadly speaking that of altering inequitable dis-tributions of economic, cultural and political goods in contemporary societ-ies" (Kress, 1996, p. 15). CDA/S does this dialectically, what Collin (2015) calls a "back-and-forth movement as the analyst asks how a text's content and form shape and are shaped by the text's economic, social, cultural, and political con-texts" (pp. 3–4). Clearly, the goals of the CDA/S program align with the project at hand, that is analyzing far-right authoritarian populist discourse in conser-vative media platforms in the context of the rise of right-wing extremism and neofascism.

In my analysis of authoritarian far-right discourses in social media, I draw particularly on the Discourse-Historical Approach (DHA) as established by Ruth Wodak (2001) that combines "linguistic analysis with historical and socio-logical approaches" (Reisigl & Wodak, 2016, p. 31), analyzes and integrates the historical context in the interpretation of discourses and texts. This approach has been used in a wealth of studies on far-right discourses (Boukala, 2021; Wodak & Krzyżanowski, 2017; Wodak, 2001, Wodak et al., 2013), discourses of national identity and anti-Semitism (Reisigl & Wodak, 2001; Wodak, 2001; Wodak & Pelinka, 2002a, 2002b; Wodak et al., 2009), and racist discourses (Krzyżanowski & Wodak, 2009; Richardson, 2004; Wodak & vanDijk, 2000).

The DHA is an interdisciplinary approach that adheres to the socio-philosophical orientation of critical theory (Wodak, 2001) using a wealth of discursive data to investigate different discourses, fields of action, genres intertextual and interdiscursive relationships to connect genres, topics, and arguments (topoi). DHA starts from a social problem and "determines the categories and tools of analysis according to its own steps and procedures" (Catalano & Waugh, 2020, p. 124) to explore its linguistic realizations.

In DHA, linguistic realizations are structured through discursive strategies. Strategies are systematic types of language use, recruited to achieve a particular goal. According to Wodak et al. (2009) "strategic action is oriented towards a goal but not necessarily planned to the last detail or strictly instrumentalist; strategies can also be applied automatically" (p. 32). Reisigl and Wodak (2001) have identified five types of discursive strategies that might be present in the texts under analysis. These include (a) *referential/nomination strategies* (how are social actors named/referred to, and the construction of in/out-groups), (b) *predication* (the positive or negative labeling of social actors), (c) *argumentation* (justification of positive/negative labeling and the use of 'topoi'), (d) *perspectivation/framing* (involvement, speakers' point of view, perspective where nominations, predications and argumentations are expressed) and (e) *intensification/mitigation* (modification of the epistemic status of a proposition by explicitly or implicitly articulating utterances). A topos (borrowed from argumentation theory) is the 'glue' that connects, implicitly or explicitly, the argument(s) in the argument scheme with the conclusions and/or goals.

The hybridity, genre-, discourse- and style-mixing found in authoritarian, far-right discourses lend themselves to a nuanced analysis following the parameters of the DHA. Finally, the Discourse-Historical Approach has a strong grounding in Critical Theory, that lies in the core of the framework I have presented in Chapter 2. Having identified a social and political problem that has a linguistic dimension (in this case, far-right populist authoritarianism and neo-fascism), DHA looks at the problem historically, building knowledge and background; it, then, brings together the discursive data to be analyzed drawing from diverse sources; the data is analyzed based on discourse topics identified by exploring discursive strategies; finally the data and analysis articulate a critique that reveals both the discursive and sociopolitical layers of the discourse at hand, and a possibility, that is, ways moving forward that create a better understanding of the problem and prompt action upon this understanding to address the problem. Both, Critical Theory and the Discourse Historical Approach put at their core the historical dimension and look at discourses synchronically and diachronically, as products of a discursive genealogy.

3   From Twitter to Capitol Hill

The Capitol insurrection had been planned online for at least six months (Atlantic Council, 2021). Various online communities came together to urge people to go to DC for the 'Save America Rally,' helping them with registration and directing them to get to the Capitol building at a certain time. Rides were offered to people to facilitate transportation, including flights to DC on private jets. Many of the groups that stormed Capitol Hill have long been active on platforms like Gab, 4chan, and Reddit. More recently, these groups had adopted newer tools to organize, such as the lightly moderated social media site Parler and the anonymous messaging service Telegram (Heilweil & Ghaffary, 2021). This happened largely after the spreading of the 'stolen election' conspiracy theory that was accompanied by a massive exodus from what Trump supporters saw as 'liberal' Facebook, in a quest for more friendly digital lands. According to the Atlantic Council (2021), the groups that showed up on Capitol Hill maintained a vigorous online presence in social media known for their extremist content and love for far-right politics. A 2021 Report from the Program on Extremism at George Washington University confirms that charging documents for 83% of the 257 individuals charged in federal court, included some form of evidence from social media linking them to the Capitol: "One hundred and twenty (47%) are alleged to have posted evidence on their personal social media accounts, and another 76 (30%) have been possibly incriminated by evidence on the social media accounts of their friends and others in their social networks. Charging documents for 18 (7%) contain both" (p. 14). In looking at the social media activity leading up to January 6th, there has been vivid talk online about breaching police line and entering the Capitol on the day of the rally. In fact, uploaded content on Parler on the day of the Capitol siege, were so massive that it started to glitch forcing users to post on other platforms illustrating that "the challenge of online extremism is not limited to any one platform but rather an entire, largely unregulated ecosystem with very few barriers to engage or disseminate content" (Atlantic Council, 2021). Starting with the question that I posed in Chapter 1 regarding the rise of far-right extremism and neo fascism, I want to explore how conservative social media have been used as a new tool, a platform for far-right discourses; how these discourses look like; and what kinds of social practices are shaped and mobilized by them. In order to do this, I am using four different discursive moments and an actual discursive and material event: Trump's speech at the Ellipse, Parler and Telegram digital chatter, and select Twitter posts in the time period between December 31st, 2020 and January 12th 2021; Iron March (IM)

72   CHAPTER 3

platform posts; and the actual events at the Capitol as semiotic events. I have purposely left out Trump's own Twitter account, except from the two tweets that led to his permanent suspension from the platform, as it has already been the subject of many scholarly investigations and I would like to focus on a different genre for him (the Ellipse speech). In addition, I was interested in finding out how Trump's message has resonated discursively with his followers, as social agents, as well as with other groups who have been on the receiving end (neo-Nazis on Iron March).

3.1   *Iron March and the Discourse of Digital Aggressiveness*

The Iron March web forum (IronMarch.org) was launched on September 13, 2011 by Russian nationalist Alexander Mukhitdinov (posting under the pseudonym 'Slavros') as a platform of militant neo-Nazi, white supremacist and fascist groups, and was labelled as a "home for the 21st Century Fascist" by the Anti-Defamation League (2019, p. 1).

Online extremism is not new, and it does not always reside, as it is often thought, in the darker places of the web. It, rather, hides in plain sight. Since the resurgence of the modern far-right in the United States in the late 1970s and early 1980s, the Internet has served them as a hospitable space. In Winter's (2019) historical account of far-right extremism, it was former Texas Klansman and Aryan Nations ambassador and strategist Louis Beam who, in the Spring 1984 issue of his magazine announced, 'Aryan Nations Liberty Net,' the "first white supremacist online system and bulletin board" (p. 41). Beam claimed that technology would allow those who love this country to save it from an 'ill-deserved fate' (Winter, 2019).

Stormfront, the first far-right website in the United States was created by former Alabama Klansman Don Black in 1995. Black learned IT in prison "while serving time for plotting to overthrow a Caribbean Island" (Winter 2019, p. 43). On the day right after Obama's 2000 election to office, 2,000 new users joined Stormfront, according to its founder. Obama's presidency seemed to have increased far-right activism, recruitment and online activity (Anti-Defamation League, 2019). Klan Grand Wizzard David Duke claimed that Obama served "as a 'visual aid' that helped attract interest and recruits, claiming that [the] website saw traffic by 'unique users' increase from 15,000 to 40,000 a day" (Winter, 2018, as cited in Winter, 2019, p. 46). In the meantime, the 9/11 terrorist attacks brought the insurgence of Alex Jones' InfoWars and other disturbing Internet conspiracy theories.

Between 2012 and 2016, according to a report by George Washington University's Program on Extremism, there was a 600% increase in followers of American white nationalist movements on Twitter alone (as cited in Reitman, 2018). Then in 2019 alone, a total of 42 domestic extremism-related deaths in 17

FROM TWITTER TO CAPITOL HILL

separate incidents were reported in Anti-Defamation League's annual *Murder and Extremism* report, the sixth deadliest year since 1970, with three of the previous four years also in the top six (Anti-Defamation League, 2020a). From 2018 to 2019, the number of incidents of white supremacist propaganda doubled—from 1,214 to 2,713, making it the highest number of incidents the organization has recorded (Anti-Defamation League, 2020b).

Iron March's content and communications were mostly unknown to the larger public until September 24, 2017, when the site mysteriously went down. Two years later, in 2019 an anonymous massive data leak to the Internet Archive exposed domains used in email registration, IP addresses, usernames, and over 150,000 posts and even private messages. While active, the Iron March never really became a visibly popular online forum and managed to hide in the shadow of more well-known neo-Nazi meeting sites like Stormfront, 4chan, 8chan, and Reddit. Its covert action was instrumental in extending its influence beyond the digital forum. The website was either affiliated with or supported by, at least, nine real-world neo-Nazi groups spread all over North America and Europe: Vanguard America, Action of Serbia, Casa Pound of Italy, Golden Dawn of Greece, Antipodean Resistance of Australia, Skydas of Lithuania, and Azov Battalion of Ukraine, among others (Bray III & Singer-Emery, 2020; Hayden, 2019a). The lack of visibility and popularity gave space for the forum "to 'thrive' and take a different direction from the other neo-Nazi and white supremacy communities, which received a lot more media attention and were generally more tame in the content they published" (Cimpanu, 2019).

Priding itself as the "Internet's premium purity spiraling website" on its welcome page, Iron March showcased quotes such as Hitler's "if freedom is short of weapons, we must compensate with willpower" with the Führer's picture on the background. Its extremist content made Iron March an illustration of a "Nazi Facebook" (the Sun, UK), "a shadowy online fascist forum" (Boston Metro, USA), "[an] alternative network that promotes race war" boasting "hundreds of ultra-radical dedicated followers around the world" (Daily Post, UK) and encouraging "people to register so they could interact with, quote 'fellow fascists' by simply clicking on a swastika" (WFTV9, abc News, Orlando Florida, USA) as proudly featured on its landing page (see Figure 3.1); or as the Anti-Defamation League called it "among the most extreme and violent of these [far-right extremist] websites" (Bray III & Singer-Emery, 2020). Screen names for users included @American Blackshirt, @American_Federalist, @Blackshirt_Matt, @Blood and Iron, @Elegos, @Hellenic Skeleton, @Rape, @WidowMaker, @Woman in Black, and thousands of others.

Discussion fora listed, among other, Fascist History, Italian Fascism, Falangism, Fascist Discussions, Fascist Foreign Policy, Fascist Economics, Fascist Social and Cultural Issues, Fascism and the Left, Fascism and Racialism,

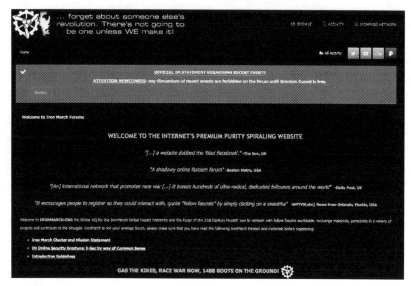

FIGURE 3.1   Iron March website landing page (Internet Archive, n.d.)

Philosophy, Third Reich, Historic Movements, NOOSE, and the Jewish Question. Members were greeted with the following message on the homepage:

> (i) Welcome to IRON MARCH.ORG the Online HQ for the Iron March Global Fascist Fraternity and the Forge of the 21st Century Fascist! Join to network with fellow fascists worldwide, exchange materials, participate in a variety of projects and contribute to the Struggle. Iron March is not your average forum, please make sure that you have read the following Iron March threads and materials before registering. (Internet Archive, n.d.)

The forum did not have a typical social media structure; it was set up as a web forum/message board; it numbered between 1,200 to 1,653 active members, even though the data leak details 3,548 registered profiles. According to Cimpanu, "the last user's database ID is 15,218; however, the dump only included details on 3,548 accounts—most likely due to spam or deleted profiles" (2019, para. 16).

In its six years of operation, Iron March brought together a number of fascist groups from different countries: It was considered to be key in the birth of two of today's most extreme far-right, neo-Nazi movements—the Atomwaffen Division and SIEGE Culture (Anti-Defamation League, 2019; Cimpanu, 2019). The platform has been linked to terrorism and over 100 hate crimes across Western countries, including to as many as five murders in the United States (Anti-Defamation League, 2019). As one Iron March user notes regarding taking action and credit for Trump's election:

(ii) The masses will be the downfall of the Alt-Right. Most people are too pacifist and if they oppose something, they'll just protest against it or just try to vote against it†(which in itself has a 50% chance of failure). There's a reason why Iron March is Far-Right and not Alt-Right, because Far-Right groups like†Golden Dawn, SYDAS, Atomwaffen,†National Action (R.I.P.), etc. actually†DO SOMETHING†like beat the shit out of Antifa scum, give food and water to the homeless and sometimes even assassinate traitors. The Alt-Right does nothing other than post memes on the internet. They†AREN'T†the reason why Trump was elected nor were they the reason for Brexit. They're pointless.

In the United States, Brandon Russell, the 22-year-old founder of the neo-Nazi group Atomwaffen Division, a member of the Florida National Guard, and a member of Iron March was convicted in 2018 of charges related to building explosives found in his premises. When Russell was arrested in Texas, police found in his car illegal assault-style rifles and up to 2,000 rounds of ammunition that he claimed could have been used for hunting. Russell kept a framed photo of Oklahoma bomber Timothy McVeigh in his apartment, as well as a copy of Hitler's *Mein Kampf* (SPLC, 2019). Russel's name first emerged in the media the previous year (2017) when his two roommates were killed by a fourth roommate, Devon Arthurs, who went by the handle *TheWeissewolfe* on Iron March.

It was also Atomwaffen member Stephen Billingsley who harassed a vigil held in Crockett Park in San Antonio, Texas for the victims of the Pulse Night club shooting, carried out by Omar Mateen on June 12, 2016 in Orlando, Florida. Billingsley was photographed at the vigil wearing the skull mask while holding a sign reading, "God Hates Fags," a phrase and demonstration-style made infamous by the Westboro Baptist Church (SPLC, 2017). James Mason, Atomwaffen's ideological figurehead, at one point admitted, "with Trump winning that election by surprise—and it was a surprise—I now believe anything could be possible" (Ware, 2019, p. 12).

Iron March users are also connected to the 'Unite the Right' rally that took place in Charlottesville, Virginia, between August 11 and 12, 2017, admittedly the most visible display of white supremacy and racial hate in the United States in recent years. According to a civil complaint filed on Sept. 17, 2019, in U.S. District Court for the Western District of Virginia against 25 individuals and organizations related to the Charlottesville rally, at least "five of the individuals or organizations listed in that complaint had active accounts on Iron March" (Singer-Emery & Bray, III, 2020, para. 12). In my research, I was able to identify three fora on the platform that contained conversations about the Charlottesville rally: (1) 'charlottesville-fallout-news-thread'; (2) 'how-r-we-supposed-to-win-unless-we-go-to-charlottesville'; and (3) 'unite-the-right-rally-in-charlottesville-va.' In them, the rift between Alt-right and fascists is vividly illustrated with IM users praising the violence and condemning the more 'moderate' Alt-right stance. As user *@Kay Kay* writes on the topic of Charlottesville, "Brute force is good because it is ACTION" (Iron March post, September 10, 2017).

'Unite the Right' rally, the third such event in 2017 in Charlottesville, SC, was triggered by the decision of the City Council to remove the statue of Robert E. Lee from Lee Park as a token of Confederate symbolism. Disguised under the argument for restoring historical truth, the rally had very little to do with restoring history and a lot with revising history through white supremacist activism. Earlier that year, white nationalist Richard Spencer had led a torchlit parade through Lee Park with participants chanting 'Blood and soil' and 'You will not replace us' a popular white supremacist slogan that underscores the assumption that the white race is under threat of extinction by non-whites led by Jews. According to neo-Nazi Andrew Anglin's description of the 'Unite the Right' rally posted on the neo-Nazi website Daily Stormer on August 8, 2017, "Although the rally was initially planned in support of the Lee Monument, which the Jew Mayor and his Negroid Deputy [sic] have marked for destruction, it has become something much bigger than that. It is now an historic rally, which will serve as a rallying point and battle cry for the rising Alt-right movement" (as cited in Coaston, 2019, para. 22).

Active Iron March users were critical decision-makers behind the rally that "led to numerous instances of violence enacted by white supremacist groups against counter protesters" (Singer-Emery & Bray, III, 2020, para. 12), including the killing of activist Heather Heyer, when a vehicle plowed into the protesters. Twenty-eight more people were injured.

In the wake of the tragic events of the rally and the white supremacist and nationalist parade, then-president Trump had claimed that there were "very fine people on both sides," later adding that at the time he was talking about people who "felt very strongly about the monument to Robert E. Lee. A great general, whether you like it or not." Trump sat on the fence and stopped short of condemning white supremacists and the deadly violence that took place, trying to whitewash the crowd and absolve them from any responsibility (see Appendix C). The popular political and discursive strategy of keeping an equal distance from two projected 'extremes' works to both portray anti-fascists as extremists (in the sense that, if you want to call white supremacists 'extremists,' you have to do the same for anti-fascists) and second, legitimizes the presence of the extremist groups in the Rally using the topos of neutrality and the topos of history: White supremacists were there to rectify a historical wrong; if they did not do it, it would threaten our nation and its history.

FROM TWITTER TO CAPITOL HILL

To summarize, beyond the discursive level, Iron March and the groups affiliated with it or borne out of it, have been involved in real acts of material and physical violence, murder, and crime. This is important because, very often, in the name of the freedom of speech and, in a process of legitimization and mainstreaming, far-right extremism hides in plain sight until it becomes a legitimate entity in the political scene and an equal interlocutor at the table. An illustrative example is the case of the Greek neo-Nazi political party 'Golden Dawn,' an organization often referred in the Iron March discussions as a good example of action and with members-users of the platform.

Neo-Nazi Golden Dawn, founded in the 1980s rose from obscurity and the margins to become the third largest political party in the 2012 national election with 6.97% of the vote. Golden Dawn's leadership was charged with running a criminal organization and carrying out a spate of violent attacks largely against political opponents and immigrants. These included the murder of anti-fascist rapper Pavlos Fyssas, the attempted murder of communist trade unionists and their leader, and the attempted murder of Egyptian immigrant fisherman Abouzid Embarak in his home. In a landmark verdict in 2020, it was ruled that Golden Dawn was a criminal organization targeting immigrants and left-wing activists and its leadership was sentenced to prison. Beyond hateful language, Golden Dawn was involved in physical violence and actual crimes.

3.2 Parler: Trump Supporters' Next Refuge

Parler came to existence in September 2018, touted as a free-speech, uncensored, social media platform, as the pro-Trump Facebook, an alternative to Twitter, and a safe haven for far-rightists, white supremacists, conspiracy theorists and others who may have been banned from mainstream social media. It billed itself as a place where people can 'speak freely' without fear of being 'deplatformed,' according to its initial, now- inoperative website and App Store description. Rebekah Mercer, a prominent Republican political donor, daughter to millionaire Robert Mercer, co-founded and funded Parler with John Matze and Jared Thomson in an attempt "to provide a neutral platform for free speech" (Bond, 2020, para. 6). The Mercer family were for years key benefactors of the Conservative News outlet Breitbart and close friends with Alt-right political strategist Steve Bannon. Mercer and her father have contributed $25 million to the 2016 republican presidential campaign (Schouten, 2017).

In a letter to the Parler Community in January 2021 former Parler CEO John Matze claimed that Facebook and Twitter's suppression of election information was a catalyst, causing many people to lose their trust: "Many of you have been activists alongside us, calling out the lack of transparency and unjust, biased policies of our competitors, as part of the Twexit and Erasebook campaigns we launched earlier this year" he noted, stressing that "together we will continue to stand up to cancel culture, defy authoritarian content curation, and reclaim the Internet as a free and open town square" (Matze, 2020, para. 9). On its new, redesigned website, Parler claimed to be "the solution to problems that have surfaced in recent years due to changes in Big Tech policy influenced by various special-interest groups. Parler is built upon a foundation of respect for privacy and personal data, free speech, free markets, and ethical, transparent corporate policy" (Parler Inc., 2021).

Right after the 2020 U.S. election and the false vote fraud claims, Parler saw a surge in new users with 4.5 million new people signing up for accounts in just one week (Yurieff, 2020). As of January 2021, Parler had an estimated 13 million users, with 2.3 million of them active and 802 moderators (Cryst, 2021). On January 8, two days after the storming of the U.S. Capitol, with users calling on Parler to "burn D.C. to the ground" Google announced that it was pulling Parler from the Google Play Store, contending that its lack of "moderation policies and enforcement" posed a "public safety threat." Parler went offline on Monday, January 11th, 2020, after Amazon stopped providing it with web-hosting services, citing 98 examples of posts that encouraged violence in the wake of the January 6th Capitol insurrection. This followed Apple and Google's removal of Parler's app from their app stores. On January 12th, Parler transferred their domain name registration to Epik. Epik was hacked in September 2021 by Anonymous who dumped 180 gigabytes of data, revealing 15 million names, phone numbers, email addresses and physical addresses stored in the platform, "a decade's worth of data from the company" according to Anonymous. Epik is a domain registrar and web hosting company self-labeled as the 'Swiss Bank of Domains' for hosting far-right websites such as Gab, Infowars, QAnon, and Proud Boys and its CEO has defended the Neo-Nazi's right. After being rejected by six Web hosts, Parler found refuge in SkySilk, an obscure Los Angeles-based Web hosting company (Allyn, 2021). In the meantime, Parler Lifeboat group was created to keep users informed and/or transition them in other platforms like Telegram. Parler requires that users join with their real names and the interface is similar to a hybrid version of Tweeter and Facebook. We followed some well-known conservative commentators such as Sean Hannity, Tucker Carlson, Mark Levin, and, following their 'Parleys' (posts), we, in turn, followed people they were commenting, such as Trump family members and other supporters. By following these users, we were able to see their *Parleys* on our feed. Under each Parley there are three symbols: 'Comment,' 'Echo,' and 'Vote Up.' This was another route to identify users we could follow by monitoring their reactions.

3.3 *Telegram: A Lifeboat for Trumpism?*

Telegram is a Dubai-based messaging application that exists since 2013 and is supported 'financially and ideologically' by Pavel Durov and his brother Nikolai Durov. Telegram rose to prominence in the context of Trump supporters quitting mainstream social media. After Parler was shut down, 'Parler Lifeboat' Group was created on Telegram to welcome users from Parler and give them a new digital platform. In an announcement posted on Telegram web on 1/13/21 it was claimed that in the past 72 hours (that is, a few days after the Capitol events), more than 25 million new users from around the world joined the platform, surpassing 500 million active users globally. According to Sidney Powel, a former member of Trump's legal team working on overturning the result of the 2020 Election, and a conspiracy theorist "Pavel Durov, the CEO of Telegram, has had a brilliant record in fighting against censorship and suppression of dictatorial governments. In addition to that, the security, flexibility, and simplicity of the platform, makes Telegram a suitable replacement for other biased social medias. [...]. Don't let them break your connections. The fight has just begun" (Powell, Telegram post on 1/12/2021). It should be noted that even after the Capitol violence, there were groups frustrated with the outcome, that were on Telegram trying to organize armed militia.

Telegram was easier to join than Parler, without identification checks or an approval process and users were urged to avoid using their real names. In Telegram, communication takes place via internet calls and messaging, there is lax moderation and end-to-end encryption for chats, including the option to self-destruct messages after an exchange.

Texts in both Parler and Telegram produce similar discourses, as two conservative and far-right friendly sites. The texts under study in the Chapter come from a) the Telegram platform and, more specifically, from the Trump account between December 31, 2020 and January 12, 2021, as well as from the 'Parler Lifeboat' group activity on January 10, 2021, created to accommodate Trump supporters fleeing 'Big tech' Facebook and Twitter after the events; b) from the Parler newsfeed in the period between January 6–January 7, 2021 as well as from the Parler TeamTrump account between December 7, 2020–January, 7, 2021; c) Iron March posts that either mention Trump explicitly or hold a Trump-related discussion and d) Trump's rally speech at the Ellipse on January 6th. These texts belong to different *Fields of Action* (segments of social reality that make up and shape the discourse frame) and *Genres* (conventionalized uses of language associated with a particular activity): Fields of action are social media posts and forum posts that are largely part of the formation of public opinion and self-presentation; the rally speech belongs to political advertising marketing and propaganda. They also belong to different genres, as "discoursal aspects of

80 CHAPTER 3

ways of acting and interaction in the course of social events," (Fairclough, 2003, p. 65) even though there is a lot of genre hybridity and inter-leaking.

3.4 *We Are at War: Analysis*

Trump's Ellipse rally speech will be my starting point of analysis because it concentrates most of the topoi and discourse topics emerging from my data corpus and sets the stage for the analysis. These same topoi and topics can be identified in the Trumpist discourse, produced between 2006 and 2020. Topics cover (1) the stolen election (2) fight back corruption (3) save America and (4) identifying enemies (5) we are at war and (6) censorship. The topoi connect topics and discursive strategies with the goals of the discursive event, and they include: the topos of *Threat and Danger*, the topos of *Responsibility*, the topos of *Law and Order*, and the topos of *History*.

4 Trump's Speech at the Ellipse-Save America Rally

A couple of hours before the carnivalesque mob entered the Capitol, Trump held his 'Save America Rally' on the White House Ellipse. Great anticipation had been building up on the weeks prior to the event, with Trump and his supporters keeping the social media chatter hot on Twitter and on conservative social media, like Parler and Gab, making 'Stop the Steal' the central slogan. Trump tweeted about the rally on December 19th: "Big protest in D.C. on January 6th. Be there, will be wild!" calling on his supporters to be part of this "Historic day!"

Crowds had started gathering from the previous night and were up bright and early by 6 am near the Ellipse. Trump's lawyer, Rudy Giuliani and his son, Eric, opened the event threatening Republicans who would vote to certify the election results: "You can be a hero, or you can be a zero. And the choice is yours. But we are all watching. The whole world is watching, folks. Choose wisely," said Eric Trump declaring that he would be on the "lawmakers' backyard" if they certify the election, adding: "This gathering should send a message to them [Republicans]: This isn't their Republican Party anymore! This is Donald Trump's Republican Party!" Eric Trump here used the topos of responsibility: Legislators have a responsibility to choose wise because the world is watching. Embedded here is also the topos of threat: choose wise or else. Trump, then, took the stage, in a typical Trump-rally style, to belligerently address the crowd, reiterating the election fraud theory "We will never give up. We will never concede" he said encouraging rally attendees to march into the Capitol: "we are going to have to fight much harder" [...] "We fight like Hell and if you don't fight like Hell, you're not going to have a country anymore" he stressed, adding: "after this, we're going to walk down to the Capitol. [...] you'll never take back our country with weakness, you have to show strength and you have to be strong." In concluding his speech, Trump again claimed that he would join his supporters as they marched to the Capitol. "We'll walk down Pennsylvania Avenue," he said. Trump of course did not physically walk down Pennsylvania Avenue with the crowd that day, nor was he planning to do so. He was, rather, using this nomination and perspectivation strategy ('we' will walk down) to intensify his proposition to actually have the crowd walk to the Capitol. His repeated use of the pronoun 'we' (as a source of nomination) shows little perspectivation, but, at the same time, it contributes to in- and out- group construction. In a speech that lasted 1 hour, 12 minutes and 21 seconds, Trump used 'we' 224 times, while he has used 'I' 176 times. He has, further, used 'they' 245 times, only a few times referring to the crowd that was present ('they're not going to take it any longer") or his own people. The use of pronouns to construct a positive self and a negative other, further helps illuminate the relationship between social actors establishing a discursive dichotomy between 'us' and 'them.'

After pressure mounted for the outgoing president by both Republicans and Democrats to take a stance against the violence, at 4:17 pm in a tweeted video lasting just over a minute, a visibly uncomfortable Trump addressed the rioters assuring them that he knows their pain and that they are hurt and asked them to "go home now" because "We have to have peace. We have to have law and order" adding "We love you, you're very special." In this example, Trump switched to address his supporters in the second person ('*you*,' your pain, you're hurt, you have to go home). Removing himself from 'we' he took a distance from the crowd but kept them close with words that denote affect (pain, hurt, love) in a successful argumentation strategy (perspectivation) where he claimed that he is *with* them but not one of them.

Trump's speech at the Ellipse, as the featured event of the *Save America Rally*, was the culmination of all previous activity leading up to the rally, and has, essentially, set in motion the events that led to the Capitol riot. The speech can be registered as a performative event, a front-stage performance that is very typical of populist leaders. The event, further, illustrates the "'spectacularization' of political communication formats and of political discourse itself" (Mazzoleni, 2017). To put this speech in context, Trump has held 154 political rallies since his inauguration (from February 18, 2017 to November 2020) and while he was in office, keeping a state of a 'permanent electoral campaign' since his inauguration in 2016. After the onset of the global pandemic and, unable to call for massive gatherings due to public health concerns, he brought the same performative style to his infamous White House COVID briefings.

Trump's frontstage performance in rallies established relatability (he is one of us, he speaks the people's language, he is not politically correct, he says what people believe but feel embarrassed to say, he has their back), familiarity (using compliments, physical proximity, emotive language), and control over the narrative (he defines what is true and what is false). His Ellipse speech illustrates these characteristics and has all the features of his rally speeches; a discernible structure with identifiable themes, a disjointed communication form with constant back and forth and repetition, and the performative dimension—a staple of far-right populist leaders.

The themes reiterated in the speech have been prevalent in the Trump camp on social media and public discourse in the months leading to the 2020 election and afterwards: the election was stolen and there is evidence that he will provide; the media and big tech are corrupt and authoritarian and they promote fake news aligning with the Democrats; the radical Left will destroy America; the media are the people's enemy, and the goal of the rally is to take back what is 'ours,' putting pressure on the legislators to not certify the election or else.

The name of the rally already raises a number of issues, underlying assumptions and presuppositions, while at the same time, fully aligning with the Trumpist rhetoric produced between 2016 and 2020. 'Save America' crystallizes the three tropes of metonymy, synecdoche and personification: metonymically, the 'country for persons' is used in an attempt to relativize agents, 'all Americans'; synecdochically, the *totum pro parte* (whole for part) to widen the group of agents where America as an entire nation/country is used for the part (American people or more specifically, Trump supporters); finally, in a personification trope, America is threatened, it is in danger and needs to be saved from something/someone, just like a person would. This anthropomorphism is used as a referential strategy to generate relatability and emotion.

First, America is presented as one homogeneous entity. Does the use of 'America' here include *all* American citizens? We already know that Trumpism has specific in-group membership rules that are deeply polarizing. In the Trumpist discourse produced the last five years, 'membership' to America is reserved to specific groups, that are mostly defined by those excluded. It is, essentially, through the referential strategies (the naming) used for 'them' the 'others' the 'enemy' that one understands who 'we' is and creates the illusion of being in the majority. This is also a strategy to discredit opponents. 'They' are the 'emboldened radical left Democrats,' radical leftists, the 'left menace' (Boukala, 2021), 'illegal' immigrants, Republicans who won't do Trump's bidding, but also 'vicious people in the world,' fake media and big tech, China, and the list goes on. 'They' is a placeholder, a receptacle filled at will with different groups, individuals, characteristics, and specific content, depending on the context.

As an argumentation strategy, the topos of 'danger and threat,' the fallacy of threat is present in the assumption that America needs to be saved: "if there are specific dangers and threats, one should do something against them" (Wodak, 2001, p. 75). With the creation of threat, saving is legitimized. And 'saving' could mean different things, especially in light of Trump's other comments ("you'll never take back our country with weakness. You have to show strength, and you have to be strong"). Rally participants and Trump supporters at large, are prompted to get on a mission to save America fulfilling the vague 'show strength' command that can be interpreted in many different ways. The imperative mood of the slogan, which does not have a subject (imperatives are always second person) achieves three goals discursively: First, it creates the kind of ideological confusion, previously discussed, where different groups of people in the Trumpism spectrum can position themselves ('we,' the people who want to save America, patriots) and their enemies ('them,' those America needs to be saved from; democrats, stealing the election, liberals, illegal immigrants). The positioning of the two groups and the 'us' versus 'them' construct is typical of far-right populist discourses in articulating sameness and difference. At the same time, what for the in-group is a 'Save America Rally' for others (the out-groups) it has been registered as 'Capitol insurrection,' 'sedition,' a 'coup,' a 'siege' and a 'riot.' Second, Save America is agentless, the imperative 'save' functions, ideologically, as what Althusser (1970) has termed 'interpellation' or 'hailing,' that "can be imagined along the lines of the most commonplace every day police (or other) hailing: 'Hey, you there!'" (p. 29).

Imagine Trump up on a balcony shouting 'Save America!' Who would turn their head feeling like this message is addressed to them? In other words, what kinds of subjects does the transitivity of *Save America* slogan constitute ideologically and materially? What types of individual and collective identities does it produce? Interestingly, in this particular case, we do have an answer that comes from all the imagery emerging in social media from the day of the rally. Trump has 'hailed' through *Save America* and his social media and particular groups of people have responded, creating themselves as ideological subjects. The slogan uses the concept of 'common ground,' that is, the assumptions involved in decoding the specific message by the people it is addressed to. As Fairclough (2003) notes, "the capacity to exercise social power, domination and hegemony includes the capacity to shape to some significant degree the nature and content of this 'common ground,' which makes implicitness and assumptions an important issue with respect to ideology" (p. 55). The 'us vs. them' construct also creates specific actors in the two categories. Furthermore, 'Save America' aims at mobilizing the patriots, those who really care about their country, around the topos of responsibility. This could have been a slogan used in a national liberation war and yet, at the end, America in this locution is equated with Trump losing the election. Trump embodies America, Trump is threatened because he unfairly lost the election, therefore America is threatened.

Who is the enemy? This is a typical construction of in-groups and out-groups discursively in far-right discourses. Trump is turning words into weapons (Lakoff, 2016) as he articulates a discourse of 'war,' likening the rally attendees and his supporters, in general, to warriors on a mission: to save America. The crowd, at one point, cheers "Fight for Trump!" while he unfolds his narrative, as if he were describing a battle. The battle metaphor is central, as illustrated in Figures 3.2 and 3.3 and, in turn, constructs winners and losers. Considering that 'loser' has been one of the most-used words in Trump's vocabulary to insult and defame his opponents, he clearly cannot inhabit the 'loser' space. By constructing the election as a competition, rather than as a democratic process that captures the choice of the electorate, he trivializes the process of voting.

1. We *beat* them four years ago. We surprised them.
2. [...] you'll never *take back our country with weakness*. You have to show *strength*, and you have to be *strong*
3. *We fight like Hell* and if you don't fight like Hell, you're not going to have a country anymore
4. Our country has been *under siege* for a long time, far longer than this four-year period
5. And everybody had us down for *a victory*. It was going to be great. And now we're out here *fighting*.
6. I want to thank the more than 140 members of the House. Those are *warriors*.
7. Kelly Loeffler, David Perdue. They *fought* a good race.
8. Unbelievable, what we have to go through, what we have to go through and you have to get your people to *fight*. *If they don't fight*, we have to primary the hell out of the ones that don't fight.

FIGURE 3.2   The fight/battle metaphor (Trump's speech in Ellipse)

@**Sian-Anne** UK Patriot here! Supporting my American brothers and sisters as best I can! Deus Vult! [motto associated with the Crusades]
@**Donald J. Trump** @**KylieJaneKremer:** The calvary is coming, Mr. President! JANUARY 6th Washington, DC
@**Oaktree Lady** Ready for the resistance to the coup d'état?

FIGURE 3.3   The fight/battle metaphor (Parler)

FROM TWITTER TO CAPITOL HILL

War, fight and battle as metaphors are weaved through the speech and directly connect with the actual events at the Capitol on January 6th. The imperative grammatical mood further contributes to this direction. War calls were certainly answered by Telegram users as illustrated in the posts below, illustrating intertextuality: Trump speaks at the Ellipse, his supporters respond in social media.

5 One-Dimensional Discourse and the Language of Total Administration

Parler, Telegram, and Iron March are illustrative examples of 'echo chambers.' An 'echo chamber' is a digital environment where users encounter information or opinions and beliefs that reflect and reinforce their own. Cinelli et al. (2021) define echo chambers as environments where "opinion, political leaning, or belief of users about a topic gets reinforced due to repeated interactions with peers or sources having similar tendencies and attitudes" (p. 1). They note that the emergence and popularity of echo chambers might be explained by the tendency of people both to be selective on the material they are exposed, and to identify information "adhering to preexisting opinions" (p. 1).

Discourses in echo chambers have the property to carry similar types of information, as these digital places are insulated from rebuttal, differing opinions or any type of challenge to the 'truths' disseminated. Reading through the feed of Parler or messages in Telegram, it seems as if users talk to themselves and not to each other, in a monological direction of communication producing an almost hypnotic narrative fraught with repetition, and short, and empty slogans. On Iron March there is more interaction between users, as posts are longer, and users ask questions to each other, as opposed to simply use buttons to react but, still, users are exposed to limited content and are hostile to any kind of alternative narrative. According to the Anti-Defamation League, users in these extremist sites are by and large intolerant of anything "other than the most extreme ideology, and express frustration and outright disdain for the more mainstream white supremacist movement, specifically the alt right, which they refer to using derogatory terms such as soy goys [sic], a reference to 'de-masculinized' modern men" (Anti-Defamation League, 2019, para. 5).

Echo chamber discourse embodies one-dimensional discourse in an illustration of the 'flattening' of discourse: a 'rational,' linear language, permeated by magical, authoritarian and ritual elements, deprived of mediations, a functionalized language that has fully integrated conformism, unfreedom, and opposition; a language that "militates against a development of meaning" where concepts are absorbed by the word: "the thing is identified by its function"; and where "transgression of the discourse beyond the closed analytical structure is incorrect or propaganda" (Marcuse, 1964, p. 88). Hitler wrote in *Mein Kampf* that in order to achieve its purpose, propaganda must "be limited to a very few points and must harp on these slogans until the last member of the public understands what you want him to understand by your slogan. As soon as you sacrifice this slogan and try to be many-sided, the effect will piddle away." This sloganization of thought and language expressed through the one-dimensional authoritarian discourse creates polarization and fosters the spreading of misinformation: "Our attention span remains limited, and feed algorithms might limit our selection process by suggesting contents similar to the ones we are usually exposed to. Furthermore, users show a tendency to favor information adhering to their beliefs and join groups formed around a shared narrative, that is, echo chambers" (Cinelli et al., 2021, p. 1).

Digital propaganda has been a key element of Trumpism. One difference with Nazi propaganda is that users are now feeding the narrative to themselves through multiple channels and digital media, without the leader and his system having total control over the mechanism. Actually, digital propaganda is not misleading. According to historian, Aristotle Kallis (2005) propaganda is a form of truth "reshaped through the lens of regime intentions" (p. 63). Trump is, therefore, selling 'American truth' rather than, say, mainstream media and global conspiracy falsehood. Trumpism has not distorted truth. It has created truth: the Trumpist truth.

Finally, Marcuse's 'magical' aspect discussed in the previous chapter is also expressed in these texts in an apocalyptic end-of-the world discourse—the 'Cassandra strategy' (Wodak et al., 2009) with the vast circulation of conspiracy theories, as well as their linguistic realizations through predication strategies. For example, in Telegram enemies are called 'Spawns of Satan,' or 'Demonic and corrupt leaders' and on Iron March there is talk about the 'day of judgment,' the 'Apocrypha,' paganism and Nordic myths that have traditionally shaped Aryan ideology.

6   Discursive Themes/Argumentative Constructions

Thematically, one-dimensional discourse in the corpus under analysis is expressed through the following argumentation constructions:

a. *The linguistic construction of 'we' versus 'they' through the topos of danger and threat.* The analysis of 'we vs. they' in echo chambers reveals a brutal creation of in- and out- groups in a climate of absolute polarization. The deictics 'we' and 'they' further intensify the argument and function to position two

FROM TWITTER TO CAPITOL HILL

poles opposite to each other. The argumentative device of rapport between the actors producing a message (authors) and the receiver (reader) of the message is articulated through the 'we/us' vs 'them' dichotomy. Figure 3.5 illustrates this device at work on Parler and Telegram and, unsurprisingly, we find the same device throughout the Iron March platform (Figure 3.4). The construction of 'we vs. they' is articulated using different strategies. The enemy includes a wide range of groups, institutions, and people: the Left, liberals, cultural Marxists, the media, African Americans, Jews, Mexicans, non-Whites, globalists, internationalists and so forth.

> **Iron March**
>
> – This hypocrisy, idiocy, and downright PROOF of a culturally Marxist, corrupted system is and has served only to motivate me further and prove to those around me the far reaches and effects of cultural Marxism. The absurd pursuits of my absolute destruction by those identifying as the "tolerant defenders of social justice," their clear quoted motives to "bring me down completely," and their efforts to burn me have and will fail. I remain steadfast, resolute, and still peaceful.
> – What always gets me though is that the left always claims to be about tolerance, equality, freedom, and other false masks (Let's face it these words and concepts are lies to begin with) yet when it comes to us they persecute us to no end and they (ironically) uses some of the very same tactics that they claim and hate us for using.
> – its funny, a lot of furries are fanatic about the environment (the ones in my drawing class keep crying about the rainforest) yet they dye their hair with chemicals and wear plasticy jewelry. to them its just a way to look moral
> – yeah, ive sorta come to realize that I dont think liberals actually believe what they preach, they just preach it because it signals to everyone LOOK HOW GOOD A PERSON I AM! I CARE ABOUT THINGS! If society suddenly switched to become a fascist holy land I bet half these spineless cowards would start wearing black shirts

FIGURE 3.4   'Us' vs 'them' (Iron March)

In the case of Iron March 'we' gets more complicated and layered, as users are discussing identification with different white supremacist and extremist groups and almost compete about their extremism and what America really needs in terms of fascist leadership.

6.1   *'The Left Are the True Fascists' and the Dehistoricization of Discourse*
A common and fascinating pattern on Parler, Telegram and Iron March is the discursive and ideological device of flipping the argument. In this device, the

> @**Murdoc** If this group is infiltrated by liberal fascists I'm out. Infiltration is not free speech. Please thin them out constantly. Fascism is not free speech.
>
> @**EOTWAWKI68** REMEMBER we are the ones that have to remind the world of Democrat Crimes
>
> @**Sam** ... I like how we're called fascist. But yet, have to go through the hassle just to talk. Lol. I think people need to look into the definition better. Then the left wants to talk about oppression?... okay... lol
>
> @**RealPatriotPhil** Change your names hide your numbers !!! The commies will be hanging around
>
> @**Mike** The left are the real nazis, it's just them trying to smear real Americans

Parler Lifeboat

FIGURE 3.5   'Us' vs 'them' (Parler/Telegram)

left is demonized as intolerant, authoritarian, autocratic and, yes, fascist. 'Leftists' are attributed all the characteristics typically reserved for the far-right extremists. Groups are also juxtaposed in a radical reversal of historically shaped discourses around fascism, as is the case with characterizing the other side (the Democrats) as 'liberal fascists' and 'the real Nazis,' and the call for the suppression of the dictatorial government. We have here what Marcuse has called the typical unification of opposites in discourse.

This argument is epitomized in the phrase of a Telegram user: "the left are the true fascists." Except here, the user admits that fascism has a negative referent and thus, appropriates it as a negative characterization for their opponent. In constructing the 'left' as the enemy, users in these sites flip the argument made against them claiming that what is wrong with our society is the political correctness and lack of tolerance of the Left towards those they disagree with. Arguments and characterizations historically reserved for far-right extremists and Nazis are now reframed, recontextualized and directed against the Left. This device further fits in the distorted idea of the 'two extremes' that are equally responsible for atrocities and violence. The two poles in this ideological construction are the extreme Left and the extreme Right and they are compared on equal terms: if one extreme can be bad (Right) the other should also be bad (Left). This is an argument straight out of historical revisionism in Europe that emerged in Europe to absolve Nazis of their crimes by equating fascism with anti-fascist communism in the theory of the extremes. Similarly, far-right and neo-Nazi users project themselves as victims of left intolerance and hypocrisy. What is also interesting is the attempt to uncover the so-called hypocrisy of 'cultural Marxists,' the left and liberals by claiming that their anti-fascist politics are just a façade imposed by political correctness and that they would be the first ones to join the fascist bandwagon if there were a regime change. Rejection of political correctness in language is a characteristic of far-right populist discourse.

b. *The linguistic construction of war and battle through the topos of threat and responsibility* that illustrates aggressiveness, dehistoricization, and instrumentalism, manifests throughout the texts under analysis as the general feeling that emerges is a call to war. It is the responsibility of the real patriots, that is, Trump supporters and Trump voters to fight this war and he has kept them war-ready the last four years by waging battles over Twitter. The battle is also structured though dehistoricization, by presenting the election fraud as an unprecedented event in global history, ignoring for example the role of the United States in supporting real fraud in national elections in other countries (particularly in Latin America). In the Iron March data, the race war is imminent and has its own forum, as one IM user laments:

> Yeah I've overheard blacks in my area genuinely talking about starting an uprising and race war if trump wins.

This is a recurring theme and discussion that, in turn, brings calls for taking real world action to 'crush the system,' that users identify as local and federal government, law enforcement, and modern Western society. This system, they claim, is threatening white existence.

A few days before the Iron March platform went down, its creator Slavros addressed a long message to all users where he noted among other things that

FIGURE 3.6   Iron March race 'War Central' (Internet Archive, n.d.)

One can hardly deny that Iron March truly is the Forge of the 21st Century Fascist, as our track record of producing dedicated fanatics who go out and create movements of superior caliber, ones that stake their claim and force everyone to take notice, speaks for itself. (Slavros, September 13, 2017)

6.2 *Iron March Has a Love/Hate Relationship with Trump*

In Chapter 1, I explored Trumpism as a far-right authoritarian populist movement, and I have attempted to draw connections with fascism. Sorting through the Iron March data, I was able to gauge how digital neo-Nazis might feel about Trump. It turns out that this is a complicated love/hate relationship. In October 2018, Trump delivered a speech where he called himself a 'nationalist,' further energizing the country's radical right. Clearly, Trump's election in 2016 and other "significant events related to the far-right in the United States and around the world" were reflected in the IM posts and membership. Furthermore, Trump's presidential campaign and subsequent election win seem to have played a role in the platform's membership spike (Bray III & Singer-Emery, 2020; Calacci & Adjodah, 2020; Hayden, 2019a) as an opportunity for users to "connect, like, nationalism, patriotism, and fascism" (Bellingcat.com, 2019). Despite the original Atomwaffen members' disdain for some aspects of Trump, they found antiliberalism a shared interest. Overall, Trump rarely became a topic for vibrant discussions on IM. According to Singer-Emery & Bray III (2020), from June 16, 2015, when Trump announced he was running for president, until the site was discontinued in November 2017, only about 1,100 public posts mentioned him. These posts did not drive overall activity on the site, which had approximately 36,000 posts from American members alone in the same period (Singer-Emery & Bray III, 2020). The 1,100 posts discussing Trump can be divided into three categories: Approval/Positive, Critical Approval, and Rejection/Negative (as illustrated in Figure 3.7).

First, there are users who have rejoiced at Trump's election and the incidents at Trump rallies. Some dropped a few references on the site to 'God Emperor' Donald Trump during the spring and summer of 2016. These users think polarization is good and they enjoy what they call the Left's fear of having a White man in charge who is not afraid.

Then, there are users that do not think highly of Trump, but they consider him useful to advance the far-right extremist and fascist agenda. They claim to embrace him only because of the degree to which they think "he would aid in accelerating the planet to the point of collapse" (Hayden, 2019a). According to an IM post by a former chief of security at privately-operated Marion County Jail II who has since lost his job, "People should support Trump because of the (((interests))) that have aligned against him […] Trump is not literally Hitler or

Approval/Positive

- Congratulations for the election of Trump, Unfortunately the French are not the Americans. It's a jerk people, The army does not seem very motivated either.
- my family all wont talk to me because i voted trump lol
- yeah im hoping trump will spark something. hes getting alot more support from the media lately, ive noticed.
- I've been loving this election. It's polarizing everything. It's making clearly defined lines where moderates are getting push aside left and right. My only concern is Trump losing the nomination. I know he can beat Hilary, but that bird faced fuck Cruz has no chance in hell.
- If a nation has the Jews it deserves, then Medieval Europe must have been a righteous place, considering all the expulsions. It's certainly disgraceful of the U.S., but after every Trump rally-like event, more whites will be radicalised, so it all ultimately serves a higher purpose. To paraphrase someone on that thread, they're doing the heavy-lifting for you.
- It's funny how terrified they are at the very idea of having a white male president who isn't a weakling, you can really smell the fear in the cities
- Trump had his foot in the door with anti-globalism [...]; won, Alt-right has their foot in the door with anti-egalitarianism [...]; we are winning culturally, then once we get a ethno-nationalist state †in North America,† what do you think comes after that cycle of winning? FASCISM! or new systems like epistocracy!

Critical Approval

- Trump supporters which as you know have the right mind set, but far from the right path.
- Yeah, it'll take a little more to wake the American people up, but the Trump riots have at least got them thinking.
- I voted for Trump as a protest vote in California but it wasn't until after Trump won and I saw the direct contradictions rise up in the left that I entirely divorced it from having any sense of morality in my head.
- I'd rather not attack Trump, because I have been to his rallies and we can benefit from his most radical supporters, they are brownshirts that are just ignorant of National Socialism.
- Even though he has a Jewish daughter who ""converted"" along with countless other jewish politicians within the back scenes. I do give the man credit, but ultimately he is no friend of fascism when it comes to the policies and spirit of the nation.
- Jew York is the same and I don't see much change happening any time soon. Too many libtards and muds in my area, but as of late with the whole presidential shit going on there have been more rebel flags and Trump supporters which as you know have the right mind set, but far from the right path.

92 CHAPTER 3

- im hoping the riots at the recent trump rally will explode a little more, they were kinda weak from what i heard. I thought a race war was gonna start, oh well. someone tried to kill trump though, which is interesting. speaking of lifting i need to work out more for the race war. do you do any kind of training
- I just registered for voting last month. Quite easy nowadays. I'm not sure. Trump is good but i hate that he is our "best." Unfortunately any right wing politician doesn't care about our climate or earth.
- Whatever betrayal The Donald will commit is made worth it ten times over by the amount of liberal whining spewed in response to saying you like The Wall

Rejection/Negative
- Trump is the very thing that prevents some people from going full Fascist because they assume that Trump can be the easier solution.
- People have lost their faith in monarchs, but not their fear and awe of power. I heard someone say a good fascist state will eventually become a monarchy of sorts. What do you think? You're a bottomless pit of Trump puns- should have really joined his propaganda team!"
- so who are you going to vote for in the coming election i would vote for trump but he's too rich and doesn't believe in global warming maybe rand paul but definitely not clinton besides its not like there are any good fascist parties worth voting for down south
- He went back on all of his racism as soon as he got elected, like I called it from the beginning it was all rhetoric to win the vote of the poor and stupid Americans.†
- Also I think race war can actually happen, but it will happen in the non-white's terms. Like what happened to Haiti. Look at whats happening with Trump. A lot of fascists here will think it'll all blow over, but as the violence escalates the more I think Trump's presidency would destabilize the country.
- I know Trump is a cuck, I've stopped riding the /pol/ hype train and just became apathetic to it all.† What really rustles my jimmmies is how overly dramatic the lefties are about him. I'm actually pretty grateful for the left for fanning the fires of racism when Trump is trying to becoming milder. It's because of the left racial tensions are still there, they're are unwitting allies in that way.†

FIGURE 3.7   Iron March users' attitudes towards Trump

a fascist, but the enemy of my enemy is my friend. Trump rattles all the right cages" (Hays, 2020, para. 20).

Finally, there are those who find Trump too moderate, for their taste and an actual impediment to developing a fascist politics and reject him altogether. In the Rejection category we also find users who find him too rich or are disturbed by his son-in-law being Jewish and his daughter having converted to Judaism.

Throughout his presidential campaign and four years in office, Trump's rhetoric "helped fuse the various factions of the far right" (Miller, 2020, para. 16). The far-right gained in power and visibility because of the political cover provided by the White House. During his administration, Trump not only excused far-right violence, by deflecting blame, he actually provided a friendly environment. Trump's positive impact on the far-right was epitomized when lawyers for three Kansas militia members who plotted to bomb homes belonging to Somali immigrants tried to argue the offenders should receive lenient terms because they were inspired by the President's "rough-and-tumble verbal pummeling," which had "heightened the rhetorical stakes for people of all political persuasions" (Reuters Staff, 2018, para. 2). Similarly, in a manifesto published shortly before the far-right attack on mosques in Christchurch, New Zealand in March 2019, the assailant praised Trump "as a symbol of renewed white identity and common purpose" (Hayden, 2019b).

7 Conclusion

The exploration and critical analysis of the discursive manifestations of far-right authoritarian populism and Nazism on social media reveals disturbing patterns. In the obscurity and anonymity of social media and often in plain light, deeply dehumanizing ideologies are becoming normalized. The vehicle is usually a language of aggressiveness that annihilates and dehumanizes the other. Given that social media are originally conceived as entertainment tools, politics becomes performative and hollow; it becomes amusement where everything is permitted. As a result, it veils the historical and social weight and consequences of discursive and physical violence and aggression on real people. For example, a common pattern in most pictures and videos taken from inside the Capitol building during the insurrection is performativity. Rioters are brazen enough to either take selfies or pose for their picture to be taken. Subsequently, rioters are posting videos and photos of themselves essentially engaging in illegal acts on their social media accounts boasting about their acts.

There are two issues at play here: The first is the politics of the self and the fact that 'self' is always broadcasted and embodied in a text: a video, a photo, a short post, an emoticon, a meme. Self is always recorded in text; self is always textual in multimodality thanks to social media. The second aspect has to do with the entertainment character of social media that is now shifting to redefine how information and news are produced and disseminated. Social media as amusement outlets are explicit political tools. Cinelli et al. (2021) stress that

94   CHAPTER 3

feed algorithms mediate and influence the content promotion accounting for users' preferences and attitudes. Such a paradigm shift affected
the construction of social perceptions and the framing of narratives; it
may influence policy making, political communication, and the evolution of public debate, especially on polarizing topics. Indeed, users
online tend to prefer information adhering to their worldviews, ignore
dissenting information, and form polarized groups around shared narratives. Furthermore, when polarization is high, misinformation quickly
proliferates. (p. 5)

As I made the case in the previous chapter, in the context of the new digitally
mediated paradigm of communication, known as Social Media Communication (SMC) content or discourse analysis are not enough. We also need to consider "the impact of the new mediation paradigm" (KhosraviNik, 2018, p. 2) and
call for a "re-problematization of the wider interdisciplinary assumptions in
CDS, e.g., why and in what way digital utterances matter in local and macro
contexts" (KhosraviNik, 2018, p. 2). KhosraviNik accurately advocates for the
reintroduction of "questions of discursive power and how it may be earned,
accumulated and enforced across SMC spaces." He urges researchers to focus
on "how the participatory web may have changed the politics of discursive
dynamics, the quality of the very content and the overall structure of discursive
participation" (2018, p. 2). In some sense, the discourse in SMC does not simply
reflect power dynamics and control; it becomes itself an instrument of power
dynamics and control, and this is an aspect that needs to be further explored.

In closing this discussion, it is important to note that the texts under study
and the discourses produced demonstrate a disturbing yet opaque lack of historicity. Dehistoricization is manifested in the instrumentalism of the 'here
and now' the 'tyranny of the moment' that comes with social media immediacy and access. It is further expressed in the multiple historical distortions and
in the production of a new 'history' that embodies the rationality of the irrational; A new 'history' that is not grounded in the labor of historical research,
a history that further 'flattens' historical facts and their discourses. How can
unflattening work through history? Chapter 5 addresses this question in detail.

References

Allyn, B. (2021, March 19). *Why SkySilk came out of nowhere to save Parler after Capitol
riot.* NPR. https://www.npr.org/2021/03/19/978210584/why-skysilk-came-out-of-
nowhere-to-save-parler-after-capitol-riot

Althusser, L. (1971). *Ideology and ideological state apparatuses. Lenin and philosophy and other essays.* New Left Books.

Anti-Defamation League. (2019, January 15). *Fascist forge: A new forum for hate.* https://www.adl.org/blog/fascist-forge-a-new-forum-for-hate

Anti-Defamation League. (2020a). *Murder and extremism in the United States in 2019.* https://www.adl.org/murder-and-extremism-2019

Anti-Defamation League. (2020b, February). *White supremacists double down on propaganda in 2019.* https://www.adl.org/media/14038/download

Atlantic Council. (2021, January 7). *Fast thinking: How the Capitol riot was coordinated online.* https://www.atlanticcouncil.org/content-series/fastthinking/fast-thinking-how-the-capitol-riot-was-coordinated-online/

Blommaert, J. (2019). Political discourse in post-digital societies. *Trabalhos em Linguística Aplicada, 59*(1), 390–404.

Bond, S. (2020). *Conservatives flock to Mercer-funded Parler, claim censorship on Facebook and Twitter.* NPR. https://www.npr.org/2020/11/14/934833214/conservatives-flock-to-mercer-funded-parler-claim-censorship-on-facebook-and-twi

Boukala, S. (2021). We need to talk about the hegemony of the left. *Journal of Language and Politics, 20*(3), 361–382. https://www.jbe-platform.com/content/journals/10.1075/jlp.19053.bou

Bray III, R., & Singer-Emery, J. (2020, April 19). Lingua ferro iter: Insights gained through linguistic analysis of Iron March. *Small Wars Journal.* https://smallwarsjournal.com/jrnl/art/lingua-ferro-iter-insights-gained-through-linguistic-analysis-iron-march

Calacci, D., & Adjodah, D. (2020, July 17–20). *Far-right forum network and LDA analysis.* 6th International Conference on Computational Social Science, MIT Media Laboratory Boston, MA. https://www.media.mit.edu/projects/investigating-the-iron-march-forums-with-computational-tools-far-right-forum-network-and-lda-analysis/overview/

Catalano, T., & Waugh, L. (2020). *Critical discourse analysis, critical discourse studies and beyond.* Springer.

Cimpanu, C. (2019, November 7). *Mysterious hacker dumps database of infamous Iron March neo-Nazi forum.* ZD Net. https://www.zdnet.com/article/mysterious-hacker-dumps-database-of-infamous-Iron March-neo-nazi-forum/

Cinelli, M., Morales, D., Galeazzi, G., Quattrociocchi, A., & Starnini, M. (2021). The echo chamber effect on social media. *Proceedings of the National Academy of Sciences, 118*(9), 1–8.

Chilton, P. (2017). "The people" in populist discourse: Using neuro-cognitive linguistics to under-stand political meanings. *Journal of Language and Politics, 16,* 582–594.

Coaston, J. (2019, April 26). *Trump's new defense of his Charlottesville comments is incredibly false.* Vox. https://www.vox.com/2019/4/26/18517980/trump-unite-the-right-racism-defense-charlottesville

Collin, R. (2015). Introducing Jameson to critical discourse analysis. *Critical Discourse Studies, 13*(2), 158–173. https://doi.org/10.1080/17405904.2015.1042393

Cryst, E. (2021, January 28). Parler's first 13 million users. *Freeman Spogli Institute News.* https://fsi.stanford.edu/news/sio-parler-contours

Enli, G. (2017). Twitter as arena for the authentic outsider: Exploring the social media campaigns of Trump and Clinton in the 2016 presidential election. *European Journal of Communication, 32*(1), 50–61. https://doi.org/10.1177/0267323116682802

Enli, G., & Rosenberg, L. (2018). Trust in the age of social media: Populist politicians seem more authentic. *Social Media + Society, 4*(1), 1–18. https://doi.org/10.1177/2056305118764430

Fairclough, N. (1995). *Critical discourse analysis: The critical study of language.* Routledge.

Fairclough, N. (2003). *Analyzing discourse: Textual analysis for social research.* Routledge.

Fairclough, N., & Wodak, R. (1997). Critical discourse analysis. In T. van Dijk (Ed.), *Discourse as social interaction* (pp. 258–284). Sage.

Flowerdew, J., & Richardson, J. E. (2018). Introduction. In J. Flowerdew & J. E. Richardson (Eds.), *The Routledge handbook of critical discourse studies* (pp. 1–11). Routledge.

Fuchs, C. (2018). Authoritarian capitalism, authoritarian movements and authoritarian communication. *Media, Culture and Society, 40*(5), 779–791. https://doi.org/10.1177/0163443718772147

Gounari, P. (2018). Authoritarianism, discourse and social media: Trump as the 'American agitator.' In J. Morelock (Ed.), *Critical theory and authoritarian populism* (pp. 207–227). University of Westminster Press.

Gounari, P. (2021). One-dimensional social media: The discourse of authoritarianism and authoritarianism discourse. In J. Morelock (Ed.), *How to critique authoritarian populism* (pp. 431–454). Brill.

Hayden, M. E. (2019a, February 15). *Visions of chaos: Weighing the violent legacy of Iron March.* Southern Poverty Law Center.

Hayden, M. E. (2019b, March 15). *New Zealand terrorist manifesto influenced by far-right online ecosystem, hate watch finds.* Southern Poverty Law Center. https://www.splcenter.org/hatewatch/2019/03/15/new-zealand-terrorist-manifesto-influenced-far-right-online-ecosystem-hatewatch-finds

Hays, H. (2020, January 10). Ex- Marion County jail II officer loses job at Nevada facility after neo-Nazi posts found. *Indianapolis Star.* https://www.indystar.com/story/news/local/indianapolis/2020/01/10/travis-frey-suspended-iron-march-neo-nazi-posts/2837677001/

Heilweil, R., & Ghaffary, S. (2021, January 8). *How Trump's internet built and broadcast the Capitol insurrection.* Vox. https://www.vox.com/recode/22221285/trump-online-capitol-riot-far-right-parler-twitter-facebook

Internet Archive Wayback Machine. (n.d.). *Iron March.* https://web.archive.org/web/20170625223445/http:/ironmarch.org/index.php?/topic/7861-hello-all/

Kallis, A. (2000). *Propaganda and the second world war.* Palgrave Macmillan.

KhosraviNik, M. (2018). Social media techno-discursive design, affective communication and contemporary politics. *Fudan Journal of the Humanities and Social Sciences, 11,* 427–442. https://doi.org/10.1007/s40647-018-0226-y

KhosraviNik, M. (2020). Digital meaning-making across content and practice in social media critical discourse studies. *Critical Discourse Studies.* https://doi.org/10.1080/17405904.2020.1835683

Kress, G. (1996). Representational resources and the production of subjectivity: Questions for the theoretical development of critical discourse analysis. In R. Caldas-Coulthard & M. Coulthard (Eds.), *Texts and practices* (pp. 15–31). Routledge.

Kreis, R. (2017). The 'Tweet politics' of President Trump. *Journal of Language and Politics, 16*(4), 1–12. https://doi.org/10.1075/jlp.17032.kre

Krzyżanowski, M., & Tucker, J. (2018). Re/constructing politics through social & online media: Discourses, ideologies, and mediated political practices. *Journal of Language and Politics, 17*(2), 141–154. https://doi.org/10.1075/jlp.18007.krz

Krzyżanowski, M., & Wodak, R. (2009). *The politics of exclusion: Debating migration in Austria.* Transaction Publishers.

Lakoff, G. (2016). *Understanding Trump.* University of Chicago press books. https://press.uchicago.edu/books/excerpt/2016/lakoff_trump.html

Marcuse, H. (1964). *One-dimensional man.* Beacon Press.

Matze, J. (2020). A letter from Parler CEO John Matze. *Texas Border Business.* https://texasborderbusiness.com/a-letter-from-parler-ceo-john-matze/

Mazzoleni, G. (2017). Changes in contemporary communication ecosystems ask for a "new look" at the concept of mediatization. *Javnost – The Public, 24,* 136–145. https://www.tandfonline.com/doi/abs/10.1080/13183222.2017.1290743

McIntosh, J., & Mendoza-Denton, N. (2020). *Language in the Trump era: Scandals and emergencies.* Cambridge University Press.

Miller, C. (2020, June 23). *'There is no political solution: Accelerationism in the White Power movement.* Southern Poverty Law Center. https://www.splcenter.org/hatewatch/2020/06/23/there-no-political-solution-accelerationism-white-power-movement

Montgomery, M. (2017). Post-truth politics? Authenticity, populism and the electoral discourses of Donald Trump. *Journal of Language and Politics, 16*(4), 619–639. https://doi.org/10.1075/jlp.17023.mon

Ott, B. (2016). The age of Twitter: Donald J. Trump and the politics of debasement. *Critical Studies in Media Communication, 34*(1), 59–68.

Ott, B., & Dickinson, G. (2019). *The Twitter presidency.* Routledge.

Parler Inc. (2021). *Our company.* https://company.parler.com/

Program on Extremism. (2021). *"This is our House!" A preliminary assessment of the Capitol Hill Siege participants.* The George Washington University.

Reisigl, M., & Wodak, R. (2001). *Discourse and discrimination. Rhetorics of racism and antisemitism.* Routledge.

Reisigl, M., & Wodak, R. (2009). The discourse-historical approach. In R. Wodak & M. Meyer (Eds.), *Methods of critical discourse analysis* (pp. 87–121). Sage.

Reisigl, M., & Wodak, R. (2016). The Discourse-Historical Approach (DHA). In R. Wodak & M. Meyer (Eds.), *Methods of critical discourse studies* (pp. 23–61). Sage.

Reitman, J. (2018, May 2). *All-American Nazis: How a senseless double murder in Florida exposed the rise of an organized fascist youth movement in the United States.* Rolling Stone. https://www.rollingstone.com/politics/politics-news/all-american-nazis-628023/

Reuters Staff. (2018, October 30). Kansas militia men blame Trump rhetoric for mosque attack plan. *Reuters.* https://www.reuters.com/article/us-kansas-crime-somalia/kansas-militia-men-blame-trump-rhetoric-for-mosque-attack-plan-idUSKCN1N500O

Richardson, J. (2004). *(Mis)Representing Islam: The racism and rhetoric of British broadsheet papers.* John Benjamins Publishing Company.

Ross, A., & Caldwell, D. (2019). Going negative: An APPRAISAL analysis of the rhetoric of Donald Trump on Twitter. *Language & Communication, 70,* 13–27. https://doi.org/10.1016/j.langcom.2019.09.003

Schouten, F. (2017, March 7). Who are mega-donors Bob and Rebekah Mercer and why are they influential? *USA Today.* https://eu.usatoday.com/story/news/politics/2017/03/07/who-are-trump-donors-bob-and-rebekah-mercer/98812284/

Sclafani, J. (2017). *Talking Donald Trump: A sociolinguistic study of style, metadiscourse, and political identity.* Routledge.

Singer-Emery, J., & Bray III, R. (2020, February 27). The Iron March data dump provides a window into how white supremacists communicate and recruit. *Lawfare.* https://www.lawfareblog.com/iron-march-data-dump-provides-window-how-white-supremacists-communicate-and-recruit

SPLC. (2017). *Donning the mask: Presenting 'The face of 21st century fascism.'* https://www.splcenter.org/hatewatch/2017/06/20/donning-mask-presenting-face-21st-century-fascism

Transnational White terror: exposing Atomwaffen and the Iron March Networks. (2019, December 19). *Bellingcat.* https://www.bellingcat.com/news/2019/12/19/transnational-white-terror-exposing-atomwaffen-and-the-iron-march-networks/

Twitter Inc. (2021, January 8). *Permanent suspension of @realDonaldTrump.* https://blog.twitter.com/en_us/topics/company/2020/suspension.html

Ware, J. (2019). Siege: The Atomwaffen division and rising far-right terrorism in the United States. *ICCT Policy Brief,* 1–19.

Wignell, P., Tan, S., O'Halloran K., & Chai, K. (2020). The Twittering presidents: An analysis of tweets from @BarackObama and @realDonaldoTrump. *Journal of Language and Politics*, 20(2), 197–225 https://doi.org/10.1075/jlp.19046.wig

Winter, A. (2019). Online hate: From the far-right to the 'Alt-Right' and from the margins to the mainstream. In K. Lumsden, & E. Harmer (Eds.), *Online othering. Palgrave studies in cybercrime and cybersecurity* (pp. 39–63). Palgrave Macmillan.

Wodak, R. (2001). The discourse-historical approach. In R. Wodak & M. Meyer (Eds.), *Methods of critical discourse analysis*. (pp. 63–94). Sage.

Wodak, R., de Cillia, R., Reisigl, M., & Liebhart, K. (2009). *The discursive construction of national identity*. Edinburgh University Press

Wodak, R., KhosraviNik, M., & Mral, B. (Eds.). (2013). *Right-wing populism in Europe: Politics and discourse*. Bloomsbury.

Wodak, R, & Krzyżanowski, M. (2017). Right-wing populism in Europe and USA: Contesting politics and discourse beyond 'Orbanism' and 'Trumpism.' *Journal of Language and Politics, 16*(4), 471–484.

Wodak, R. & Meyer, M. (2009). Critical discourse analysis: History, agenda, theory and methodology. In R. Wodak & M. Meyer (Eds.), *Methods of critical discourse analysis* (pp. 1–33). Sage.

Wodak, R., & Pelinka, A. (Eds.). (2002a). *The Haider phenomenon*. Transaction Press.

Wodak, R., & Pelinka, A. (2002b). Introduction: From Waldheim to Haider. In R. Wodak & A. Pelinka (Eds.), *The Haider phenomenon* (pp. vii–xxvii). Transaction Press.

Wodak, R., & van Dijk, T. (2000). *Racism at the top: Parliamentary discourses on ethnic issues in six European states*. Drava Verlag.

Yurieff, K. (2020, December 10). *Conservatives flocked to Parler after the election. But its explosive growth is over*. CNN. https://www.cnn.com/2020/12/10/tech/parler-downloads/index.html

CHAPTER 4

Against Critical Pedagogy

For a Critical Pedagogy with a Radical Political Project

> Thought is subversive and revolutionary, destructive and terrible; thought is merciless to privilege, established institutions, and comfortable habits; thought is anarchic and lawless, indifferent to authority, careless to the well-tried wisdom of ages. Thought looks to the pit of hell and is not afraid. It sees man [sic], a feeble speck, surrounded by unfathomable depths of silence; yet bears itself proudly, as unmoved as if it were lord of the universe. Thought is great and swift and free, the light of the world, and the chief glory of man.
>
> BERTRAND RUSSEL (cited in Erich Fromm, 1981)

⁝

1   Introduction

Education is a battlefield, a contested terrain where different forces are seeking to establish hegemony over its vision, content, role, and goals. The neoliberal, neoconservative, capitalist restructuring of the last 40 years has prompted important shifts, as part of a broader assault on the public good. The neoliberal attack on public education has thrived in the now-unbroken alignment of capital's needs with educational goals, the implementation of protracted austerity, the use of schools as a mechanism for social control, the intensification of their sorting function, and their commercialization and privatization coupled with centralization of power. High-stakes, standardized testing and tracking for students, punitive evaluation for teachers, expansion of student choice with vouchers and charter schools, pressuring schools into accepting funding from large foundations in exchange for 'reforms' (Russom, 2012) are only some of the items on the neoliberal educational agenda. In this agenda, education is instrumentalized and operationalized in order to serve a capitalist system that depends on the production and exploitation of disposable, obeying bodies and minds, disposable labor, disposable knowledge and ideas, and disposable politics.

© KONINKLIJKE BRILL NV, LEIDEN, 2022 | DOI: 10.1163/9789004510470_005

Schools are a primary site for the production of human disposability. Ideologies currently shaping the very structure of public education and school curricula coerce public schooling to operate as a funnel for students getting into different categories: dropouts, community college and Ivy League, U.S. Army, prison, labor and so forth. Education takes shape in capitalism based on the type of laborers needed by the capital at any given historical moment; laborers who adapt to the changing labor conditions, often in need of constant training, retraining and specialization that, in turn, legitimizes different training sites, including Institutions of Higher Education. Degrees earned in these institutions are, unfortunately, disconnected from the right to work. Capitalism addresses this phenomenon with the creation of 'gig economy' (flexible/disposable, free-lance, temporary jobs) and what the late David Graeber (2013) has called *bullshit jobs*,

> the ballooning of the administrative sector, up to and including the creation of whole new industries like financial services or telemarketing, or the unprecedented expansion of sectors like corporate law, academic and health administration, human resources, and public relations. And these numbers do not even reflect on all those people whose job is to provide administrative, technical, or security support for these industries, or for that matter the whole host of ancillary industries (dog-washers, all-night pizza delivery) that only exist because everyone else is spending so much of their time working in all the other ones. (para. 4)

Schooling, as a ritualistic, authoritarian site, is central to the creation of a new type of human being: the 'neoliberal subject.' As Richard Seymour (2014) notes, neoliberals are aware that human beings are not naturally predisposed to embrace the market and other neoliberal myths. He claims that "people must be compelled to embrace their 'entrepreneurial' selves, to treat every aspect of their lives as a self-maximizing quest, and to embrace the calculus of risks and rewards in the market, including the inequalities that come with it, rather than seeking to control it" (p. 9). The neoliberal subject is schooled and socialized to perceive knowledge as a commodity, as something external to them, and to value only 'useful' knowledge; it has a limited horizon of understandings that are usually dehistoricized and decontextualized.

The fact that the neoliberal program has survived for as long as it has (since the 1980s) is due, in part, to the creation and shaping of this new human type (with their matching consciousness) through schooling, who, as an adult, becomes part of a competitive, highly hierarchical society that values the survival of the fittest, marginalizes the weak, and has low tolerance for the poor and the oppressed, often attributing their 'condition' to issues of character or lack of adequate individual effort, as opposed to systemic problems and socio-political structures. This notion further aligns with the typical liberal logic of meritocracy that alleges that "we are all individuals... structural and institutional inequalities don't really exist—because in our society, if you just work hard enough as an individual, you will be successful in school and elsewhere" (Au, 2018, p. 58). We, then, have the following paradox, noted by Au:

> On the one hand, the school must assist in accumulation by producing both agents for a hierarchical labor market and the cultural capital of technical/administrative knowledge. On the other hand, our educational institutions must legitimate ideologies of equality and class mobility, and make themselves be seen as positively by as many classes and class segments as possible [...] What we see is the school attempting to resolve what may be the inherently contradictory roles it must play. (p. 81)

In that sense, schools do more than simply reproducing the social order. They must legitimize their very existence and ideological construction as a leveling, equalizing apparatus, where students supposedly have equal choices and options. However, as Aronowitz (2008) stresses "'Equality of opportunity' for class mobility is the system's tacit recognition that inequality is normative" (p. 19).

Capitalism's idea of education has always been a dystopian one. However, the last twenty years, we have clearly moved even further into a market-driven, theocratic, ethnocentric, militarized, authoritarian, punitive model that holds firm capitalist and neoconservative values, where middle and, particularly, working class students and students of color are taught obedience, compliance, and conformity and remain relegated to the margins (Fine & Weis, 2003). I am talking about an education where both students and educators have been slowly robbed of autonomy and control over their own bodies and minds; an education where, as consumers of information (not knowledge) they can buy their living (or rather, survival) by selling their skills and/or their bodies as labor. Increasingly, schools in poor neighborhoods and neighborhoods of color train their students in discipline, obedience, and subordination, using a pre-packaged commercial curriculum that kills imagination, creativity and intellectual curiosity. Along these lines, we are witnessing what De Lissovoy (2008) calls an "intensifying authoritarianism of educational culture" (p. 4). Authoritarianism, by definition, entails obedience to authority that limits individual and collective freedoms; oppressive control of people, and the centralization of an unregulated use of power to maintain a repressive social order.

AGAINST CRITICAL PEDAGOGY 103

Authoritarianism in education functions on different planes. From the organization and standardization of curricula and the control of forms and content of knowledge to the physical control and discipline, the ritualistic organization of school routines and the regulation of student bodies, authoritarianism registers overtly and covertly as a main driving force. This authoritarian control instills fear in students' consciousness making safety a central matter.

Often, in the name of safety and discipline, schools literally function like prisons or military camps and their chief function becomes repression (Aronowitz, 2012, as cited in Giroux, 2013, p. 459). Capitalism and authoritarianism mix well in the educational battlefield to socialize students, who are told they can conquer the world if they work hard enough, but who aren't truly 'free to choose' as the famous neoliberal dogma posits. They are, rather, conditioned to grasp reality in predetermined ways, where knowledge is hollow, enslaved in a pragmatic, utilitarian notion, and their bodies conditioned to experience the world through restrictions, prohibitions, and containment. Aronowitz (2008) challenges schooling that is all about control: "Institutions want you to demonstrate your subordination by taking more and more courses and acquiring more credentials [...] Students know that getting credentials is simply an endurance test, and most have no expectation of receiving a critical education" (p. 13). In our profoundly anti-intellectual culture, there is no place where students from oppressed and marginalized groups, working-class students and students of color can find a liberatory education. This way, schools 'process' both people and knowledge (Apple & Weis, 1983).

A different way of understanding the world in general, and in education in particular, comes from what has been known as Critical Pedagogy. Critical Pedagogy, since its inception, has been asking different kinds of questions, inspired by a radically different vision and goal for education and society. In this chapter, I provide an overview of the historical roots and theoretical foundations of Critical Pedagogy, and I present, analyze, and contextualize the core questions it posits in relation to our current far-right, authoritarian historical moment. Finally, I suggest some new directions for future theory and research, particularly in the context of critical public pedagogy.

2   Historical Roots and Main Concepts of Critical Pedagogy: Making the Pedagogical Political

Tracing the map and defining the borders of what has come to be known as Critical Pedagogy is a particularly complex task, and it continues to be "something of a sliding signifier" (Apple & Au, 2009, p. 63). Critical Pedagogy as a distinct theoretical tradition of intellectual production and educational practice emerged in North America in the late 1970s and early 1980s. It was Henry Giroux who, inspired by the work of Brazilian educator Paulo Freire, along with that of American progressive education philosopher John Dewey, and others in the progressive education tradition, first linked education with concepts from Critical Theory coming out of the Frankfurt School for Social Research. He termed this theoretical 'encounter' the "critical foundation for a theory of radical pedagogy" in 1983, and, in his seminal *Theory and Resistance in Education* he set the foundations of Critical Pedagogy through a proposal for a radical democracy that involved the effort to expand the possibility for social justice, freedom, and egalitarian social relations in the educational, economic, political, and cultural domains that locate men, women and children in everyday life. In this framework, he saw the critique of positivism in schools (manifested through achievement, excellence, standards, high stakes tests, the standardized curriculum, measurability, and predictability) as central in the educational arena and posited the need for developing historical consciousness where dialectical thought would replace positivist forms of social inquiry. He presented a theory with a radical view of knowledge that would put schools and pedagogy on the sociohistorical map while at the same time infusing other disciplines with the pedagogical, making the pedagogical political and the political pedagogical.

Between 1980 and 1990, Critical Pedagogy as a new theoretical direction in educational studies in North America witnessed important intellectual output that established the field, as illustrated in the work of Henry Giroux, Stanley Aronowitz, Michael Apple, bell hooks, Peter McLaren, Maxine Greene and Michelle Fine, Lois Weis, and, later, Antonia Darder, Joe Kincheloe, and Roger Simon, among others.

The timing of this intellectual development is by no means coincidental, and it should be understood against a historical and sociopolitical context unfolding in the post-war period (Gounari & Grollios, 2010). The time between 1945 and 1960 in the United States was marked by what appeared as great economic prosperity and affluence. This period saw population growth coupled with an increase in productivity, the use of technological advances in production and the doubling of the Gross Domestic Product. However, this prosperity was not shared by all Americans, making instead economic inequalities even more pronounced. African Americans, Latinos, women, and other minoritized groups continued to be largely excluded from the 'American Dream,' as was the case before the war. On the political plane, the Cold War and the competition of the United States with the Soviet Union generated the notorious 'red scare' and brought anti-communist sentiments to new heights with political persecutions, union busting, censorship, and so forth.

The second phase of the post-war period extending from 1960 to 1980 brought a lot of movement, or rather, many movements. What was perceived until then as a sense of internal stability in the nation was severely challenged. The 60s were a tumultuous time for the United States marked by important historical events but it was, above all, the decade of movements: the Civil Rights movement, the anti-war protests, the student movement, as well as the women's rights and gay rights movements, and the environmental movement. Widespread mobilizations and protests during that time brought to the surface the systemic inequalities hidden under the glossy image of prosperity of the previous years. The nation was then shaken by the assassinations of Martin Luther King and John F. Kennedy. Programs such as Lyndon Johnson's 'Great Society' and the 'War on Poverty,' as well as granting some rights to African Americans, did not curb the dynamic of the movements. It led to the 'long hot summer of 1967' that saw 159 'race riots' erupting across the country. Violent protests took place across America in Los Angeles, Chicago, Cleveland, and Detroit, among other cities. The anti-war movement, resistance to the draft and massive demonstrations inside and outside the universities illustrated the heightened degree of dissatisfaction of the population. On August 26th, 1970, the women's rights movement, active since the early 60s, organized their first successful national women's strike with a massive march down New York's Fifth Avenue. The Women's Strike for Equality March came with demands that, up to that time, were considered taboo for the American society: repeal of anti-abortion laws, equal opportunity in jobs and education and establishment of child-care centers. Unfortunately, partial victories during this vibrant activist time did not eradicate sexism, much in the same way that the gains of the Civil Rights movement did not eradicate racism.

The social unrest and turmoil culminated in the tragic events in Kent State Ohio on May 4th, 1970, where police shot and killed four students while another nine were wounded during a protest against the Vietnam War. American troops started withdrawing from Vietnam in 1973. By the time of their full withdrawal, thousands of American soldiers had been killed or wounded. The United States and coalition forces were defeated but, in the meantime, they had committed untold atrocities against the population, poisoning the crop and forests in Vietnam, Cambodia and Laos, an area equal to the State of Massachusetts; they had dropped 7.5 million tons of bombs resulting in thousands of civilian deaths and destruction (Gounari & Grollios, 2010).

In the mid and late 70s, the U.S. economy was still in recession, unemployment was on the rise, and stagflation (high inflation and slow economic growth) was the central issue of the economy. The Watergate scandal eventually brought Jimmy Carter to power, and, despite the initial relief, he was not able to handle the economic crisis that ultimately cost him his re-election.

The 1980s brought to power Ronald Reagan, signaling the beginning of neoliberalism in the United States. Reagan was sworn in promising a 'revolution of ideas' that would set the capitalist spirit free from the tyranny of federal bureaucracy and government regulations. His famous Reaganomics consisted of tax cuts, government deregulation, and a model of market freedom that reflects the interests of private property owners, businessmen, multinational corporations, and financial capital. Reagan would reestablish the old morals that were severely challenged during the 60s and 70s, stopping abortions, bringing back religious values to schools, fighting crime and student movements in the universities. Reagan opposed an expanded role for the federal government in education, going as far as suggesting that the U.S. Department of Education should be abolished. He would reinstate the 'pride' of the nation, that would, in turn, regain international respect with the increase of military spending and a tour de force against the Soviet Union. Appealing mostly to the middle class and gaining the support of evangelical Christians whose influence was growing, Reagan won the election by a landslide. Reagan's victory was also due to the failure of American liberalism and its political representative, the Democratic Party, to absorb the shocks and tribulations of the 60s. At the same time, a coordinated effort of ideological disorientation was under way by Republicans to establish mechanisms of ideological hegemony known as neoconservatism: Think Tanks, publishing houses, and radio and TV stations (Gounari & Grollios, 2010). Proponents of neoconservatism held an aversion to communism and left-wing radical politics, as well as to the culture of the 1960s movements and their disdain for authority and tradition.

From the 1990s on, a violent neoliberal and neoconservative restructuring of education took place to meet the needs of capital. This restructuring has been implemented by Democrat and Republican administrations alike, as amply demonstrated in the political agendas for education between 2001 and 2016. George W. Bush's 2001 *No Child Left Behind*, Clinton's *Goals 2000*, and Obama's *Race to the Top* and *Every Student Succeeds* followed in the same standards-based accountability, educational entrepreneurship, exhaustive student, teacher, and school evaluations, and school choice with the unwavering support for charter schools, largely refunneling funding away from public schools and into private hands.

Against the historical background presented, the emergence of Critical Pedagogy in the late 1970s and early 1980s was grounded in the concerns and issues of that time. As a complex, multilayered intellectual and educational project, it brought together several different theoretical traditions around a specific political and pedagogical project. At the core of the theory lies the premise that educational issues are necessarily political. Critical Pedagogy questions the purported political neutrality of educational institutions that, supposedly, makes them unbiased sites where students simply acquire knowledge and skills. Further, it challenges prevailing notions that schools are level playing fields and that education functions as the great equalizer, pointing to widespread inequalities and injustices that are produced and reproduced through schooling (Apple, 2004, 2012; Au, 2019; Fine & Weis, 2003; Knopp, 2012; Shor & Freire, 1987).

Critical Pedagogy has its roots in the progressive educational movements and theorists seeking to connect education with social transformation. Its precursors were progressive education theorists like John Dewey and the social reconstructionists Theodore Brameld, George Counts, and Harold Rugg in the 1930s (Grollios, 2011; Kliebard, 1995, 2002); also Myles Horton and Herbert Kohl in the 1960s. Most importantly, Critical Pedagogy was inspired by and grounded in Paulo Freire's seminal radical work, particularly his iconic *Pedagogy of the Oppressed* (1970, 2005), and his notions of the historicity of knowledge, pedagogy as revolutionary praxis versus a banking model of education, the development of critical consciousness (*conscientização*), problem-posing education, and the view of students as historical subjects of the educational process. It is also important to note some political roots, such as the "efforts by some subaltern groups to challenge dominance in education" (Apple & Au, 2009, p. 995) that included African American and Afro-Caribbean communities and their struggle over curricula for Blacks, the Harlem Committee for Better Schools in NYC in the 40s, critical feminist critiques of education, and Socialist Sunday Schools (Apple & Au, 2009).

Critical Pedagogy's intellectual history is far-reaching and diverse. It owes its 'critical' name to Critical Theory produced in the Frankfurt School of Social Theory of the late 1950s, 60s, and 70s in Germany (Fromm, 1973, 1976; Horkheimer & Adorno, 1947; Marcuse, 1964). Critical Theory was juxtaposed to 'traditional theory' that sought to address social issues following the lead of the natural sciences; traditional theory embraced positivism and provided a neutral account for social phenomena with the goal of making society more productive. Critical Theory, on the contrary, was motivated

> by the effort [...] to transcend the tension and to abolish the opposition between the individual's purposefulness, spontaneity, and rationality, and those work-process relationships on which society is built. Critical thought has a concept of man as in conflict with himself until this opposition is removed. If activity governed by reason is proper to man, then existent social practice, which forms the individual's life down to its least details, is inhuman, and this inhumanity affects everything that goes on in the society. (Horkheimer, 1982, p. 210)

108   CHAPTER 4

Other intellectual traditions integrated in early Critical Pedagogy literature include Marxist and neo-Marxist theory, Antonio Gramsci's political writings (his notions of *hegemony* and *common sense*) and the work of Louis Althusser (his notion of *relative autonomy* and the role of schools as a dominant *Ideological State Apparatus*).

Critical Pedagogy further built on the Sociology of Education of the late 1970s and 1980s, as it critically capitalized on theories of social and cultural reproduction (Bowles & Gintis, 1976; Bourdieu & Passeron, 1977). In a social reproduction theoretical framework, schools use their material and ideological resources to reproduce the social relations and attitudes needed to sustain the social divisions of labor necessary for the existing relations of production. Bowles and Gintis (1976) posited that schools serve two functions: first, they reproduce the labor power, and second, they reproduce those forms of consciousness, dispositions, and values necessary for the maintenance of the existing social order. According to Bowles and Gintis's *correspondence principle*, hierarchically structured patterns of values, norms, and skills that characterize the workforce are mirrored in the social dynamics of everyday classroom life. Early Critical Pedagogy theorists challenged this correspondence principle, arguing that it leads to what they saw as a one-sided economistic and deterministic approach in education. They proposed, instead, that school knowledge is a product of conflicts and negotiations between different social groups inside and outside education. These conflicts do not determine mechanistically but rather condition or limit social actors (students, teachers, and other stakeholders). Wayne Au rebukes Left critiques of Bowles and Gintis' correspondence principle stressing that they never stripped teachers or students from their power. While critics have discussed agency and consciousness as missing from Bowles and Gintis' work, Au (2018) raises, instead, a different kind of critique that speaks to their "lack of a developed analysis of the interplay of race and educational inequality within the context of capitalist schooling" and their use of IQ test scores (p. 68).

In contrast to social reproduction, in cultural reproduction theories, also part of the theoretical grounding of Critical Pedagogy, schools are seen as relatively autonomous institutions only indirectly influenced by more powerful economic and political institutions. Cultural reproduction theories are largely based on the work of French sociologists Pierre Bourdieu and Claude Passeron, who analyzed the reproduction of dominant cultural norms, values, cultural capital, and discourses through the schooling process (Bourdieu & Passeron, 1977). A sociology of curriculum linked culture, class, and domination with schooling and knowledge. Bourdieu considered traits of individuals' everyday way of life to make up what he termed *cultural capital* (Bourdieu, 1986).

AGAINST CRITICAL PEDAGOGY

Cultural capital results from a person's long-lasting engagement in and socialization with family, culture, education, as well as neighborhoods, peers, and so forth. The school affirms, rewards, and legitimizes the cultural capital that, by and large, resonates with dominant values and is further exhibited and transmitted in school. Along these lines, when the school devalues the cultural capital of disadvantaged and oppressed students by promoting and rewarding a White, middle-class cultural norm, it reproduces unequal relations in the form of educational inequalities. Cultural reproduction theories had an important impact on Critical Pedagogy in that they highlighted the role of culture, language, and discourses in the schooling process.

By identifying the limitations of reproduction theories, and capitalizing on theoretical constructs from Marxist and neo-Marxist theory and progressive education, early Critical Pedagogy theorists in North America set the ground for important discussions around what counts as knowledge and its social construction (Apple, 1993, 2004; Aronowitz, 2008; Aronowitz & Giroux, 1985; Giroux, 2011); the role of culture as a lived experience and a main pedagogical force (Giroux, 1997, 2000a, 2000b, 2013); teacher autonomy and student agency (Giroux, 1983a, 1983b; McLaren, 1993, 1998); student resistance (Apple, 2004; Aronowitz & Giroux, 1985); school ideologies (Apple, 1993, 2004, 2012; Giroux, 1983a, 1983b); the hidden curriculum (Apple, 2004); and control exercised through forms of meaning (Apple, 2004; Giroux, 1983a, 1983b). Other directions in this theoretical tradition brought richness and complexity to the discussion, namely racial politics, and feminist thought (hooks, 1994), liberatory meaning making through education (Greene, 1988); and racism, political economy, and social justice (Darder, 1991).

3 Critical Pedagogy: Where Are We Today?

Over 40 years after the first works in Critical Pedagogy saw the light, educators and scholars in the field are still struggling with many similar issues as they were in the 80s. While the theoretical discussion is now richer and more nuanced, the conditions on the school ground have, in fact, been deteriorating for teachers, students and their communities. Schools are not 'better' than they were in the 80s. This speaks to the pervasiveness of capitalist ideologies and politics, the struggle ahead for progressive educators, as well as to the possible limitations of Critical Pedagogy as we know it, in addressing some of the pressing educational problems of our times. Critiquing and identifying limitations presents an opportunity for new pathways for research, intellectual production, and school-based practices. Critique articulated here "should not be considered as part of a methodology of disposal" that is "a field procedure for the displacement of theories of others" (Bernstein, 1990, p. 145) but rather as a reflective space for development, moving forward and constructing better theories.

Critical Pedagogy during the last 40 years has been used to describe a multitude of concepts, currents, orientations, and practices in the field of education. In a massive body of work spanning since the mid-80s that self-identifies as Critical Pedagogy, there is a variety of directions, definitions, theoretical foundations, research goals, and social visions that are far beyond the scope of this chapter. As the field of Critical Pedagogy is constantly expanding with new work, it is also being redefined, challenged, deconstructed, and reconstructed, distorted, and misinterpreted. Given its disciplinary liquidity and renewed popularity, particularly during the four years of the Trump administration, it is not surprising that Critical Pedagogy is a much contested and, at the same time, appealing concept in that it tends to be appropriated by conservative and 'progressive' scholars alike, albeit for the wrong reasons. While disciplinary liquidity may lend Critical Pedagogy the richness and theoretical nuance often needed, at the same time, it blurs its boundaries and assimilates a whole host of work that lacks theoretical grounding, radicalism, and political and ideological clarity. At this juncture, it is clear that Critical Pedagogy has not settled its accounts with other theories claiming to be progressive, or with scholars claiming to be progressive. Superficial progressivism has often worked to obscure both the ideological lines and the political project at hand with works that claim to be progressive but have no roots in the theory itself. This has created a degree of theoretical murkiness that has gotten away wrapped in safe radicalism. Pseudo-radicalism and conservative co-opting of radical theories resonate with Giroux's (2000b) discussion on Harold Entwistle and E.D. Hirsh's appropriation of the ideas of Marxist philosopher Antonio Gramsci in their work, respectively. Giroux, following Gramsci, cautions critical intellectuals to use "their education in order to both know more than their enemies, and to make such knowledge consequential by bringing it to bear in all those sites of everyday life where the struggle for and against the powerful was being waged" (Giroux, 2000b, p. 130). He further encourages progressive educators to develop a language of critique and possibility as necessary for articulating a truly radical project. Unfortunately, scholars writing in Critical Pedagogy often do not follow Giroux's admonition. Work in Critical Pedagogy is at times superficial, pretentious, unnecessarily polemic, theoretically thin, and often used as the signifier for radical work when the signified is liberalism or progressivism at best.

The intellectual production in the broadly defined Critical Pedagogy field in the United States, while often progressive or, at least, well-intentioned, has at times shied away from becoming truly radical and remained at the level of reformist proposals. By radical, here, I mean the literal meaning of the word: a project that starts at the roots of schooling, a project that is grounded in real educational sites; and by extension, a project outside the existing sociopolitical imaginary, imagining the possibilities off the borders of liberal democracy. A kind of humanist radicalism that "goes to the roots and thus to the causes," that seeks to liberate people from the chains of illusions (Fromm, 1973, p. 485).

There has been a reluctance on the part of many prominent theorists to truly articulate a political and pedagogical project outside 'progressive' politics or 'social democracy' that, unfortunately, seems to underestimate the force of capitalism and neoconservative ideologies and is, instead, treating it with some revolutionary romanticism, if not naiveté. At the same time, self-proclaimed critical pedagogues, including those who have done important work in the field, have every so often fallen in the neoliberal trap of academic stardom, opportunism, and the very division of labor they are critiquing, becoming largely disconnected from the communities they proclaim to advocate for. A politics of personal branding and celebrity has won over socially committed scholarship, aiming to bring some change in the world. Michèle Foster is right on target when she writes, paraphrasing Gramsci (2005), that "for too many academics being an intellectual consists merely of eloquent discourse about equity, rights, and social justice, a fleeting appeal to feelings, passions, and intellect, rather than active participation in practical day-to-day life struggles against inequality and oppression" (p. 175). Foster claims that academics rarely connect their theory with their own practice:

> For although much of scholarship academics have undertaken in education over the past thirty years has promoted a sense of social justice as well as an activist narrative, this scholarship merely pays lip service to these ideals. The result is that while academics easily problematize and critique the practices and institutions of others, they do not act in ways that are compatible with their critique nor do they engage in day-to-day actions within their own oppressive sites. Not only does this situation illuminate the elitist nature of the academy, it erodes academia's already waning credibility. (Foster, 2005, p. 175)

A second problem in the existing work has been the appeal on Critical Pedagogy to address or speak to every possible issue connected with education, to the degree that in some versions, it has become trivialized and disconnected from its theoretical and political roots. The typical question for panelists on Critical Pedagogy is "What does Critical Pedagogy say about [*fill in here anything you may imagine*]?" Critical Pedagogy has a theoretical (political and pedagogical) agenda, and this agenda cannot be stretched in every possible direction to provide answers for all educational and sociopolitical problems and ills of the capitalist society. Critical Pedagogy is not and should not be used as an umbrella term and theory for everything progressive and educational under the sun.

Third, Critical Pedagogy has yet to seriously make race and racism central in the analyses and engage scholars of color. This critique has been articulated by a host of scholars in the Critical Race Theory tradition who have forcefully argued against 'race neutral' and 'color blind' approaches to education (Allen, 2005; Leonardo, 2002; Lynn, 2004; Parker & Stovall, 2004). Some of the question raised include for example, "how do domination and hegemony work in a system of global white supremacy? What are the racialized barriers to solidarity both within and between racial groups? How can critical education act as a form of empowerment within and against a white supremacist context?" (Allen, 2005, p. 54). Allen, building on Ladson-Billings, points out that Critical Pedagogy "has had a difficult time gaining acceptance among people of color on the U.S. educational left, who are more likely to be concerned about white power and privilege and suspicious of critical theory" (Allen, 2005, p. 54). Ladson-Billings (1997) goes on to claim that critical pedagogy has failed to address adequately the question of race and that scholars of color have been challenging the assumption that critical theory/pedagogy has universal applicability. While Critical Pedagogy has peripherally addressed race, race and Whiteness have yet to acquire a central role in the analyses, particularly as systemic racism persists in violent and pervasive ways in the United States. This may be, in part, because White male scholars have largely dominated the field, especially in the original formulation of the theory, potentially alienating "those who do not have the privilege to ignore white supremacy—no matter what economic form it takes" (Allen, 2005, p. 54). A similar critique is coming from Apple (2012) who notes that capitalism is not the root of all contemporary issues, even though it is "implicated in so many of the crucial inequalities we face and certainly makes them even more difficult to overcome" stressing that "among the roots of capital accumulation during the growth of capitalism as a global economic system was the enslavement and trade in black persons" (p. 152). While I do not fully agree with Apple's perspective about capitalism here, I want to resonate with the need for more nuanced discussions that address systemic institutional racism on the two axes that Keeanga Yamahtta-Taylor (2016) has suggested: first, "a full accounting of the myriad ways that racial discrimination factors in and shapes the daily lives of African Americans, in particular working-class and poor African Americans" as a way to "fundamentally undermine America's continual efforts to project itself as the moral leader of the world" (p. 46). And second, "a massive redistribution of wealth and resources to undo the continuing damage" (Yamahtta-Taylor, 2016, p. 46). By

AGAINST CRITICAL PEDAGOGY

making race central here I do not mean simply discussing the oppressive and discriminatory experiences of students and educators of color in the nation's schools. I rather argue for nuanced theoretical analyses that attempt to explain why "African-American students, regardless of their economic standing and/or gender, suffer the pernicious effects of a racist society. [...] issues of class and gender represent 'additive' means of oppression for African Americans. The growing African-American middle class is still subject to, and likely to encounter, racism" (Ladson-Billings, 1997, p. 131).

All things considered, the core issues on the critical education agenda remain intensified: What are the role, vision, mission and goals of education in the context of capitalism? How does the political nature of schooling define educational theory and practice? How do schools work to produce and reproduce racial, social, gender and other inequalities? What new kinds of knowledges are legitimized and reproduced through school curricula? What role can Critical Pedagogy praxis (theory and practices) play in the current explosive sociopolitical landscape?

The historical period we traverse brings to the fore new, additional questions: With the rise of the far right and the increasing authoritarianism worldwide, what is the role of schools in this context? What are the connections between school curricula and the increasing popularity of fake news and of right-wing conspiracy theories, such as the extravagant QAnon claims? What are different sites of public pedagogy and what are the kinds of knowledge they produce? How are social media producing new kinds of 'legitimate' knowledge that rival 'official' school knowledge? In what ways is EdTech redefining the field of education through new forms of control and content creation? Where might the Critical Pedagogy project have missed the point until today and how can it be reoriented? How do we as scholars, educators, activists define the struggle ahead of us, and through what means can we achieve some gains? What is the role of educator unions? How can Critical Pedagogy inspire and capitalize on educational and broader movements and, in turn, generate research and knowledge on these movements? How have progressive politics been co-opted by conservatives to support the very system we are supposed to fight? Thinking through these questions, I would like to suggest a few paths for future research.

4 Moving Forward

4.1 Neoliberalism in Education and New Disruptive Models as 'Opportunity'

Neoliberalism as an ideology, an economic doctrine and a social practice has demonstrated remarkable resilience and superior survival power. Its ability to rebrand and adapt itself over and over, expanding into yet unexplored public spaces to identify new markets has also been possible through the production of a dominant discourse that softens the rough edges of its violent human consequences. Take for example the authoritarian right-wing populist neoliberalism, also known as Trumpism of 2016–2020, that built on white nationalism to promote the same old capitalist agenda; or the COVID-ridden neoliberal political plan of the year 2020 that capitalized on illness and death to increase the wealth of U.S. billionaires by half a trillion dollars. In both cases the human consequences were harrowing and yet the discourse used has often normalized them.

Generally, neoliberalism promotes the idea that human well-being can be best advanced by liberating individual entrepreneurial freedoms and skills within an institutionalized framework characterized by strong private property rights, free markets, and free trade (Harvey, 2007). Here, I am talking about a set of economic, political, ideological, cultural, and discursive practices that give primacy to the market order, where profit and consumption are the defining factors of human reality. In a neoliberal world there are no citizens, only consumers; there are no societies, only markets; there is no civic life but only making the market move. Neoliberalism presents itself as an economic doctrine that professes free markets, deregulation, and freedom from government restrictions and trade controls. At the same time, it renders invisible the effects of this economic theory on real people or the social costs of implementing such an economic order. As Harvey (2005) notes, "the theoretical utopianism of neoliberal argument has primarily worked as a system of justification and legitimation" for either restoring or creating the power of an economic elite (p. 19). According to this justification system, social problems are issues of character, and social concerns are private troubles. Neoliberalism takes the political ideals of 'human dignity' and 'individual freedom' as the central values of civilization.

As far as U.S. education is concerned, one can easily discern the multiple waves of neoliberal reform implemented covertly or unapologetically over the last 30 to 40 years. These have redefined the purpose and nature of the school by both transforming it into a market and by running schools like businesses, where market values triumph in the struggle of everyday school life. A reality where the market is the one that dictates its values in society and in schools and not the opposite. Capitalism sets as a priority a different type of education where austerity and privatization determine federal and state policies; an education that aims at mechanization, automation, and quantification of the educational process, and, at the same time, imposes a new regime of oppression, authoritarianism, and loss of autonomy for both students and teachers.

At stake is also gaining control over "what students are taught so as to mold the new workforce" (Weiner, 2019, para. 4). This is all part of the "corporate elite's plan to eliminate jobs on a scale never seen before" (Weiner, 2019, para. 4). Chronic underfunding, the expansion of charter schools, the dismantling of teachers' pay and the lack of job security, as well as cuts in pensions and benefits, overcrowded classes, antiquated books, lack of materials, dilapidated buildings, cuts in programs and services, lack of support staff, such as nurses and school counselors, are all symptoms of undermining public education across America, under both Democrat and Republican administrations.

While these issues are known and discussed in the respective literature, scholars working in a Critical Pedagogy framework need to revisit neoliberalism to understand how dominant ideologies have been prevailing in the ideological struggle around schooling the last 40 years and to explore how neoliberalism has managed to do this through specific discourses and practices. It would be important to see how neoliberal discourses and practices have been reinvented and rebranded, and in what particular ways they are leading the shift in the role and vision of education.

An illustrative example of this latter point is the schooling model that has emerged because of the pandemic. COVID-19, a pandemic of historical proportions, dealt a blow to a society already shaken by multiple attempts at full capitalist restoration, ongoing immiseration, impoverishment and oppression of large masses of people, coupled with authoritarianism and repression. COVID came to illustrate with terrifying precision what Naomi Klein (2007) has termed the *shock doctrine*; a natural disaster, a pandemic, an apocalyptic scene creates those conditions of insecurity, precarity and emergency, that in turn, serve as a vehicle for a new reality, for implementing new kinds of repressive politics and policies as part of a violent capitalist assault that aims at further wealth redistribution at the top. Suffice to note here that less than a year after the onset of the pandemic in March 2020, U.S. billionaire wealth had surpassed $1.1 trillion gain (Collins, 2021). At the same time, over 73 million people lost their jobs between March 21st and December 26th, 2020, with 16 million Americans collecting unemployment in January 2021; some 100,000 businesses have permanently closed; as of August 2020, 12 million workers had likely lost employer-sponsored health insurance (Collins, 2021).

The pandemic came at a moment of crisis, to rupture in a violent way any sense of normalcy we thought existed, redefining the value and meaning of human life, of human relationships, labor, public space, public health, public education, educational process and knowledge itself. As a moment of public health emergency, the COVID-19 pandemic will not last forever, but it can, nevertheless, serve as an important pedagogical moment that illustrates vividly what happens when the market runs schools and when the state abandons its social and welfare functions.

The current pandemic embodying isolation, sickness, death, loss of income for many, appears as an opportunity for others, such as the global education technology industry that established "crisis as the catalytic opportunity for educational transformation" (Williamson & Hogan, 2020, p. 1). Since March 2020, the EdTech market has been booming; predictions for a fertile market ground will further attract private investments and "investors seeking profit from new disruptive models of education" (Williamson & Hogan, 2020, p. 2). EdTech has been central in pandemic education at different levels, including online school platforms, school and learning management platforms, AI-based technologies, student monitoring and safeguarding, and online learning resources. Already back in 2017, Pearson, as the second-largest provider of virtual schools in the United States, had identified the need to capitalize on a rapidly growing 1.5 billion market (Williamson & Hogan, 2020). Something similar happened after Hurricane Katrina in New Orleans where, through a radical education reform, the city's lower performing schools were turned into charter schools in possibly the largest handover of public education and its funding to private hands.

In a 2020 report exploring the commercialization and privatization of education during the COVID-19 global public health crisis and the consequences for education after COVID, Williamson and Hogan identify important and profound shifts in the educational terrain—trends that are here to stay post-COVID, and beyond the state of emergency. These include the private global EdTech industry making its way into schools to provide 'solutions' that are then turned into long-terms reforms; the establishment of powerful partnerships, coalitions, and networks between the private and public sector that affect educational delivery and governance. Note here that "some of the most influential promoters of EdTech solutions... include the World Bank, OECD and UNESCO" (p. 2); The Gates Foundation and the Chan Zuckerberg initiative are among the technology philanthropies providing financial support and political advocacy for EdTech solutions. Financial support comes with strings attached, as these philanthropists and their organizations are now asked to provide expert opinion and shape the educational agenda. The "private re-infrastructuring of public education" refers to companies such as Google and Amazon that have "integrated school, teachers and students into their global cloud systems and online education platforms" creating the need for long-term dependencies (p. 2). Finally, online schooling platforms have been promoted as long-term alternative models of education/personalized education, moving to a teaching model without teachers, and with the heavy use of surveillance technologies (Williamson & Hogan, 2020).

4.2   *Surveillance and Militarization*

Digital surveillance is now "part of a booming, nearly $3bn-a-year school security industry in the United States" (Beckett, 2019, para. 10) developed out of safety fears. After Columbine, a new market emerged to cater 'security' to public schools in the country. Lewis (2003) has termed this phenomenon *post-Columbine amplification*: security technology companies that, until then, were working with large traffic areas like airports, now target schools as a new market for their products. Among the products targeted for schools: closed surveillance systems, cameras, metal detectors, clear backpacks for students including bulletproof backpacks and notebooks, school lockdown products, as well as entire 'safety solutions' packages that include training and seminars for faculty and students, crisis response kits, and school emergency response plans. More recently, after the school shooting in Parkland, Florida, more tech companies entered the competition to offer schools "free, automated, 24-hour-a-day surveillance of what students were writing in their school emails, shared documents and chat messages, and sending alerts to school officials any time the monitoring technology flagged concerning phrases" (Beckett, 2019, para. 2). The educational Big Brother "doesn't turn off when the school day is over: anything students type in official school email accounts, chats or documents is monitored 24 hours a day, whether students are in their classrooms or their bedrooms" (Beckett, 2019, para. 7). Tech companies have also been working with schools to monitor students' web searches and internet usage, and, in some cases, to track what they are writing on public social media accounts.

The general model of surveillance pedagogy currently promoted in education sees schools functioning as military camps, in alignment with the concept of *education as enforcement* that understands militarized public schooling to be part of the broader "militarization of civil society" (Saltman, 2003, p. 48). In this scenario, schools function like an army base, creating a dystopian daily reality for students and educators. Schools are developing closer collaboration with the military as well as local law enforcement. In some schools, there have been cameras directly connected with the local police department broadcasting video from the school in real time (Lewis, 2003). There are indicative examples of school architecture that developed after the 1999 Columbine massacre; some schools have been built in a panopticon model where the principal, from a central place (a 'tower'), can have visual access to 70% of the school site. The principal can watch in hiding but students don't know whether they are being watched so they regulate their behavior assuming they are always watched (Lewis, 2003).

Is this the kind of school we are envisioning for our children? Children who resemble the slaves in Plato's allegory of the cave: chained from a very young age as prisoners with their legs and necks restrained, unable to turn their heads and only able to see the wall in front of them. Behind them, there is a path, a raised walkway where puppeteers cast shadows carrying simulacra/effigies of animals and objects, and occasionally talking. Thanks to a fire burning behind the puppeteer path, prisoners are able to see the puppeteers' shadows on the wall in front of them. The prisoners see nothing but moving shadows of unseen objects and people and hear only echoes reverberating from the walls of the cave. This is the way they come to understand shadows as reality. Students as prisoners, caught in a dark world of simulacra, are given particular visions of knowledge as Truth. Thinking outside their dark world is not permitted and they come to accept reality as an ambiguous shadow. This reality later becomes part of their socialization through media, and as evidenced in the previous chapter, in social media. They are deprived from the ability to see around them, experience the world with all their senses outside the predetermined mode. They are educated and socialized as prisoners of their thoughts, prisoners of pre-determined knowledge and prisoners of a repressive school system that further makes them prisoners of a labor system of exploitation as adults.

The prisoner metaphor is not exaggerated when one considers that in the name of safety, schools have now been employing invasive surveillance technologies, such as facial recognition. According to the Electronic Frontier Foundation, school districts across the country have, in recent years, expanded their efforts to surveil their students (Wang & Gebhart, 2020). Some schools have installed "microphones equipped with algorithms that often misinterpret coughs and higher-pitched voices with 'aggression'" (Wang & Gebhart, 2020, para. 4). Schools are further "watching students online, and on their phones. Social media monitoring company Social Sentinel offers software to monitor students' social media accounts, not unlike what the Department of Homeland Security regularly does to immigrants and Americans" (Wang & Gebhart, 2020, para. 5). There are designated surveillance vendors such as "Bark, Qustodio, and AirWatch who encourage schools and families to install spyware on their children's phones [...] Qustodio, one of many companies marketing to both schools and parents, earnestly encourages parents to 'monitor your kid's Internet use NSA-style'" (Wang & Gebhart, 2020, para. 5). With COVID, student surveillance technologies have been further adopted to monitor students' virtual attendance, assess social-emotional learning and well-being, and enable schools to fulfill their safeguarding responsibilities. These developments will extend the reach of edu-businesses to new areas of schooling and heighten their long-term influence in classrooms due to continuous monitoring of their online learning activities (Majeed et al., 2017).

There is a side, multi-million- dollar economy that is booming off schools' worse fears. On the other hand, there are explicit efforts to expand and legitimize military training in public schools by recruiting school-aged students. The incorporation of military values and practices into school curriculum, and the amplified presence of military leaders in school space, make up a new kind of school for military education that grooms students for the U.S. Army. In the context of these institutional arrangements, the military often shapes daily life in U.S. public schools, especially those serving poor and working-class youth of color in rural and urban communities. By targeting "African American and Latinos to fight this country's wars," the American military industrial complex continues to grow their forces "without creating the mass dissension that a draft may provoke" (Furumoto, 2005, p. 208). Military education illustrates the taking over of school curriculum by the U.S. Military, Homeland Security, Border Patrol, ICE, and other law enforcement organizations to train mostly poor, and students of color for a career in one of their respective agencies to the degree that it is not an exaggeration to talk about a school-to-military pipeline. To add insult to injury, these organizations recruiting poor, and students of color are the dominant mechanism of repression of these same populations (as is the case of police violence against Blacks and ICE violence against immigrants).

4.3 *Education Is Still Political and the Struggle over Meaning*

Forty years after the advent of Critical Pedagogy that has put at its core the political nature of schooling, we are, sadly, still debating today whether schools are political sites. Building on the work of Cornelius Castoriadis and Raymond Williams, Giroux (2004) has argued that "Education, in the broadest sense, is a principal feature of politics because it provides the capacities, knowledge, skills, and social relations through which individuals recognize themselves as social and political agents" (p. 81). The corporate and conservative agenda still wants to present schools as neutral temples of knowledge and skills, disconnected from a broader sociopolitical and historical context where decisions are largely taken independently of the students' best interests in mind.

In their zeal to rid education of politics, conservatives and neoconservatives have tried hard to save schools from what they term 'leftist propaganda.' Donald Trump himself has, at one point through his now defunct 1776 Project, proclaimed that "The Left has warped, distorted, and defiled the American story. We want our sons and daughters to know they are the citizens of the most exceptional nation in the history of the world" (Trump, 2020, para. 2). The rewriting of history taught in schools is a politicized project aligned with a capitalist vision of schooling.

120   CHAPTER 4

Schools are not neutral sites of learning, objective temples of knowledge. Public education is not the mechanism that opens the doors of social mobility, individual development, and political and economic power to disadvantaged and oppressed students:

> It would be tremendously naive to ask the ruling class in power to put into practice a kind of education which can work against it... from the point of view of the ruling class, of those in power, the main task for systematic education is to reproduce the dominant ideology. (Shor & Freire, 1987, p. 36)

In this antagonistic ideological context, too many hopes are placed on the schooling process, while capitalism adds thousands of people in the ranks of poor, unemployed, low-waged exploited workers. According to Aronowitz and Giroux (1993), schools are something other than transmitters of humanist values. Instead, school knowledge is instrumental for the reproduction of capitalist social relations which are not confined to preparation for hierarchically arranged occupational and class structures, but also transmit the discourse of domination.

Critical pedagogues want to "rescue the notion of the 'political' from its conservative and liberal advocates by arguing that its meaning should include the entire way we organize social life along with the power relations that inform its underlying social practices" (Aronowitz & Giroux, 1985, p. 140). In this case, curriculum theory becomes "both a form of representation and a set of social practices that are inextricably related to specific cultural and social forms as well as particular ideologies" (Aronowitz & Giroux, 1985, p. 140). In opposition to the conservative notion of depoliticization, the real political task in a society is

> to criticize the workings of institutions, which appear to be both neutral and independent; to criticize and attack them in such a manner that the political violence which has always exercised itself obscurely through them will be unmasked, so that one can fight against them. (Foucault, 1974, as cited in Chomsky & Foucault, 2006, p. 41)

The task, then, for Critical Pedagogy is to bring politics back to schools as a way through which people intervene in the world that necessarily signals a sense of agency, a force for awareness, conscientization, and transformation. Against traditional educational theory's long-standing emphasis on the management and administration of knowledge, Critical Pedagogy should position a critical concern with the historical and social determinants that govern the selection of such knowledge forms and attendant practices. However, Critical Pedagogy posits that against training for skills and competencies, knowledge and competitiveness in the job market, schools should be first and foremost places for developing critical agency and historical thinking, for socializing individuals into radical forms of social organization where exploitation, symbolic and material violence, authoritarianism and unequal distribution of wealth and power have no place. Schools should teach a discourse of inquiry and analysis not consensus, dissent rather than complacency, and they should encourage students to explore the translation tools necessary for their developing agency. Deconstructing schools as neutral training sites is part of Critical Pedagogy's critique of positivism and instrumental rationality as it is manifested in schools through the fragmentation and standardization of the curriculum, high stakes testing, the instrumental pragmatic character of public education, and the quantification of all aspects of school life. Critical Pedagogy contests the conservative language of positivism and the emphasis on 'excellence' via more punitive evaluation or 'rigorous' science and math curricula as if the mastery of technique is equivalent to knowledge.

Along these lines, it is important to further research the ongoing debate and struggle over meaning in educational discourse and to challenge the capitalist neoconservative agenda of usefulness, pragmatism, and evidence-based results. This can also be a critical linguistics project that calls for critically analyzing dominant educational discourses (neoliberal, neoconservative) produced and explore their function in the construction of consent and common sense. The battle against neoliberalism does not manifest only on the material plane, but also on the symbolic, and this also needs to be explored.

4.4   *Education and the Discourse and Practices of Authoritarianism*

Authoritarian politics embodied in right-wing populism and far-right extremism have been on the rise across the world. As presented in detail in Chapter 1, from Europe to the Americas and beyond, authoritarianism is gaining new ground together with the rebirth of new forms of fascism. After four years of a presidency filled with racially charged rhetoric, fake news, and the degrading of public discourse and debate, schools can serve as a unique site that both reflects and reproduces what is going on in the broader society. Some work in Critical Pedagogy has already tackled similar issues (Giroux, 2015, 2018) but it would be useful to now ground it in school ethnographies and other field work in collaboration with educators on the ground.

The effect of the Trump presidency on education has been documented in the *Teaching in the Age of Trump* in education literature (Costello, 2016; Dunn et al., 2019; Gewertz, 2019; Hamann & Morgenson, 2017; Huang & Cornell, 2017; McNeela, 2017; Rogers et al., 2017; Rogers et al., 2019, Sondel et al., 2018) with alarming findings. From verbal harassment, the use of slurs and derogatory language directed at minoritized students of color, and Nazi insignia at school, to real violence, assaults, and property damage, "a drastic increase in post-election hate speech" in schools has been reported (Rogers et al., 2017, 2019; Wallace & Lamotte, 2016, as cited in Au, 2017). At the same time, we have also witnessed cases of educators who have felt emboldened to express their discriminatory views and perpetuate a rhetoric of hate. A Fort Worth, Texas teacher was fired after writing a series of tweets addressed to former President Trump under the impression she was sending him private messages. In these tweets she claimed that her school was "loaded" with "illegal students from Mexico" and asked Trump to "remove" them from her school because they "refuse to honor our flag" (Mack, 2019, para. 4). As I have documented elsewhere (Gounari, 2020) numerous incidents of violence and hatred have taken place in schools in the name of former President Trump. In this context, Dunn et al. (2019) talk about the need for a *pedagogy of political trauma* and ask a very important question: "What does it mean to work for justice and equity in a context where basic human rights are increasingly framed not just as political but also as partisan?" (p. 470). Educators can be at the forefront of making the present meaningful and the past relevant, of making history come alive in the context of a historicized critical public pedagogy. Bringing in schools the discussion about authoritarianism and its embodiments in political life is not optional anymore. The historical time we live through requires it. We need to "anchor our pedagogy to a justice and equity framework" in order to "determine how best to respond to contextual pressures and meet the needs of all students given the multiple forms of oppression our students currently experience" (Dunn et al., 2019, p. 446). I further elaborate on this idea in Chapter 5 proposing a historical pedagogy as a political and educational response to the rise of far-right authoritarianism.

4.5   *Teaching for Black Lives*

Building on the dynamic of the Black Lives Matter movement and other grass-roots organizations, as well as work coming out of schools (i.e., Watson et al., Teaching for Black Lives, 2018), critical pedagogy scholarship must put the struggle against anti-Blackness and white supremacy at the core of its analyses and connect it organically with the demands for a critical liberatory education. Given the ongoing systemic racism and the way it affects Black students in our nations' schools, authoritarianism, police brutality and constructions of Blackness in education must be part of a critical pedagogy theory and analysis that moves beyond representation and recognition and puts at the core access to symbolic and material resources, as well as the very humanity of Black students. We know that "from the north to the south, corporate curriculum lies to our students, conceals pain and injustice, masks racism, and demeans our Black students" (Watson et al., 2018). It is not just the curriculum; it is real physical violence and the construction of the Black body as a threat. It is the rewriting of African-American history, it's the school-to-prison pipeline, police brutality and mass incarceration. As Watson et al. (2018) note,

> Not only is it critical that we teach about the systemic violence against Black people and the travesty of Black deaths, it is also important for students and teachers to understand their roles in organizing in support of Black life and Black communities, and against anti-Black racism. (p. 37)

4.6   Critical Pedagogy and Language Learning and Teaching

As someone who works in the intersection of education and applied linguistics, I have recently made the case about teaching and learning language in a Critical Pedagogy framework (Gounari, 2020). Language teaching and learning are neither politically neutral, nor ahistorical, nor free of ideological considerations. On the contrary, language as a site of power, ideological tensions, political and financial interests, hierarchies, and symbolic and material violence, is most definitely a *war zone* (Ngũgĩ wa Thiong'o, in Inani, 2018, para. 17) especially in the current historical moment. War is being waged over which languages have more 'value' or are 'worth learning;' which languages are at the core and the periphery and how they got there; what the goals of language learning should be; what counts as knowledge and what should be taught; in what ways particular theoretical, curricular, methodological, and other choices marginalize and oppress certain languages, their speakers, and their interests, reproducing racism, sexism, classism, ableism, and so forth; and how language learning is connected to political economy, to name just a few of the 'battlefields.' How are we, as academics, researchers, and language educators, engaging with this social and political reality? How do we educate and raise educators' and students' critical consciousness, so that they will always find themselves on the right side of history? If we want to claim doing socially engaged scholarship that truly aims at improving the lives of students, their families, their communities, and our society, we must be ready to talk about the workings of power and power asymmetries, the unequal distribution of wealth and power, racism, and the role of schooling in all this. As Lourdes Ortega (2019) has so powerfully argued, "our 21st-century world looks fraught with real threats to human difference, and many language learners and multilinguals are under siege. The worrisome present times demand responses at all levels, not only personal and civic but also scholarly" (p. 23). In the current historical juncture, researchers and educators are compelled to discuss how languages (cultures, identities, lived experiences, and discourses) of subjugated and oppressed people can earn their space and get legitimacy in the language classroom; Or to explore how identities and representations of otherness are embodied and enacted in language. Given that World Language curricula continue to be Eurocentric (Glynn & Wassel, 2018) with a focus mostly on French, German, Italian, and Spanish (cf. ACTFL Language Connects, 2020), there is a need to discuss the asymmetry in symbolic and economic power at play, while constructing a critical, de-colonial agenda. What might be the implications for the teaching of other World Languages? What would it mean to decenter English as the sole focus of critique and/or celebration and look at other languages as well? How can the language classroom be reinvented as a space for decolonization, transformation, and the development of critical consciousness? Language researchers and educators should not shy away from taking up these issues, as part of a critical language pedagogy. This is the *Critical Pedagogy* I would like to talk about here. A pedagogy that names, interrupts, challenges, critiques, and has a proposal for a different kind of language classrooms, curricula, schools, and communities that in turn affect societies and human life as a whole.

4.7   *Social Media, Digital Technologies, and Critical Public Pedagogy*

Public pedagogy is an interesting conceptual construction in the context of Critical Pedagogy scholarship that includes multiple sites of practice as pedagogical spaces. Public pedagogy is understood as educational activity and learning in extra-institutional spaces and discourses (Sandlin et al., 2010). Occurring beyond formal schooling, it involves learning in institutions such as museums, zoos, and libraries; in informal educational sites such as popular culture, media, commercial spaces, and the Internet; and through figures and sites of activism, including public intellectuals and grassroots social movements (Sandlin et al., 2010, 2011). However, public pedagogy is not simply the process of learning through exposure to public spaces. As Brady (2006) notes, "public education... is activism embedded in collective action, not only situated in institutionalized structures, but in multiple spaces, including grassroots organizations, neighborhood projects, art collectives, and town meetings (p. 58) providing a forum for dialogue, questioning, rage, humor, and ultimately action. This public pedagogy should therefore be *critical*: it sees public spaces as sites for political action that have the potential to disrupt common sense, inertia, and passivity and to create opportunities for the expression of complex perspectives and the organization of political interventions.

Here I want to suggest that social media as sites of communication, interaction and sharing information have a powerful educational function; "they

AGAINST CRITICAL PEDAGOGY 125

are a crucial source of education and may, in comparison to schools, exercise a greater influence on children and youth" (Aronowitz, 2008, p. 31). While Aronowitz is referring simply to the media in the above quote, one can understand how social media's influence is further amplified and their impact is such that 'knowledge' produced in these sites rivals 'official' school knowledge. For instance, conspiracy theories that are becoming increasingly popular in far-right populism are produced and disseminated in social media. Or far-right extremists find willing interlocutors in dark digital spaces. Algorithms are defining the context people get exposed to, relegating them in echo rooms where they are unable to read an alternative narrative. Content produced online in 2020 amounted to 2.5 quintillion bytes of data *per day*. How are users to sift through the content they are exposed daily and with what tools are they to decode it? As illustrated in Chapter 2, people now more and more turn to social media for every aspect of human life and social media, in turn, colonize an increasingly larger space in our daily lives.

Social media have been playing an important role in COVID-19 pandemic education, even creating content for educational institutions. To reiterate from my discussion from Chapter 2, social media are privately owned companies and are sites of specific discourse production.

Social media platforms like YouTube and TikTok have "sought to grow their presence in education through content creation partnerships for students learning at home, thereby increasing their revenue through attracting advertisers and turning education into a vehicle for the commercial advertising industry" (Williamson & Hogan, 2020, p. 3). TikTok is a new entry into the EdTech market, an involvement due to the COVID pandemic. TikTok announced in June 2020 partnerships with "universities, experts and charities to create educational content for the platform after recording millions of views of content on the *#LearnOnTikTok* hashtag during the pandemic" (Williamson & Hogan, 2020, p. 48). TikTok is anticipated to build content creation partnerships in order to deliver what they call "high-quality 'microlearning' videos through the platform," a development that was initiated before the pandemic but was "fast-tracked in response to users' own creation of educational content during the COVID-19 emergency" (Williamson & Hogan, 2020). Analyzing content production in social media for educational purposes and its alignment with an instrumentalist view of the curriculum and education is another important avenue for research.

4.8   *Critical Pedagogy and Historical Thinking*

Last but not least, Critical Pedagogy scholarship must engage with the core matter of thinking historically and put historical knowledge at the core of our pedagogical and theoretical practices as part of a liberatory project. As I

126   CHAPTER 4

mentioned earlier, often the very analyses in Critical Pedagogy literature are, themselves, superficial and dehistoricized and mostly serve as a vehicle for disposable progressive politics. An important attempt has been made by De Lissovoy (2007, 2008) who distinguishes history (as a linear dominant narrative) from historicity (that redefines history as a site of possibility). Drawing on Paulo Freire's work, De Lissovoy structures historicity as part of the fulfillment of the historical vocation of humanization by the oppressed where "history is a human learning and a human teaching toward liberation" (De Lissovoy, 2018, p. 12).

Exploring and challenging historical revisionism and the demise of historical thinking by authoritarian far-right capitalism, is an important project in the framework of critical public pedagogy. It is also important to articulate a critique against forms of 'progressive' politics that are only willing to accept non-threatening versions of history or that adapt to an already hegemonic narrative about class, race, gender and so forth. This project is outlined in detail in the next chapter.

References

Allen, R. L. (2005). Whiteness and critical pedagogy. In Z. Leonardo (Ed.), *Critical pedagogy and race* (pp. 53–69). Blackwell Publishing.

Apple, M. (1993). *Official knowledge: Democratic education in a conservative age*. Routledge.

Apple, M. (2004). *Ideology and curriculum*. Routledge.

Apple, M. (2012). *Can education change society?* Routledge.

Apple, M., & Au, W. (2009). *Critical education*. Routledge.

Apple, M., & Weis, L. (Eds.). (1983). *Ideology and practice in schooling*. Temple University Press.

Aronowitz, S. (2008). *Against schooling*. Paradigm Publishers.

Aronowitz, S., & Giroux, H. (1985). *Education under siege*. Bergin & Garvey.

Aronowitz, S., & Giroux, H. (1993). *Education still under siege*. Bergin & Garvey.

Au, W. (2017). When multicultural education is not enough. *Multicultural Perspectives, 19*(3), 147–150. http://dx.doi.org/10.1080/15210960.2017.1331741

Au, W. (2018). *A Marxist education*. Haymarket.

Au, W. (2019). Racial justice is not a choice: White supremacy, high-stakes testing, and the punishment of Black and Brown children. *Rethinking Schools, 33*(4). https://www.rethinkingschools.org/articles/racial-justice-is-not-a-choice

Beckett, L. (2019, October 22). Under digital surveillance: How American schools spy on millions of kids. *The Guardian*. https://www.theguardian.com/world/2019/oct/22/school-student-surveillance-bark-gaggle

AGAINST CRITICAL PEDAGOGY

Bernstein, B. (1990). *The structuring of pedagogic discourse: Class, codes & control.* Routledge.

Bourdieu, P. (1986). The forms of capital. In J. G. Richardson (Ed.), *Handbook of theory and research for the sociology of education* (pp. 241–258). Greenwood Press.

Bourdieu, P., & Passeron, J.-C. (1977). *Reproduction in education, society and culture.* Sage.

Bowles, S., & Gintis H. (1976). *Schooling in capitalist America: Educational reform and the contradictions of economic life.* Basic Books.

Brady, J. F. (2006). Public pedagogy and education and leadership: Politically engaged scholarly communities and possibilities for critical engagement. *Journal of Curriculum & Pedagogy, 3*(1), 57–60. https://doi.org/10.1080/15505170.2006.10411575

Chomsky, N., & Foucault, M. (2006). *The Chomsky-Foucault debate: On human nature.* New Press.

Collins, C. (2021, February 24). *Updates: Billionaire wealth, U.S. job losses and pandemic profiteers.* Inequality.org. https://inequality.org/great-divide/updates-billionaire-pandemic/

Costello, M. B. (2016). *The Trump effect: The impact of the 2016 presidential election on our nation's schools.* Southern Poverty Law Center. https://www.splcenter.org/sites/default/files/the_trump_effect.pdf

Darder, A. (1991). *Cultural and power in the classroom: A critical foundation for bicultural education.* Bergin & Garvey.

De Lissovoy, N. (2007). History, histories, or historicity? The time of educational liberation in the age of empire. *Review of Education, Pedagogy, and Cultural Studies, 29*(5), 441–60.

De Lissovoy, N. (2008). *Power, crisis, and education for liberation rethinking critical pedagogy.* Palgrave Macmillan.

Dunn, A. H., Sondel, B., & Baggett, H. C. (2019). "I don't want to come off as pushing an agenda": How contexts shaped teachers' pedagogy in the days after the 2016 U.S. presidential election. *American Educational Research Journal, 56*(2), 444–476. https://doi.org/10.3102/0002831218794892

Fine, M., & Weis, L. (2003). *Silenced voices and extraordinary conversations: Re-imagining schools.* Teachers College Press.

Foster, M. (2005). Race, class, and gender in education research: Surveying the political terrain. In Z. Leonardo (Ed.), *Critical pedagogy and race* (pp. 175–183). Blackwell.

Freire, P. (2005). *Pedagogy of the oppressed.* Continuum. (Original work published in 1970)

Fromm, E. (1973). *The anatomy of human destructiveness.* Holt, Rinehart & Winston.

Fromm, E. (1976). *To have or to be?* Harper & Row.

Fromm, E. (1981). *On disobedience.* Harper Perennial.

Furumoto, R. (2005). No poor child left unrecruited: How NCLB codifies and perpetuates urban school militarism. *Equity & Excellence in Education, 38*(3), 200–210.

Gewertz, K. (2019, March 13). Principals dealing with hostility and division in the age of Trump, survey shows. *Education Week.* https://www.edweek.org/leadership/principals-dealing-with-hostility-and-division-in-the-age-of-trump-survey-shows/2019/03

Giroux, H. (1983a). *Theory and resistance in education: A pedagogy for the opposition.* Bergin & Garvey.

Giroux, H. (1983b). Theories of reproduction and resistance in the new sociology of education: A critical analysis. *Harvard Educational Review, 53*(3), 257–293.

Giroux, H. (1997). *Pedagogy and the politics of hope: Theory, culture, and schooling.* Westview Press.

Giroux, H. (2000a). *Impure acts: The practical politics of cultural studies.* Routledge.

Giroux, H. (2000b). *Stealing innocence.* St. Martin's Press.

Giroux, H. (2004). Cultural studies and the politics of public pedagogy: Making the political more pedagogical. *Parallax, 10*(2), 73–89. http://dx.doi.org/10.1080/1353464042000208530

Giroux, H. (2011). *On critical pedagogy.* Continuum.

Giroux, H. (2013). *Public spaces, private lives: Beyond the culture of cynicism.* Rowman & Littlefield.

Giroux, H. (2015). D*angerous thinking in the age of the new authoritarianism.* Routledge Publishers.

Giroux, H. (2018). *American nightmare: The challenge of U.S. authoritarianism.* City Lights Publishers.

Glynn, C., & Wassell, B. (2018). Who gets to play? Issues of access and social justice in world language study in the US. *Dimension, 11,* 18–32.

Gounari, P. (2020). Teaching and learning language in dangerous times. Introduction to the special issue on rethinking critical pedagogy in L2 teaching and learning. *L2 Journal, 12*(2), 3–20.

Gounari, P., & Grollios, G. (Eds.). (2010). *A reader of critical pedagogy.* Gutenberg Publishers.

Graeber, D. (2013). On the phenomenon of bullshit jobs: A work rant. *Strike Magazine.* https://www.strike.coop/bullshit-jobs/

Greene, M. (1988). *The dialectic of freedom.* Teachers College Press.

Grollios, G. (2011). *Progressive education and the curriculum.* Epikentro.

Hamann, E. T., & Morgenson, C. (2017). Dispatches from flyover country: Four appraisals of impacts of Trump's immigration policy on families, schools, and communities. *Anthropology & Education Quarterly, 48*(4), 393–402. https://doi.org/10.1111/aeq.12214

Harvey, D. (2005). *A brief history of neoliberalism.* Oxford University Press.

Harvey, D. (2007). Neoliberalism as creative destruction. *Annals of the American Academy of Political and Social Science, 610*(1), 22–44.

AGAINST CRITICAL PEDAGOGY 129

hooks, b. (1994). *Teaching to transgress: Education as the practice of freedom.* Routledge.

Horkheimer, M. (1982). *Critical theory: Selected essays.* Continuum.

Horkheimer, M., & Adorno, T. (1947). *Dialektik der Aufklärung.* Amsterdam.

Huang, F. L., & Cornell, D. G. (2017). Student attitudes and behaviors as explanations for the Black-White suspension gap. *Children and Youth Services Review, 73,* 298–308. https://doi.org/10.1016/j.childyouth.2017.01.002

Klein, N. (2007). *The shock doctrine: The rise of disaster capitalism.* Macmillan.

Kliebard, H. M. (2002). *Changing course: American curriculum reform in the 20th century.* Teachers College Press.

Kliebard, H. M. (1995). Why history of education? *The Journal of Educational Research, 88*(4), 194–199.

Knopp, S. (2012). *Education and capitalism: Struggles for learning and liberation.* Haymarket Books.

Ladson-Billings, G. (1997). I know why this doesn't feel empowering: A critical race analysis of critical pedagogy. In P. Freire (Ed.), *Mentoring the mentor: A critical dialogue with Paulo Freire* (pp. 127–144). Peter Lang.

Leonardo, Z. (2002). The souls of white folk: Critical pedagogy, whiteness studies, and globalization discourse. *Race, Ethnicity & Education, 5*(1), 29–50.

Lewis, T. (2003). The surveillance economy of contemporary schooling. *The Review of Education, Pedagogy and Cultural Studies, 25*(4), 335–355.

Lynn, M. (2004). Inserting the 'race' into critical pedagogy: An analysis of 'race-based epistemologies.' *Educational Philosophy and Theory, 36*(2,) 153–165. https://doi.org/10.1111/j.1469-5812.2004.00058.x

Mack, D. (2019, June 5). A Texas teacher was fired after asking Trump via Twitter to "remove the illegals" from her school. *BuzzFeed News.* https://www.buzzfeednews.com/article/davidmack/texas-teacher-fired-tweeting-trump-illegal-immigrants

Majeed, A., Baadel, S., & Haq, A. U. (2017). Global triumph or exploitation of security and privacy concerns in E-Learning systems. *Communications in Computer and Information Science, 630,* 351–363.

Marcuse, H. (1964). *One-Dimensional man.* Beacon Press.

McLaren, P. (1993). *Schooling as ritual performance.* Routledge.

McLaren, P. (1998). *Life in schools: An introduction to critical pedagogy in the foundations of education.* Longman.

McNeela, C. (2017). Creating space for student voice after the election. *Perspectives and Provocations, 6*(2).

Ortega, L. (2019). SLA and the study of equitable multilingualism. *The Modern Language Journal, 103*(S1), 23–38.

Parker, L., & Stovall, D. O. (2004). Actions following words: Critical race theory connects to critical pedagogy. *Educational Philosophy and Theory, 36*(2), 167–182. https://doi.org/10.1111/j.1469-5812.2004.00059.x

Rogers, J., Franke, M., Yun, J. E., Ishimoto, M., Diera, C., Geller, R. C., Berryman, A., & Brenes, T. (2017). *Teaching and learning in the age of Trump: Increasing stress and hostility in America's high schools*. UCLA's Institute for Democracy, Education, and Access. https://idea.gseis.ucla.edu/publications/teaching-and-learning-in-age-of-trump

Rogers, J., Ishimoto, M., Kwako, A., Berryman, A., & Diera, C. (2019). *School and society in the age of Trump*. UCLA's Institute for Democracy, Education, and Access. https://idea.gseis.ucla.edu/publications/school-and-society-in-age-of-trump/

Russom, G. (2012). Obama's neoliberal agenda for education. *International Socialist Review, 71*. https://isreview.org/issue/71/obamas-neoliberal-agenda-education

Sandlin, J. A., O'Malley, M. P., & Burdick, J. (2011). Mapping the complexity of public pedagogy scholarship: 1894–2010. *Review of Educational Research, 81*(3), 338–375. https://doi.org/10.3102/0034654311413395

Sandlin, J. A., Schultz, B. D., & Burdick, J. (2010). Understanding, mapping, and exploring the terrain of public pedagogy. In J. A. Sandlin, B. D. Schultz, & J. Burdick (Eds.), *Handbook of public pedagogy: Education and learning beyond schooling* (pp. 1–6). Routledge.

Saltman, K. J. (2003). The strong arm of the law. *Body & Society, 9*(4), 49–67. https://doi.org/10.1177/1357034037736684649

Seymour, R. (2014). *Against austerity: How we can fix the crisis they made*. Pluto Books.

Shor, I., & Freire, P. (1987). What is the "dialogical method" of teaching? *Journal of Education, 169*(3), 11–31.

Sondel, B., Baggett, H. C., & Dunn, A. H. (2018). "For millions of people, this is real trauma": A pedagogy of political trauma in the wake of the 2016 U.S. presidential election. *Teaching and Teacher Education, 70*, 175–185. https://doi.org/10.1016/j.tate.2017.11.017

Trump, D. (2020, September 17). *Remarks by President Trump at the White House conference on American history*. White House Archives. https://trumpwhitehouse.archives.gov/briefings-statements/remarks-president-trump-white-house-conference-american-history/

Wang, M., & Gebhart, G. (2020, February 27). Schools are pushing the boundaries of surveillance technologies. *Electronic Frontier Foundation*. https://www.eff.org/deeplinks/2020/02/schools-are-pushing-boundaries-surveillance-technologies

Watson, D., Hagopian, J., & Au, W. (Eds.). (2018). *Teaching for Black lives*. Rethinking Schools.

Weiner, L. (February 10, 2019). What a teachers movement can look like. *JACOBIN*. https://www.jacobinmag.com/2019/02/los-angeles-teachers-union-strike-education-reform?fbclid=IwAR09MZeNxDnHZ5GPpXej17wCmMoRkqq_lQEyRkCiV7TuEByPjwC7WBtlv34

Williamson, B., & Hogan, A. (2020). *Commercialization and privatization in/of education in the context of Covid-19*. Education International Research. https://www.researchgate.net/profile/Ben-Williamson-2/publication/343510376_Commercialisation_and_privatisation_inof_education_in_the_context_of_Covid-19/links/5f2d6fo5a6fdcccc43b2cf99/Commercialisation-and-privatisation-in-of-education-in-the-context-of-Covid-19.pdf

Yamahtta-Taylor, K. (2016). *From Black lives matter to Black liberation*. Haymarket Books.

CHAPTER 5

Emergency Time as a Pedagogical Project

Historical Thinking and Critical Consciousness

1   'Actions Committed in the Past'

In March 2021, Republican Florida Governor Ron DeSantis attacked Critical Race Theory (CRT) calling it a politicized academic 'fad' that reflects "what's really ideology, not actual facts" asserting that there is no room (and no funding) for theories that teach "kids to hate their country and to hate each other." During a press conference where he presented a proposal that would commit $106 million from pandemic-related federal funding to support civic education, he supported the teaching of "foundational knowledge to understand what makes America unique" and "the principles that people have fought for." He further argued that we should not treat each other "based on race" but rather "as individuals." Our schools, he said, "are supposed to give people a foundation of knowledge, not supposed to be indoctrination centers, where you're trying to push specific ideologies." DeSantis used the well-known conservative argument discussed in detail in Chapter 4, that schools should be neutral temples of knowledge and criticized the educational push for anti-racist ideologies, but not the white supremacist, exceptionalist, ethnocentric ideologies that have dominated the curriculum, generating, in turn, even more racism in educational institutions and beyond. Clearly, for DeSantis the analysis and understanding of race and racism in the United States, and the ways they have maintained and perpetuated systems of oppression and symbolic and material violence against people of color, is what's truly 'divisive.' The underlying assumption is that there is, in fact, a 'unifying' version of history ("what makes America great") and this version is, somehow, not ideological. The educational neutrality argument and the 'divisiveness' concern reveal what's in the root of the issue: It is not that conservatives do not want ideology in the schools; they simply want *their* ideology. And they want to use neutrality on their terms as they re-write the past, reducing history to 'actions committed in the past.' However, choices about which histories count and are legitimized and taught is not a simple educational issue; it is a deeply political one.

DeSantis's statements illustrate part of the problem with racism in America: the 'White norm' against which everything else must be measured. The White norm is a common-sense construct that, as such, is always invisible and

© KONINKLIJKE BRILL NV, LEIDEN, 2022 | DOI: 10.1163/9789004510470_006

EMERGENCY TIME AS A PEDAGOGICAL PROJECT

stands above and beyond criticism; it is, in fact, transparent. The White norm is the placeholder for all debates and discussions. It does not only define what should be legitimized and valued on many different realms of public life (political, educational, legal, and discursive) but it also dictates *in what terms* these issues should be talked about; *how* the discourse should be structured. DeSantis's 'foundational knowledge' in schools is whitewashed and color-evasive, and any reference to race is seen as contaminating the illusionary hegemonic narratives of happy consciousness sustained for centuries in school curricula, public discourse, and collective memory.

The relationship between race, racism, and power that Critical Race Theory scholars have been uncovering and analyzing, seems to pose a threat to this dominant narrative. Critical Race Theory has put race at the core of its analyses, presenting the history of white supremacy and revealing the systemic, legal, and other mechanisms that have maintained and continue to maintain racial division and discrimination. For instance, through CRT, students might be able to grasp the context behind the nine minutes and twenty-nine seconds Minneapolis police officer Derek Chauvin was kneeling on George Floyd's neck resulting to his death.

Early CRT theorists focused on the role law played in establishing, maintaining, and perpetuating racial discrimination, segregation (including housing segregation) as well as racist practices in bank loans, discriminatory labor practices, inequities in education, and so forth (Crenshaw, 1989; Crenshaw et al., 1995; Delgado & Stefancic, 2001; Solórzano, 1997; Solórzano & Yosso, 2002). DeSantis's solution to avoid going into systemic issues that would have to name oppressors and oppressed, colonizers and colonized, is to treat people as 'individuals' in a colorblind capitalist construction, where there are no groups, no collectives, no alliances, no solidarity, just people working hard or not working 'hard enough,' trying to fight for their spot in the 'American dream.' In this picture, race is seen as 'divisive.' Fully aligned with the individualistic capitalist ideology and the construction of the neoliberal subject (discussed in Chapter 4), the focus is on the individual student, disconnected from their historicity as members of particular groups that may have been historically oppressed, marginalized and robbed off the symbolic and material resources other groups have enjoyed by virtue of their skin color.

And yet, Black students have been disproportionately at the receiving end of school discipline or they are more likely "to be seen as problematic and more likely to be punished than white students are for the same offense" (Riddle & Sinclair, 2019, p. 8255); Black males disproportionately make up prison population being six times more likely to be imprisoned than Whites (Gramlich, 2020; Yamahtta-Taylor, 2016); Black families disproportionately live in low-income

134   CHAPTER 5

neighborhoods (Solomon et al., 2019) and are (disproportionately) stricken with poverty (Creamer, 2020); the poverty rate for African Americans is more than double that of Whites; African Americans are disproportionately affected by the 'wealth gap' regardless of households' education, marital status, age, or income; the median wealth for Black households with a college degree equaled about 70% of the median wealth for white households without a college degree (Hanks et al., 2018); police killings continue unabated, at 2.5 times the rate for Black men as for White men; 1 in 1,000 Black men and boys can be expected to be killed by police at some point in their lifetime; and dying at the hands of law enforcement is a leading cause of death among young Black men (Edwards et al., 2019). All these facts, in DeSantis and other Republican conservatives,' and neoconservatives' vision of human societies, must be isolated accidents of history, rather than manifestations of systemic racism. But how exactly is it to live one's life always *disproportionately* to the White norm?

In a similar vein, former president Trump, cracked down on diversity training at federal agencies that were using Critical Race Theory, demanding that these trainings 'cease and desist' because they "not only run counter to the fundamental beliefs for which our Nation has stood since its inception, but they also engender division and resentment within the Federal workforce" (Vought Memorandum, 2020, para. 3). Trump's openly racist directive came in September 2020, after a summer of heightened racial tensions and the massive wave of protest and demonstrations across the United States, following the murder of George Floyd in May 2020 by Minneapolis police. Clearly, in Trump's and the Republican party's account, it is the mere acknowledgment of diversity dividing the country and not the fact that diversity is built on difference, power asymmetry, violence, and pervasive systemic racism, as delineated in the wealth of inequity patterns presented earlier (and many more—too many to list). In Trump's directive, diversity training is, similarly to HB 377, called 'divisive,' 'false,' 'anti- American,' 'un-American' and 'demeaning' propaganda (Vought Memorandum, 2020, para. 5). As such, it must be eradicated. But diversity is not just a term. It is a word that refers to multiple and diverse groups of human beings. Therefore, if diversity is the problem, the underlying assumption is that we should render the people making it up invisible, or worse, eradicate them. This should hardly be a surprise coming from the President who built his alliances playing nice with and giving space to white supremacists for four years. Faithful to the Trumpist manual, the former administration bluntly rejected the violent history of racial inequality, blaming instead the victims of this violent history for making their co-workers feel 'resentful' and 'uncomfortable.' As previously discussed, Trumpism has largely built on race divisions and on a racialized version of patriotism, to create the ideological confusion necessary for its sustenance, particularly with white working-class voters. This perverse race-based patriotism has been at the core of the former president's far-right authoritarian politics and discourse.

Trump's hate relationship with Critical Race Theory (with people of color, really) is better illustrated in his talk on Constitution Day at the National Archives Museum in the context of the first White House Conference on History, where he announced that he would create a commission to promote Patriotic Education through a grant to develop a "pro-American curriculum that celebrates the truth about our nation's great history" (Trump, 2020, para. 23). The singular 'truth' in his pronouncement creates the assumption that there is in place an untruthful anti-American curriculum that is not teaching the United States' great history but a different version: a "twisted web of lies" (para. 2) promoted by the Left and other radicals: "Teaching this horrible doctrine to our children is a form of child abuse, in the truest sense" (para. 16) Trump said referring to Critical Race Theory. Arguing against what he termed 'toxic propaganda,' 'ideological poison,' 'indoctrination' and 'cancel culture' from the 'radical movement,' he further attacked the New York Times' Pulitzer Prize-winning '1619 Project,' a historical analysis of how slavery shaped American political, social, and economic institutions. The 1619 Project is a collection of essays that present the country's history from when the first enslaved Africans were brought to America's shores and explores African Americans' contributions. Trump's 'Patriotic Education' instead, proposed to focus and celebrate the legacy of 1776, when American Colonies declared independence from Great Britain. Trump singled out the late progressive historian Howard Zinn, author of *A People's History of the United States*, a groundbreaking, radical, historical account that focuses more on the contributions of ordinary people, unsung heroes and questions the hegemonic whitewashed male version of history. Trump went so far as to threaten to withhold federal funding from public schools that used materials from the 1619 project. Clearly, the 'race problem' in America is *also* a history problem.

The patriotic curriculum was presented as an antidote to the hot summer of civil unrest and massive protests across the country that Trump was hoping to quell. For him, to talk about racial violence was unpatriotic and divisive and a "hateful and destructive message" (Trump, 2020). In a perfect social dystopia, the struggle over historical knowledge and meaning becomes, once again, a simple Manichean binary where one side is the *de facto* the norm: un-American, toxic propaganda that will "dissolve the civic bonds that tie us together" and will "destroy our country" on one side, against the 'patriots' on the other. The construction of an (internal) imminent threat is, once more, used discursively to articulate a reactionary far-right populist and racist project that is the

136

CHAPTER 5

true divisive force. In conservatives' version of history, the U.S. society is exceptionally just, equal, democratic, and tolerant.

Trump and DeSantis are hardly the only Republicans taking aim at CRT in education curricula and/or promoting a revisionist version of U.S. history. Conservative Republican South Dakota Governor and Trump ally Kristi Noem blamed the U.S. Capitol insurrection on 'inadequate education in American civics.' In her own State, legislature approved Noem's $900,000 request to support a new civics and history education initiative for public K-12 schools across the state. Noem claimed that the goal of the curriculum was to teach students that the United States "is the most unique nation in the history of the world" (Groves, 2020, para. 7) and to give all state residents the knowledge needed to "pursue their own American dream" (Woodiel, 2021, para. 13).

In line with Trumpism's racist legacy, in April 2021, Idaho lawmakers advanced a bill that would prohibit public schools and public universities from teaching that "any sex, race, ethnicity, religion, color, or national origin is inherently superior or inferior," tenets that, according to the bill, are "often found in 'critical race theory.'" The bill also prohibits teaching that "individuals, by virtue of sex, race, ethnicity, religion, color, or national origin, are inherently responsible for actions committed in the past by other members of the same sex, race, ethnicity, religion, color, or national origin" (HB 377, lines 22–42). In the all-out war against Critical Race Theory, in April 2021 the Oklahoma Senate has overwhelmingly approved legislation (HB 1775) that would prevent schools from teaching CRT as part of the curriculum, using identical language as Idaho HB 377. Once more, the argument here was that CRT is racist. House Bill 1775's supporters argued that the legislation upholds the "principle of a colorblind society where people are judged based on their individual merits and character, not their skin color or other characteristics" (Carter, 2021, para. 19). As of August 2021, twenty-seven States were proposing legislation that would prevent educators from teaching the role of racism, sexism, and oppression throughout U.S. history to K-12 students across the country. Language in all these bills has been similar, if not identical to Trump's executive order discussed earlier. The move to impose a far-right reactionary agenda in schools that suppresses the histories and lived experiences of minoritized groups is hardly new. The 2012 initiative originating in Arizona to ban ethnic studies was promoting the idea that ethnic studies are teaching Latino students that they "are an oppressed minority" (para. 4), and that public schools should treat students as individuals, rather than endorsing "ethnic solidarity" (DiVirgilio, 2010).

What all the post-Trump bills point to is a new American racist historical revisionism. Much in the way that European historical revisionism attempted to absolve fascism of its crimes, the new American historical revisionism is attempting to absolve (White) America from enslavement, white supremacy, and violent racism. Anti-CRT state legislation is arguing against the teaching of slavery as 'hard history:' "It is hard to comprehend the inhumanity that defined it. It is hard to discuss the violence that sustained it. It is hard to teach the ideology of white supremacy that justified it. And it is hard to learn about those who abided it" (Jeffries, 2018, p. 5). According to research conducted by the Southern Poverty Law Center in 2018, schools have been failing to teach the history of African enslavement. After surveying U.S. high school seniors and social studies teachers, analyzing a selection of state content standards, and reviewing ten popular U.S. history textbooks, findings were telling about U.S. students' relationship with their past. High school seniors struggled on even the most basic questions about American enslavement of Africans and only 8% of high school seniors surveyed could identify slavery as the central cause of the Civil War. Two-thirds of respondents (68%) did not know that it took a constitutional amendment to formally end slavery. States have their own share of responsibility: of the 15 sets of state standards under analysis, "none addresses how the ideology of white supremacy rose to justify the institution of slavery (p. 9); most fail to lay out meaningful requirements for learning about slavery, about the lives of the millions of enslaved people, or about how their labor was essential to the American economy" (SPLC, 2018, p. 29).

What are these 'actions committed in the past' that conservatives want to exculpate? Enslavement of people and cotton fields? Lynching, nooses, and white robes? Stealing native lands and annihilating native populations? Boarding schools for Indian children? Segregated schools? What is left to teach if we erase 'actions committed in the past' by members of specific groups, when human history is a history of violence and oppression of some groups over others? Who could propose such a bill, if not the group made up of the oppressors who also has hegemony over the discourse? How do violent facts of recent history become issues of discomfort and who is uneasy about them? What is left to learn if we sterilize our teaching from the struggles and fights of the past? And at the end, who benefits from erasing 'actions committed in the past' from our collective memory? Instead of addressing the pervasive racial segregation of schools, almost 70 years after Brown v. Board of Education, and using the law to not only protect civil rights and securing racial equality, but also to undo these legal structures that still maintain and feed systemic racism (the core of CRT theory), far-right conservative legislators are simply using it to erase race so that they do not have to address it.

In this Chapter, in the context of conservative backlash against CRT, I want to explore the features of historical narratives and their role in supporting and strengthening the authoritarian far-right Trumpist rhetoric, as well as the new strong discourses emerging out of Trumpism. The control over the collective historical narrative is central in far-right politics and Trumpism has successfully integrated a dangerous historical revisionism into their muddy ideological mix. However, this is not just Trumpism at work here. It is racism rooted in the very fabric of this country, from settler colonialism to Jim Crow, to the Prison Industrial Complex, to police brutality against Blacks. The whitewashing and distortion of history has traditionally been at the core of all ideological struggles. There is a version of the past that is better left forgotten. Wounds can be painlessly healed with a beautiful star-spangled, red-white-and-blue, shiny BandAid. This is historical remembrance *a la carte* that does not disturb neither neoconservative happy consciousness nor liberal fantasies of equality and social justice. If something is going to be remembered, it can't be painful or uncomfortable. This Chapter looks at the hard and painful facets of historical narrative in U.S. authoritarianism, and the themes of historical revisionism in an attempt to articulate a Critical Pedagogy project as a deeply historical project.

2   Emergency Time: Unsettled Accounts with History

German philosopher and Frankfurt School affiliate Walter Benjamin wrote *On the Concept of History* in Paris, in the early days of 1940, shortly before his attempt to escape from Vichy France, where Jewish and/or Marxist German refugees were handed over to the Gestapo by the authorities (Lowy, 2016). When his escape failed and he was intercepted by Franco's police at the Spanish border, Benjamin committed suicide by ingesting morphine pills.

   In this fragmented and enigmatic document that was not meant for publication, Benjamin challenges positivistic notions about history and the thesis that the past is a predictable continuum towards progress into the present, and that "the arc of history bends naturally toward justice" (Penny, 2020, para. 15), cautioning on the danger of the return of fascism in the human life scene. "The tradition of the oppressed" he writes in Thesis VIII, "teaches us that the 'emergency situation' in which we live is the rule." This is the view of history from a class struggle perspective, where the norm is "oppression, barbarism and violence of the victors" (Lowy, 2016, p. 204). On the other hand, he presents the positivistic view, according to which the historical norm stipulates that evolution brings progress, the realization of full human potential and the "development of societies towards more democracy, freedom or peace" (Lowy, 2016, p. 134). "Fascism has a chance" he claims because "in the name of

EMERGENCY TIME AS A PEDAGOGICAL PROJECT

progress, its opponents treat it as a historical norm. The current amazement that the things we are experiencing are 'still' possible in the twentieth century is not philosophical" (Lowy, 2016, p. 134). This is to mean that fascism, while seen as an exception to the norm of progress or an accident of history for positivistic historiography, it is for Benjamin nothing but *a violent expression of the permanent state of emergency*. As I made the case in Chapter 1, after the end of World War II, the Nazi atrocities, violence, and the sentiments of aversion these provoked in the mainstream collective imaginary, seemed to have created a 'never again' narrative that suggested that the progress human societies have been making, coupled with the knowledge of atrocities, would relegate fascism in the trashcan of history. I noted that this famous trashcan was, after all, for recyclables. Clearly, neither progress and human development nor 'knowledge' of the atrocities prevented the reinvention of far-right extremist and neo-Nazi movements and the symbolic and material violence they have generated anew. Benjamin concluded that "the astonishment that the things we are experiencing in the 20th century are 'still' possible [...] is not the beginning of knowledge" unless this astonishment makes us question the view of history that perceives fascism as a historical norm (Lowy, 2016, p. 134).

The rise of authoritarianism, far-right politics and the emboldened revival of neo-Nazi ideologies, as discussed in previous chapters, are still perceived as accidents of history, as stains in the human progress and they illustrate Benjamin's thesis that 'progress' is not a linear path towards the improvement of human societies but, rather, the platform for the emergence of human atrocities. If progress is supposedly where humans are unequivocally headed to, how can we explain the dark historical landscape of far-right populism since the 80's that culminated in the last five years of Trumpism as a far-right authoritarian movement? History is a permanent state of emergency, and such movements are not exceptions; they are embedded in history's violent fabric. In the revisionist historical narrative of far-right movements, progress and moving forward are used as ideological devices to either uproot people from their historical grounding or to whitewash and smooth out violent histories, as is the case with racism in America presented earlier. In the name of 'progress' and 'harmony' conservatives are legislating the eradication of CRT from school curricula. For the creation of the desired homogeneous harmony, societies are put in a false state of emergency through the creation of imaginary threats, while the true state of emergency, that, is the emboldening of dehumanizing forces, neoliberal ideologies, and politics, particularly in the context of liberal democracies, goes unacknowledged. Far-right authoritarian ideologies are further normalized and function through historical narratives in complex ways

140   CHAPTER 5

and using a variety of ideological devices. What follows is a discussion of different features of historical narratives that frame history as a critical pedagogical
project and pedagogy as a historical project.

2.1   *Instrumentalism of History and Historical Knowledge*

"And it's as good as if it never happened," utters the Devil in Goethe's *Faust*,
revealing his innermost principle: the destruction of memory (Adorno, 2005,
p. 91). And we know well that the Devil is in the details, as this phrase sum-
marizes the hegemonic conservative view of history; it speaks to the 'actions
committed in the past' discussed earlier, where these are seen disconnected
from their effects, the agents who have 'committed' them (verb in the passive
voice at work) and the sociopolitical context where they took place (vaguely
and generally 'the past'). Memory is destructed and select historical narratives,
as linear sequences of privileged events, are neatly tucked into boxes, attached
to dates and to heroic figures, as they are washed, sterilized, and polished to
articulate and complement the official national narrative around 'one country,
one nation, one culture.' At the same time, many other events and actions are
'as good as if they never happened,' the same way that many people and groups
of people never existed. The "erasure of huge swaths of humanity is a fundamental feature of the school curriculum, but also of the broader mainstream
political discourse" (Bigelow, 2018, para. 6). Or as Adorno (2005) has powerfully argued, "the murdered are to be cheated out of the single remaining thing
that our powerlessness can offer them: remembrance" (p. 91).

     All these make up the instrumentalist and positivistic character of official
histories, and their construction in one dimension. Their intention is to "close
the books on the past and, if possible, even remove it from memory" (Adorno,
2005, p. 89). The appeal to 'objectivity' and ideological purging serves as the
excuse for the imposition of Western knowledge and the exclusion of peripheral,
subjugated knowledges, the erasure of "countless voices and contributions from
the rest of the world" (Yako, 2021, para. 52). In the context of rationalization, as
a form of social organization, "social action is no longer oriented toward meanings, values, and beliefs, but toward strategies, no longer toward the questions 'Is
it true?' 'Is it good?' but toward the questions 'Does it work?' 'Does it achieve its
purposes?" (van Leeuwen, 2008, p. 3). Consequently, history is proceduralized,
becoming a step-by-step linear methodology or a manual to describe the world.

     The assumptions here are first, that there is such a thing as objectivity
and second, that objectivity holds a full degree of neutrality, and is neither
shaped ideologically, nor is it value laden. Paulo Freire (1970) in *Pedagogy of
the Oppressed* forcefully argued that there cannot be objectivity without subjectivity and that to deny the importance of subjectivity "in the process of

transforming the world and history is naïve and simplistic. It is to admit the impossible: a world without people" (p. 59). He further juxtaposed this with subjectivism, "people without a world." Human beings and the world exist in a dialectical relationship, the same way objectivity and subjectivity must be mutually conceived and never dichotomized. Any claim to the purity of subjectivism or objectivism is disingenuous (Freire, 1970). If we apply this conception of history to school curricula, we realize that the way students are been socialized through national historical narratives in public schools is multifaceted, complex, and ideologically loaded.

First, students from minoritized and racialized groups are forced to understand history as something outside of them, their communities, and their lives. More often, they are observers of other people's history or witnesses to the distortions of their own history. As such, they are uprooted by or annihilated from their very history. Historical narratives are taught in a decontextualized, narrow, instrumentalist mode, focusing on what might be perceived as positive, or glossing over the negative. In this history, students are never the subjects but rather, the objects of historical processes.

Second, students are taught to think about history in Manichean terms: the good and the bad; the positive and the negative; winners and losers; 'we' and 'they'; always a dichotomy where the two categories need to be filled in with specific traits, characteristics, and values. This accumulation of historical facts resonates with the Freirean banking model of education, where knowledge is deposited onto students with education functioning as an instrument of oppression. In the banking concept of history, historical knowledge is transferred in fragments through different venues of hegemonic discourse and ideologies such as curricula, media, etc. The banking concept of education, in turn, perceives people as adaptable, manageable containers to be filled. The more students accumulate deposited 'knowledge' the more they are disabled from developing the critical consciousness that would arise from their intervention in the world, as transformers of that world. In this scenario, students can never transform their world; they are simply 'implements' in the educational process. In sum, history is something that happens *to* students, not rooted *in* or developed *with* students.

Our school pedagogies focus on addressing standards and on pushing students to meet the demands of high-stakes tests, where knowledge becomes fragmented, dehistoricized and irrelevant. Teaching history is being narrowed down, watered down, broken down into comfortable segments from the past, where the "disturbing elements of Time & Memory" tend to be liquidated as an "irrational rest" (Marcuse, 1964, p. 99). This version of history provides answers rather than asking questions. Memory is disturbing because in neoliberal

142   CHAPTER 5

societies time is only 'the here-and-now.' Time is colonized and robbed away from humans. Thinking of the past in capitalism is a rather dangerous waste of time, it is unproductive; the past helps only if it can be useable or motivate people to be more productive, more 'patriotic,' or more 'American,' as illustrated in the discourse of Trump, DeSantis, and other Republicans.

The teaching of history has a polarizing effect because the values, beliefs, ideologies, and practices, as well as the desires and fears of large groups of people depend on and are shaped through their relationship to the past, through their gaze upon it. Adorno (2005) notes that there is much "that is neurotic in the relation to the past: defensive postures where one is not attacked, intense affects where they are hardly warranted by the situation, an absence of affect in the face of the gravest matters, not seldom simply a repression of what is known or half-known" (p. 90). In this relationship, humans are registered as subjects or objects in the stories told. History is our relationship to ourselves, our families, our communities, our societies, and the world. However, knowledge of the past, is not in and of itself empowering or moves people to subjectivity positions. It takes a degree of critical consciousness to do that: "Knowledge emerges only through invention and re-invention, through the restless, impatient, continuing, hopeful inquiry human beings pursue in the world, with the world, and with each other" (Freire, 1970, pp. 88–89). An instrumentalist view of history fails to take into consideration that "there is no historical reality which is not human. There is no history without humankind, and no history for human beings; there is only history of humanity" (Freire, 1970, p. 169). In far-right authoritarian populism, where humanity is selectively attributed as a special status to specific groups of people, we have in place the construction of a history of (in)humanity. All this is not to suggest that the past should be worshipped. Working through the past, according to Adorno (2005), does not mean doing so "through a lucid consciousness breaking its power to fascinate" (p. 89). It means that "we need history, but we need it differently from the spoiled lazy-bones in the garden of knowledge" (Nietzsche, as cited in Benjamin, 1974, para. XII).

2.2   *Historical Revisionism*

Historical revisionism is a contested term that has taken distinct content in different continents and historiographical traditions. For the project at hand, it is important to define it, understand it, and identify its iterations in Trumpism as a far-right populist movement.

Enzo Traverso in the *New Faces of Fascism* (2019) presents a short genealogy of the term that reveals that it is, in fact, historiographical, as much as it is political. It is borrowed from political theory, where it was used to either characterize reformist politics or those deviations from orthodoxy, based on wrong interpretation. When transposed in historiography, it maintained a negative connotation, designating "the abandonment of canonical interpretations and the adoption of new, politically controversial views" (p. 118). It should be noted that historical revisions per se, are a legitimate process of historical inquiry, necessary to unearth and add new pieces to existing historical knowledge. The writing of human history is an ongoing, unfinished project, as is human life. Traverso notes that "each society has its own regime of historicity—its own relationship with the past" (p. 117). Revisionism is, in turn, putting both this relationship with the past and the regime of historicity into question (Traverso, 2019). Because we always write history from the present, our present gaze can change our relationship with our past. This relationship is shaped by new perspectives, different ways of thinking, and different frameworks of conceptualizing the past. In this sense, the regime of historicity also comprises our relationship with the present, in that history is also taking place now or, as I discuss later in this Chapter, *history is the present*. In essence, revisionism is really about "the political and ideological goals of revisions" because "many historical revisions usually accused of 'revisionism' imply an ethical and political turn in our vision of the past" (Traverso, 2019, p. 124).

In European historiography, revisionism emerged as an attempt to revisit and rehabilitate fascism to equate it with communism, by looking at both as popular revolutions of the two extremes. A good example can be found in the discussion in Chapter 3 on far-right, one-dimensional discourse in the phrase "the Left are the true fascists." This version of historical revisionism has further built tolerance to fascism, downplaying its atrocities after World War II, thus shifting people's perceptions and feelings about them. Far-right populist leaders in Europe capitalized on this shift, self-labeling as holocaust deniers and Nazi worshippers. As Grigoropoulos (2019) suggests, this type of historical revisionism has not only contributed to exonerating fascism, but it has also shifted the focus if its agenda in the post war period. For instance, in the classical fascist agenda, an authoritarian state was necessary (even in the context of a bourgeois democracy) in order to 'resolve' issues such as the fear of social decadence and degeneration, the defense of national and cultural identity, the threat of 'contaminating' national identity by the massive influx of foreigners, religious hate, and homophobia. Contemporary far-right populist rhetoric puts at its core hostility towards immigrants, border protection from intruders, and the deportation of immigrants back to their countries of origin since they do not qualify as asylum seekers. This type of anti-immigrant rhetoric lies at the core of far-right populist parties and is part of the reason they have become so popular (Grigoropoulos, 2019).

144   CHAPTER 5

The same rhetoric has been front and center in Trumpism. In the United States context, White America has been anxious to revise its own recent history that has been particularly violent with non-Whites. Examples of such revisionist narratives have been presented in the beginning of this Chapter with the curricular interventions against Critical Race Theory or with Trump's Patriotic Education. In these revisionist versions there is plenty of room for present-day white supremacy, digital aggression (as presented in Chapter 3) and the rise of neo-fascism. Familiar examples of the two extreme poles are used to equate anti-racist movements with far-right extremists, as vividly illustrated in the Charlottesville Rally discussed in Chapter 3.

Historical revisionism has, in turn, produced historical relativism. Historical relativism has been legitimizing an individualistic approach to history that presents subjective understandings or marginal opinions as a historical dimension of an event. This historical relativism borne out of historical revisionism has given rise to the phenomenon of producing highly individual versions of history. For instance, in the digital media land, historical production became the purview of every individual who owns a social media account, giving shape to a post-truth grand narrative, where everything is relative or up for challenge. In this context, fake news, cancel culture and conspiracy theories have found fertile ground becoming a core element of Trumpism and reaching an ever-growing audience.

A digital walk around social media can quickly reveal a host of misinformation that points to widespread ideological confusion. With Trumpism, came the proliferation of a host of outrageous conspiracy theories. Pro-Trump QAnon is the most popular of them. According to it, a secret cabal of Satan-worshiping cannibalistic pedophiles controls the Democratic Party, Hollywood, and the American government. QAnon adherents believe, among other, that Hillary Clinton and George Soros are drinking the blood of innocent children. In the QAnon narrative, Donald Trump will save America from this cabal, as he appears like God on earth. QAnon draws its beliefs from an anonymous writer posting cryptic posts on a message board who claims that he has access to high-level government intelligence. A 2020 NPR/Ipsos poll recorded that fewer than half (47%) of respondents were able to correctly identify that this statement is false: "A group of Satan-worshipping elites who run a child sex ring are trying to control our politics and media" (p. 1). Thirty-seven percent of respondents were unsure whether this theory backed by QAnon is true or false, and 17% believe it to be true (NPR/Ipsos, 2020).

Trump, on his end, has said of QAnon supporters that they are simply "people who love our country." The former President has not been the only Republican

EMERGENCY TIME AS A PEDAGOGICAL PROJECT   145

embracing QAnon, even though one can safely claim that his opinion weighs quite a bit. The Republican Party, clinging to far-right populism, has become, unapologetically, home to conspiracy theorists, far-right extremists, and white nationalists. Several Republicans have either refrained from condemning QAnon or have openly supported it, as is, for instance, the case of Republican congress-woman from Georgia, Marjorie Taylor Greene. Greene, who is an avid QAnon supporter, praised by Trump as the "future Republican star." While QAnon may have started in the dark corners of the web, it has now become mainstream with a large presence on social media. On January 12th, 2021, after the Capitol insurrection, Twitter suspended 70,000 accounts linked to QAnon, with some accounts having literally millions of followers. Groups which promote QAnon on Gab, have added tens of thousands of followers in the same time period, and in January 2021 boasted more than 400,000 followers in total (BBC, 2021).

Revisionism has received a great boost through social media, particularly in the form of widespread conspiracy theories that are reaching larger numbers of people and acquiring new fans. According to the 2020 NPR/Ipsos poll men-tioned earlier, misinformation mostly around COVID-19, QAnon, and recent Black Lives Matter protests, is becoming more mainstream. Forty percent of Americans believe it is true that COVID-19 was created in a lab in China; sim-ilarly, nearly half (47%) believe the majority of Black Lives Matter protests in the summer 2020, were violent, while just 38% correctly indicated that this is a false statement. Challenge revisionism as a distortion of historical narratives that is part of a conservative agenda seeking to normalize far-right extremism, racism, and dehumanization is a pedagogical project.

2.3   *Decolonial Historical Knowledge: Learning to Unlearn*
My argument throughout this Chapter sets at its core the power and value of historical thinking as pedagogical thinking, where the critical becomes ped-agogical and the pedagogical critical. A different kind of historical thinking means to critically reflect on our relationship with dominant narratives, in this case Western narratives, and to understand decoloniality as an ongoing pedagogical project. This is not a proposal to dispose of Western knowledge altogether; it, rather, means to revisit our exclusive relationship with the West (with privileged versions of the West, more accurately) at the expense of other knowledge production and producers. The West, while not "a homogeneous construction is held together by the narratives and rhetoric of modernity, including the variation of postmodern narratives and the logic of coloniality." Consequently, argues Mignolo (2017), "the westernization of the world touched upon many different histories and memories. Each local history and memory

was disturbed by the intervention and domination of Western civilization, with the collaboration of elites in each local history" (para. 9).

Colonial constructions of history are stubborn and enduring, despite the growing body of literature on decoloniality (Mignolo, 2017; Mignolo & Walsh, 2018). In this discussion, Walter Mignolo's work is illuminating with its focus on delinking from Western narratives and relinking to affirm other modes of existence we want to preserve and promote as an important pedagogical process that challenges the Colonial Matrix of Power (CMP): a structure of management (composed of domains, levels, and flows) that controls and touches upon all aspects and trajectories of our lives (Mignolo, 2017). The invisibility of CMP sustained Western civilization as a visible narrative.

The decolonial project is not exclusively a scholarly endeavor; it includes decolonial thinking and doing. Decolonization is a pedagogical project of unlearning narratives, ways of thinking and doing, deeply steeped in oppressive systems of knowledge and identity production. The first step in this decolonial project would be to decolonize the self: for scholars and educators who have been socialized, educated, and conditioned in particular ways of learning, knowing, teaching, and talking about knowledge and disciplinary ways of inquiry, unlearning is a long and painful process; it is about uneducating ourselves from the "colonial shackles of knowledge production" (Yako, 2021, para. 8). With unlearning, comes re-learning, that is, rescuing, articulating, and enriching a vision of knowledge that does not limit itself in the confines of the West. A vision of knowledge embodied in different groups of human beings in the World "to rebuild all that has been damaged by the colonial wounds and the disciplinary institutions we dealt with throughout our lives" (Yako, 2021, para. 9).

Another important process in the project of decoloniality is that of constant humanization to counter dehumanization. Colonization dehumanizes people, it devalues their mind, psyche, and body. This process works on two levels: for scholars/educators who are colonized subjects it means reclaiming their value and authority in making meaningful contributions. As Yako (2021) notes, "coloniality puts colonized people in such a position that they must validate everything they do through the criteria and measurements of the apparatus put in place by Europe and North America" (para. 10). It is then, vital that colonial subjects/scholars reclaim their value and reconnect "with that deeply buried voice of knowledge inside of us that has been silenced by the wreckage of wars, sanctions, racism, violence, sexism, and other forms of divisions, classifications manufactured and imposed by coloniality" (para. 10). Second, it is important that as scholars and educators we hold and preserve the core of what makes us human refraining from reproducing dehumanizing ideologies

EMERGENCY TIME AS A PEDAGOGICAL PROJECT

and practices in our lives and in our work; and that we constantly engage in the delinking and relinking process suggested by Mignolo.

2.4 History Is the Present and the Present as History

> History is the object of a construction whose place is formed not in homogenous and empty time, but in that which is fulfilled by the here-and-now [Jetztzeit]. (Benjamin, 1974, para. XIV)

Earlier in this chapter, I presented the disturbing Trumpism-inspired movement to eradicate discussions of race and other forms of oppression from school curricula. Contextualized at a time of heightened racial tensions, a momentum for the Black Lives Matter movement, calls for police reform and defunding, and an ongoing awakening regarding racial issues in America, this movement really speaks to the present, rather than the past. Particular histories become dangerous because they have bearings on the present. These histories are too powerful to simply be rewritten so they have to be annihilated. James Baldwin (2010) in a speech at Wayne State University in 1980 had powerfully claimed that "history is not the past. It is the present. We carry our history with us. We are our history. If we pretend otherwise, to put it very brutally, we literally are criminals" (p. 158).

To think critically means to think historically. But history is the present. So, to think historically means to think about the present in ways that are emancipatory, agential, and liberating. Thinking historically does not simply mean to 'know' history. Or to read the past through the lens of the present and the present through the lens of the past. It means to realize the continuities and ruptures of history, the interconnectedness and difference. It also signifies the ability to realize ourselves as historical beings with a developing critical consciousness. History in the sense of historiography should not be an exercise in narrative but rather bear use to the 'here and now:' 'We need history for life and action...' claims Nietzsche (Lowy, 2016, p. 110). History is not a prison of the past through which we can look at the present only through bars; it is not a mechanism that confines our thinking, but it can surely function this way. Marcuse (1964) is illuminating once more here when he notes that the recognition and relation to the past as present "counteracts the functionalization of thought by and in the established reality. It militates against the closing of the universe of discourse and behavior; it renders possible the development of concepts which de-stabilize and transcend the closed universe by comprehending it as historical universe" (p. 103).

2.5   *Trauma and Healing*

In the Preface of this book, I briefly talked about the potential trauma inflicted upon scholars when they study violence against humanity, in what was referred to as a process of 'vicarious traumatization.' I also discussed earlier the purported discomfort that conversations about racism and enslavement potentially inflict on people in the far-right conservative view. The 'traumatizing' dimension of history aims neither at forcing humans to relive the trauma, nor to play the blame game. It is the ability to look at the horror and struggle straight in the face, to allow oneself to be affected by other peoples' lives and histories. It aims at connecting humanity with their kin, to relate at the most fundamental level: affect, the perishability and fragility of human actions. What the mind and intellect might resist understanding, affect can record in the language of humanity. It speaks to the ability to imagine, to put together the picture of that which occurred and use it pedagogically. The reconstitution also requires a degree of imagination in recreating not only lives bygone but also the ambience, atmosphere, feeling about space and people: a kind of *historical aura*. This can be achieved through imagination. Hannah Arendt (1953) claimed that imagination "enables us to see things in their proper perspective, to put that which is too close at a certain distance so that we can see and understand it without bias and prejudice, to bridge abysses of remoteness until we can see and understand everything that is too far away from us as though it were our own affair. This 'distancing' of some things and bridging the abysses to others is part of the dialogue of understanding" (p. 392). Imagination for Arendt (1953) is understanding; it is our 'inner compass' "if we want to be at home on this earth, even at the price of being at home in this century, we must try to take part in the interminable dialogue with its essence" (p. 392). Imagination creates distance and closeness that makes understanding possible.

3   History: A Critical Public Pedagogy Project of Recontextualization

> *Unidentified user*: I recall reading a post from you in which you revealed that you are a 1st year psychology student at university. I used to write essays in high school pretending to be leftwing so as to satisfy the teachers and stay out of trouble. It worked and my psych/anthro/sociology teacher said that he thought I was his best student. If you are not already, I would strongly suggest that you do the same or switch to a different major. Leftists can be very nasty people and psychology departments are filled with such obnoxious leftists.

EMERGENCY TIME AS A PEDAGOGICAL PROJECT

Ethno Nationalist (1D40): Thanks for the uni[versity] advice too. I've been towing the line a lot so far. We're actually starting off with 'The Authoritarian Personality' and Adorno's anti-racist, psychoanalyctic nonsensence [sic] and other Frankfurt school rubbish. They start early to feed the agenda in university it seems. (Iron March user exchange under the forum topic *Interested in your Ideology*)

This dialogue between two users on the neo-Nazi Iron March platform, resonates once again with the Trumpist far-right discourse built around the idea of the enemy from the 'Left.' The creation of a permanent enemy is structured on the perspective of historical revisionism outlined earlier. If an alien landed in the United States today and was only exposed to these far-right populist narratives, they would probably think that there is some sort of imminent 'red threat' ready to unleash their vicious mobs to take over politics, education, and every realm of human life. Those of us who have not only been inspired by 'Frankfurt school rubbish' but have used it over and over in our teaching, writing, and thinking, would be unquestionable enemies. The above exchange also points to a persistent myth on the left takeover of the academy, a myth that cannot be further from the truth. In the name of that myth, there are organizations such as the notorious ultra conservative Campus Reform, an online platform self-labelled as the "#1 Source for College News" and whose stated mission is to expose "liberal bias and abuse on the nation's college campuses" (Campus Reform, 2021, Mission section, para. 2) Campus Reform was created in 2009 as a hub for conservative students in U.S. colleges to provide them with "weapons in their fight for the hearts and minds of the next generation of citizens, politicians, and members of the media" (Speri, 2021, para. 15). In the words of Campus Reform's publisher, the Leadership Institute, the site aims to train "freedom fighters" to "effectively defeat the radical Left." The Leadership Institute, is a nonprofit that has trained conservative activists for over forty years (since 1979) with funding received by billionaire donors, including foundations connected to the Koch family. The institute reported more than $16 million in revenue in 2018 alone, and offers a rich program with a heavy focus on media and communications (Speri, 2021). What Campus Reform does casually is to identify and target hundreds of college professors who have expressed progressive stances, by publishing 'articles' that lead to "online harassment campaigns, doxxing, threats of violence, and calls on universities to fire their faculty" (Speri, 2021). The site gives users the option to send a 'confidential tip' about what they call "liberal abuse or wrongdoing taking place on an American College." The war against progressive curricula and historiography becomes

150   CHAPTER 5

more violent and ugly, considering the resources organizations like Campus
Reform have at their disposal.

3.1   History, Discourse and Recontextualization

> Language can turn into a prison or a set of wings that can help us fly.
> (Yako, 2021, para. 20)

How do events acquire meaning? How are historical narratives filled with
meaning over and over? As Heer et al. (2008) observe, history as a retrospective-
ly-composed and meaning-endowed narrative is always construction and fic-
tionalization. Historical phenomena as the result of social processes are borne
out of contradiction, conflict, and the struggle over meaning. In this struggle,
some events "will become carriers of consensual values and ideals" and will
"therefore have value as objects in collective memory" (p. 1). The process of ret-
rospective attribution of meaning, includes conflict, since decisions are being
made on inclusions and exclusions and the production of specific discourses.
Historical narratives are carried and reproduced through discourses in history
books, films, documentaries, political speeches, and other sites, such as social
media. The different discourses produced in diverse sites through a multiplicity
of texts make up collective memory. History, written or oral, official, or unofficial, distant, or recent, is always a 'text' of some sorts, oral, written, or other—it
is impossible to escape its textual nature. Historical narratives are constantly
made and remade, thought and rethought, discursively. As we have seen, in the
far-right authoritarian context, one central process is that of 'dehistoricization.'
Dehistoricization manifests in the production of discourses that lack a historical dimension and are carried through one-dimensional language that in turn,
produces a one-dimensional historical narrative. According to Marcuse (1964)
"the functional language is a radically anti-historical language: operational
rationality has little room and little use for historical reason" (p. 101). Among
many different competing historical narratives, one is to become dominant,
or hegemonic not because of some inherent qualities it engenders, but rather
because of the structure and power of the evaluative process involved.

The decisions on attributing meaning to select historical narratives impacts,
in turn, the discursive construction of national identities (Wodak et al., 1999,
2009) drawing on a wide range of collective and individual memories. As Pennebaker and Banasik note, "history defines us just as we define history. As our
identities and cultures evolve over time, we tacitly reconstruct our histories.
By the same token, these new collectively defined historical memories help to
provide identities for succeeding generations" (Pennebaker & Banasik, 1997, as
quoted in Strath & Wodak, 2009, p. 19).

EMERGENCY TIME AS A PEDAGOGICAL PROJECT

Finally, and in connection with the previous discussion on decoloniality, discourses as constitutive of knowledge need to be decolonized, we must

> examine why we say the things we say and how we get to internalize and express the things that shape our lives. In fact, language is truly the only home that remains even in exile when all else is lost. (Yako, 2021, para. 20)

From my discussion so far, the pedagogical character, dimension and value of history and historical narratives is evident. I want to further elaborate on this pedagogical dimension by drawing on educational sociologist Basil Bernstein's (1990) theoretical concept of 'recontextualization' in the context of his discussion on cultural reproduction and the pedagogic device and pedagogic discourse. First, for Bernstein, pedagogy is not just the content of the formal curriculum, but also the way in which knowledge is transmitted and evaluated. He critiques the focus on *what* is reproduced in and by education and the view that the specialized discourse of education is only a voice through which others speak (class, gender religion, race). It is as if pedagogic discourse is, itself, no more than a relay for power relations external to itself; a relay whose form has no consequences for what is relayed. He reorients the discussion on how the pedagogic discourse is reproduced. For Bernstein, pedagogic discourse is a "principle for appropriating other discourses and bringing them into a special relation with each other for the purposes of their selective transmission and acquisition" (Bernstein, 1990, p. 159). He is, therefore, more interested in the analysis of the medium of reproduction, the nature of the specialized discourse. Towards this goal, he presents the pedagogic device as the hierarchical rules of distribution, recontextualization and evaluation for specializing forms of consciousness. Pedagogic discourses operate in the context of the pedagogic device by selectively creating which pedagogic subjects will be created and which discourses will be selected and appropriated for transmission. 'Context' is where knowledge is first produced, while 'pedagogical context' is where this knowledge is reproduced and disseminated. So, for example, knowledge produced originally in a biology lab, is reproduced for use in the classroom. In the process of production, reproduction and dissemination knowledge is reframed, or rather 'recontextualized.' For instance, similarly to the previous example, historical knowledge taught through schools is already recontextualized in the following sense: a historical narrative in the form of discourse is first chosen, and subsequently removed (delocated) from its "substantive practice and context" (that would be historiography) and is relocated "according to its own principle of selective reordering and focusing." In the relocation process the social basis of its practice and the power relations are removed. Bernstein (1990) is worth quoting at length here:

152   CHAPTER 5

In the process of the de- and relocation, the original discourse is subject
to a transformation which transforms it from an actual practice to a virtual or imaginary practice. Pedagogic discourse creates imaginary subjects. We must sharpen our concept of this principle which constitutes
pedagogic discourse. It is a recontextualizing principle which selectively
appropriates, relocates, refocuses, and relates other discourses to constitute its own order and orderings. In this sense, pedagogic discourse cannot be identified with any of the discourses it has recontextualized. In
this sense it has no discourse of its own, other than a recontextualizing
discourse. We have now made the move from the distributive rules to the
recontextualizing rules, the rules which constitute pedagogic discourse.
(p. 159)

The process of recontextualization from delocation to relocation is useful,
both because it allows us to understand the ways historical narratives get
transformed for pedagogical practices along the interests, goals, and values
of the schooling process as these are embodied in specific semantic shifts;
and because it focuses on the particular form of discourses as constitutive of
the pedagogical historical narratives. According to Wodak and Van Leeuwen
(1999), there are four main transformations involved in this type of recontextualization: rearrangement, deletion, addition (such as purposes or justifica-
tions) and substitution of elements; these are important transformations that
one should consider when studying the discursive construction of historical
narratives. At stake in the recontextualization process is what's added and left
out, as well as the shifts in content, discourse and meaning. It further raises the
issue of different 'loci' where historical narratives are produced, the purpose
and audience. This resonates with van Leeuwen's (2008) discussion of discourse as a recontextualized practice, that is "a socially constructed knowledge
of some social practice" (p. 6). Discourse, as such, develops in specific social
contexts, and in ways that are appropriate to these contexts.

4   Making the Pedagogical Historical and the Historical Pedagogical

In the beginning of this chapter, I presented Walter Benjamin's notion of
'emergency situation' where fascism is understood as a violent expression of
the permanent state of emergency. Emergency situation crystallizes the ongoing struggle over historicity, collective memory, meaning and human practices.
Because "Fascism is always, apparently, the alternative future struggling to be
born" (Penny, 2020, para. 8) there is another struggle for different alternative

futures to be fought. And this struggle is also deeply pedagogical. In the context of emergency time and drawing on Chapter 4 of this book, I want to articulate my proposal for a pedagogical project that puts historicity at its core.

Historicity in this context resonates with understanding humans as actors/agents of history and looking at all knowledge and learning, whether 'official' and 'unofficial,' inside, and outside schools and in multiple sites as deeply historical; It is historical in that it is a substantial element of an agentive process that has the potential to develop critical consciousness in humans. Historicity also suggests reading the past as present in a process that neither worships the past nor annihilates it, in the name of the tyranny of the present. This is a pedagogical project that challenges one-dimensionality in historical thinking in educational sites and in public discourse and debates and brings the 'disturbing elements' of time at the core of our analyses. One-dimensional historical narratives limit our thinking and embody authoritarianism and conformity, as evidenced in the far-right discourses presented and discussed in Chapter 3.

I am proposing a pedagogy that always exists in historical terms, as a liberatory project, very much along the lines that Paulo Freire envisioned in his work. The pedagogical historical project is, therefore, a humanizing project. Educational theorists and educators need to develop a solid historical formation made up of multiple and diverse narratives, a formation that is rarely offered through institutions of higher education. This type of historical knowledge and developing consciousness might create the conditions where they acknowledge themselves as historical beings and therefore, realize their roles and function in education institutions, while they challenge their own assumptions and values. Historicity, further, would empower them to rethink teaching and learning historically. Among the important challenges for scholars and educators is to understand and historicize the public debates and discourses emerging in multiple sites inside and outside schools. This would entail the inclusion of multiple histories and experiences that reflect the lives, struggles, aspirations, and dreams of historically subjugated groups. As a result, these subjugated groups could move from the periphery into a center stage, where they will be able to recount their own histories while at the same time questioning, redefining and, in the end, uprooting the dominant versions.

Along the same lines, a fundamental element in this pedagogy would also be the historicization of social conflicts. Students (and educators) should have historical and current knowledge about social struggles, the ways these have been shaped historically and what they mean for their lives today. These narratives of collective memory might enable people to read the world and position themselves in it, make the appropriate choices and decisions, and assume responsibility for themselves and the societies they live in. Reflecting on our societies and social practices, we can witness critical thought becoming historical consciousness. It is this consciousness that navigates as a compass looking at the history of humans "for the criteria of truth and falsehood, progress and regression. The mediation of the past with the present discovers the factors which made the facts, which determined the way of life, which established the masters and the servants; it projects the limits and the alternatives." This is a critical consciousness that "speaks 'le langage de la connaissance'[1] (Roland Barthes) which breaks open a closed universe of discourse and its petrified structure. The key terms of this language are not hypnotic nouns which evoke endlessly the same frozen predicates. They rather allow for "an open development; they even unfold their content in contradictory predicates" (Marcuse, 1964, p. 103). And they structure a discourse and narratives breaking the instrumentalism and common sense of one dimension.

For example, educators would find value in exploring the analogy of current authoritarian regimes around the world with fascism and analyzing their common characteristics, as an interesting and powerful pedagogical and political tool. It often takes an extreme analogy for people to realize the severity of a sociopolitical situation, especially in the context of a democracy, that is in reality, the embodiment of a mutated form of capitalism. The study of authoritarianism, far-right populism, and neofascism can illuminate the polarization in schools and the hatred-filled political rhetoric in public-school climate; but more importantly, it can illuminate the state of political life today, locally and globally. Similarly, a solid grounding in history coupled with a genuine awakening of epistemological curiosity, would challenge dangerous versions of historical revisionism that attempt to make authoritarianism relevant or to legitimize racism.

One of the characteristics of fascism, according to Max Horkheimer (1939) is that it robs people of their minds. In authoritarian states people stop thinking. But minds can develop, grow, get challenged, stimulated, and opened up in educational institutions. And while I have made the case in my Preface that schools don't change societies, they have the capacity to create spaces for radical thinking. This could be part of a problem-posing education, an anti-pedagogy to the oppressive educational culture of the banking concept of education. A problem-posing pedagogy is generated through "dialectical engagement of teacher and students, where teaching and learning are understood inseparable to a (subjective-objective) revolutionary praxis within schools and communities that supports conscientização—a communal process of evolving social consciousness" (Darder, 2018, p. 142). The Freirean notion of 'conscientização' or critical awareness grows out of understanding our relationship with/in the world and with history. It is the development of social consciousness as "both

EMERGENCY TIME AS A PEDAGOGICAL PROJECT

a historical phenomenon and a human social process, linked to our emancipatory necessity as human beings to participate as both cognitive and narrative
subjects of our destinies" (Darder, 2018, p. 143).

One of the biggest challenges that arises from the school neutrality myth
is the fragmentation and de-historicization of knowledge (is it knowledge or,
rather, information?). The critical public pedagogy I propose here is deeply
historical and therefore, *real*: It is anchored in reality, in everyday life, in the
daily struggles of educators, students, parents, and communities to fight the
far-right conservative authoritarian backlash. And yet, these struggles must
always be situated historically, as is the knowledge of this world. And only by
knowing our social world, can we act upon it through a dialectical process of
reflection and action that leads to transformation. It is the knowledge of this
world that, for example, has been rewritten in multiple sites in the far-right
authoritarian context. Which takes me to another dimension of critical public
pedagogy. Public pedagogy should not be limited to making pedagogy public,
but to make the public, a core element of pedagogy. In the same way that learning can take place in so many public (and private) sites, the 'public'—what
is going on in public life, should be part of learning. The public must enter
schools and classrooms, instead of building high walls to block out 'unofficial'
discussions and 'unofficial' knowledge. For instance, it would be important
and worth exploring the multiple ways students engage with social media, the
narratives produced there, and the kinds of identities produced; and demystify
their structure and discourses, as I have done in Chapters 2 and 3.

Finally, it is important to capitalize on the lessons from an 'anti-pedagogy;'
create our counter pedagogies with courage, honesty, humility, and commitment by revisiting our relationship with the past: "The past will have been
worked through only when the causes of what happened then, have been elim-
inated. Only because the causes continue to exist does the captivating spell of
the past remain to this day unbroken" (Adorno, 2005, p. 34). To break the 'captivating spell of the past,' we need to develop an honest, consistent, humble
radicalism that, according to Freire (2005) is committed to human liberation,
and "does not become the prisoner of a 'circle of certainty' within which reality
is also imprisoned" (p. 39). On the contrary, it is our dwelling in reality, that
prompts us to understand it and transform it.

As Marx has so powerfully argued, "the weapon of criticism cannot, of course,
replace criticism of the weapon, material force must be overthrown by material force; but theory also becomes a material force as soon as it has gripped the
masses. Theory is capable of gripping the masses as soon as it demonstrates
ad hominem, and it demonstrates *ad hominem* as soon as it becomes radical.
To be radical is to grasp the root of the matter. But, for man [sic], the root is

156   CHAPTER 5

man himself. [...] *man is the highest essence for man*—hence, with the *categoric imperative to overthrow all relations* in which man is a debased, enslaved, abandoned, despicable essence" (Marx, 1843/1994).

Note

1   The language of knowledge.

References

ACLED. (2020). *Demonstrations and political violence in America.* https://acleddata.com/acleddatanew/wp-content/uploads/2020/09/ACLED_USDataReview_Sum2020_SeptWebPDF_HiRes.pdf

Adorno, T. W. (2005). *Critical models: Interventions and catchwords.* Columbia University Press.

Arendt, H. (1953). Understanding and politics. *Partisan Review, 20*(4), 377–392.

Baldwin, J. (2010). Black English: A dishonest argument. In R. Keenan (Ed.), *The cross of redemption: Uncollected writings* (pp. 154–160). Pantheon.

BBC. (2021, January 12). Twitter suspends 70,000 accounts linked to QAnon. *BBC News.* https://www.bbc.com/news/technology-55638558

Benjamin, W. (1974). *On the concept of history* (D. Redmond, Trans.). Suhrkamp Verlag

Bernstein, B. (1990). *The structuring of pedagogic discourse: Class, codes & control* (Vol. IV). Routledge.

Bigelow, B. (2018, October 2). Whose history matters? Students can name Columbus, but most have never heard of the Taíno people. *Zinnedproject.org.* https://www.zinnedproject.org/if-we-knew-our-history/whose-history-matters-taino

Campus Reform. (2021). *Mission.* https://campusreform.org/about

Carter, R. (2021, April 29). *Ban on racist instruction sent to governor.* Oklahoma Council of Public Affairs. https://www.ocpathink.org/post/ban-on-racist-instruction-sent-to-governor

Creamer, J. (2020, September 15). *Inequalities persist despite decline in poverty for all major race and Hispanic origin groups.* Unites States Census Bureau. https://www.census.gov/library/stories/2020/09/poverty-rates-for-blacks-and-hispanics-reached-historic-lows-in-2019.html

Crenshaw, K. (1989). Demarginalizing the intersection of race and sex: A Black feminist critique of antidiscrimination doctrine, feminist theory and antiracist politics. *University of Chicago Legal Forum, 1989*(8), 139–167.

Crenshaw, K., Gotanda, N., Peller, G., & Thomas, K. (Eds.). (1995). *Critical race theory: The key writings that formed the movement*. The New Press.

Darder, A. (2018). *The student guide to Freire's 'Pedagogy of the oppressed.'* Bloomsbury.

Delgado, R., & Stefancic, J. (2001). *Critical race theory: An introduction*. New York University Press.

DiVirgilio, L. (2010, May 13). *Arizona's new law bans ethnic studies in public schools*. Syracuse. https://www.syracuse.com/news/2010/05/arizonas_new_law_bans_ethnic_s.html

Edwards, F., Lee, H., & Esposito, M. (2019). Risk of being killed by police use of force in the United States by age, race–ethnicity, and sex. *Proceedings of the National Academy of Sciences, 116*(34), 16793–16798. https://www.pnas.org/content/116/34/16793

Freire, P. (2005). *Pedagogy of the oppressed* (30th anniversary ed., M. B. Ramons, Trans.). Continuum.

Gramlich, J. (2020, May 6). *Black imprisonment rate in the U.S. has fallen by a third since 2006*. Pew Research Center. https://www.pewresearch.org/fact-tank/2020/05/06/share-of-black-white-hispanic-americans-in-prison-2018-vs-2006/

Grigoropoulos, D. (2019). The contribution of revisionism to the exculpation and rise of fascism. *Marxism Notebooks, 10*, 89–118.

Groves, S. (2021, January 15). *Noem blames Capitol insurrection on lack of civics education*. Associated Press. https://www.usnews.com/news/politics/articles/2021-01-15/noem-blames-capitol-insurrection-on-lack-of-civics-education

Hanks, A. Solomon, D., & Weller, C. (2018, February 21). *Systematic inequality: How America's structured racism helped create the black-white wealth gap*. Center for American Progress. https://www.americanprogress.org/issues/race/reports/2018/02/21/447051/systematic-inequality/

H.B. 377, 2021 Sixty Sixth Legislature, 2021 Reg. Sess. (ID. 2021). https://legislature.idaho.gov/wp-content/uploads/sessioninfo/2021/legislation/H0377.pdf

H.B. 1775 ENGR, 57th Legislature, 2021 2nd Sess. (OK. 2021). http://webserver1.lsb.state.ok.us/cf_pdf/2021-22%20AMENDMENTS/Amendment%20&%20Engr/HB1775%20SAHB%20&%20ENGR.PDF

Heer, H., Manoschek, W., Pollak, A., & Wodak, R. (2008). *The discursive construction of history: remembering the Wehrmacht's war of annihilation*. Palgrave Macmillan.

Horkheimer, M. (1939). *The Jews and Europe*. The Charnel-House. https://thecharnelhouse.org/2015/03/20/the-jews-and-europe/

Jeffries, H. K. (2018, January 31). Preface. In *Teaching hard history: American slavery*. Southern Poverty Law Center. https://www.splcenter.org/20180131/teaching-hard-history#preface

Lowy, M. (2016). *Fire alarm: Reading Walter Benjamin's on the concept of history*. Verso.

Marcuse, M. (1964). *One-dimensional man*. Beacon Press.

Marx, K., & Davis, R. (1994). A contribution to the critique of Hegel's philosophy of right: Introduction. In J. O'Malley (Ed.), *Marx: Early political writings* (pp. 57–70). Cambridge University Press.

Mignolo, W. (2017, March 7). *Coloniality is far from over, and so must be decoloniality*. Afterall. https://www.afterall.org/publications/journal/issue.43/coloniality-is-far-from-over-and-so-must-be-decoloniality

Mignolo, W., & Walsh, C. E. (2018). *On Decoloniality: Concepts, analytics, praxis*. Duke University Press.

NPR/Ipsos. (2020, December 30). *More than 1 in 3 Americans believe a 'deep state' is working to undermine Trump*. Ipsos. https://www.ipsos.com/en-us/news-polls/npr-misinformation-123020

Penny, L. (2020, November 18). The timelines of our lives. *Wired*. https://www.wired.com/story/timelines-of-our-lives/

Riddle, T., & Sinclair, S. (2019). Racial disparities in school-based disciplinary actions are associated with county-level rates of racial bias. *Proceedings of the National Academy of Sciences, 116*(17), 8255–8260. https://doi.org/10.1073/pnas.1808307116

Serwer, A. (2019, December 23). The fight over the 1619 project is not about the facts. *The Atlantic*. https://www.theatlantic.com/ideas/archive/2019/12/historians-clash-1619-project/604093/

Solomon, D., Maxwell, C., & Castro, A. (2019, August 7). *Systemic inequality: Displacement, exclusion, and segregation*. Center for American Progress. https://www.americanprogress.org/issues/race/reports/2019/08/07/472617/systemic-inequality-displacement-exclusion-segregation/

Solórzano, D. (1997). Images and words that wound: Critical race theory, racial stereotyping, and teacher education. *Teacher Education Quarterly, 24*(3), 5–19.

Solórzano, D., & Yosso, T. J. (2002). Critical race methodology: Counter-storytelling as an analytical framework for education research. *Qualitative Inquiry, 8*(1), 23–44. https://doi.org/10.1177/107780040200800103

Southern Poverty Law Center. (2017). *Donning the mask: Presenting 'The face of 21st century fascism.'* https://www.splcenter.org/hatewatch/2017/06/20/donning-mask-presenting-face-21st-century-fascism

Southern Poverty Law Center. (2018). *Teaching hard history*. https://www.splcenter.org/sites/default/files/tt_hard_history_american_slavery.pdf

Speri, A. (2021, April 10). *A billionaire-funded website with ties to the far right is trying to "cancel" university professors*. The Intercept. https://theintercept.com/2021/04/10/campus-reform-koch-young-americans-for-freedom-leadership-institute/

Strath, B., & Wodak, R. (2009). Europe-discourse-politics-media-history: Constructing 'crises'? In A. Triandafyllidou, R. Wodak, & M. Krzyżanowski (Eds.), *The European public sphere and the media* (pp. 15–33). Palgrave Macmillan.

Traverso, E. (2019). *The new faces of fascism*. Verso.

EMERGENCY TIME AS A PEDAGOGICAL PROJECT   159

Trump, D. (2020, September 17). *Remarks by President Trump at the White House conference on American history.* White House Archives. https://trumpwhitehouse.archives.gov/briefings-statements/remarks-president-trump-white-house-conference-american-history/

van Leeuwen, T. (2008). *Discourse and practice: New tools for critical discourse analysis.* Oxford University Press.

Vought, R. (2020, September 4). *Memorandum for the heads of executive departments and agencies.* Executive Office of The President, Office of Management and Budget. https://www.whitehouse.gov/wp-content/uploads/2020/09/M-20-34.pdf?fbclid=IwAR1r7Ej2VogZ8pNhIEjLtHDDNlfeYvBkzEgUfbrU3cXfot7RP2XKPwnCDe4

Wodak, R., de Cillia, R., Reisigl, M., & Liebhart, K. (2009). *The discursive construction of national identity* (2nd ed.). Edinburgh University Press.

Wodak, R., & van Leeuwen, T. (1999). Legitimizing immigration control: A discourse-historical analysis. *Discourse Studies, 1*(1), 83–119. https://doi.org/10.1177/1461445699001001005

Woodiel, C. (2021, April 9). Educators and historians want to keep politics out of new civics and history curriculum. *Kelo.* https://kelo.com/2021/04/09/152015/

Yako, L. (2021, April 9). Decolonizing knowledge production: A practical guide. *Counterpunch.* https://www.counterpunch.org/2021/04/09/decolonizing-knowledge-production-a-practical-guide/

Yamahtta-Taylor, K. (2016). *From Black lives matter to Black liberation.* Haymarket Books.

APPENDIX A

Trump's Last Two Tweets on January 8th, 2021

a. (1) The 75,000,000 great American Patriots who voted for me, AMERICA FIRST, and MAKE AMERICA GREAT AGAIN, will have a GIANT VOICE long into the future. They will not be disrespected or treated unfairly in any way, shape or form!!!

b. (2) To all of those who have asked, I will not be going to the Inauguration on January 20th.

APPENDIX B

Twitter Blog Post on the Permanent Suspension of Donald Trump's Account, January 8th, 2021

Company

Permanent suspension of @realDonaldTrump

By Twitter Inc.

Friday, 8 January 2021

After close review of recent Tweets from the @realDonaldTrump account and the context around them—specifically how they are being received and interpreted on and off Twitter—we have permanently suspended the account due to the risk of further incitement of violence.

In the context of horrific events this week, we made it clear on Wednesday that additional violations of the Twitter Rules would potentially result in this very course of action. Our *public interest framework* exists to enable the public to hear from elected officials and world leaders directly. It is built on a principle that the people have a right to hold power to account in the open.

However, we made it clear going back years that these accounts are not above our rules entirely and cannot use Twitter to incite violence, among other things. We will continue to be transparent around our policies and their enforcement.

The below is a comprehensive analysis of our policy enforcement approach in this case.

Overview

On January 8, 2021, President Donald J. Trump Tweeted:

> The 75,000,000 great American Patriots who voted for me, AMERICA FIRST, and MAKE AMERICA GREAT AGAIN, will have a GIANT VOICE long into the future. They will not be disrespected or treated unfairly in any way, shape or form!!!

APPENDIX B

163

Shortly thereafter, the President Tweeted:

> To all of those who have asked, I will not be going to the Inauguration on January 20th.

Due to the ongoing tensions in the United States, and an uptick in the global conversation in regards to the people who violently stormed the Capitol on January 6, 2021, these two Tweets must be read in the context of broader events in the country and the ways in which the President's statements can be mobilized by different audiences, including to incite violence, as well as in the context of the pattern of behavior from this account in recent weeks. After assessing the language in these Tweets against our *Glorification of Violence* policy, we have determined that these Tweets are in violation of the Glorification of Violence Policy and the user @realDonaldTrump should be immediately permanently suspended from the service.

Assessment

We assessed the two Tweets referenced above under our *Glorification of Violence policy*, which aims to prevent the glorification of violence that could inspire others to replicate violent acts and determined that they were highly likely to encourage and inspire people to replicate the criminal acts that took place at the U.S. Capitol on January 6, 2021.

This determination is based on a number of factors, including:
- President Trump's statement that he will not be attending the Inauguration is being received by a number of his supporters as further confirmation that the election was not legitimate and is seen as him disavowing his previous claim made via two Tweets (1, 2) by his Deputy Chief of Staff, Dan Scavino, that there would be an "orderly transition" on January 20th.
- The second Tweet may also serve as encouragement to those potentially considering violent acts that the Inauguration would be a "safe" target, as he will not be attending.
- The use of the words "American Patriots" to describe some of his supporters is also being interpreted as support for those committing violent acts at the US Capitol.
- The mention of his supporters having a "GIANT VOICE long into the future" and that "They will not be disrespected or treated unfairly in any way, shape or form!!!" is being interpreted as further indication that President Trump does not plan to facilitate an "orderly transition" and instead that he plans to continue to support, empower, and shield those who believe he won the election.

- Plans for future armed protests have already begun proliferating on and off-Twitter, including a proposed secondary attack on the US Capitol and state capitol buildings on January 17, 2021.

As such, our determination is that the two Tweets above are likely to inspire others to replicate the violent acts that took place on January 6, 2021, and that there are multiple indicators that they are being received and understood as encouragement to do so.

APPENDIX C

Donald Trump Talking to Reporters after the Charlottesville Rally

TRUMP: *I am not putting anybody on a moral plane, what I'm saying is this: you had a group on one side and a group on the other, and they came at each other with clubs and it was vicious and horrible and it was a horrible thing to watch, but there is another side. There was a group on this side, you can call them the left.* You've just called them the left, that came violently attacking the other group. So you can say what you want, but that's the way it is.

REPORTER: You said there was hatred and violence on both sides?

TRUMP: I do think there is blame—yes, I think there is blame on both sides. You look at, you look at both sides. I think there's blame on both sides, and I have no doubt about it, and you don't have any doubt about it either. And, and, and, and if you reported it accurately, you would say.

REPORTER: The neo-Nazis started this thing. They showed up in Charlottesville.

TRUMP: Excuse me, they didn't put themselves down as neo-Nazis, and you had some very bad people in that group. But you also had people that were very fine people on both sides. You had people in that group—excuse me, excuse me. I saw the same pictures as you did. You had people in that group that were there to protest the taking down, of to them, a very, very important statue and the renaming of a park from Robert E. Lee to another name.

[…]

No, no. There were people in that rally, and I looked the night before. If you look, they were people protesting very quietly, the taking down the statue of Robert E. Lee. I'm sure in that group there were some bad ones. The following day, it looked like they had some rough, bad people, neo-Nazis, white nationalists, whatever you want to call 'em. But you had a lot of people in that group that were there to innocently protest and very legally protest, because you know, I don't know if you know, but they had a permit. The other group didn't have a permit. So I only tell you this: there are two sides to a story. I thought what took place was a horrible moment for our country, a horrible moment. But there are two sides to the country. Does anybody have a final—does anybody have a final question? You have an infrastructure question.

Index

Adorno, Theodor XIV, XV, 5, 27, 32, 45, 140, 142, 149
affluent society 50, 55
agency 3, 10, 19, 108, 109, 120, 121
aggressiveness
 digital 41, 48, 66, 67, 72
 language of XIV, 48, 49, 66, 93
anti-Blackness XI, 3, 122
antiliberalism 90
alt-right XIII, 2, 4, 24–26, 33, 57–59, 75–77, 91
American Dream 104, 133, 136
Arendt, Hannah XIII, 5, 19, 148
argumentation strategy 81, 83
authoritarian capitalism 17
authoritarian discourse 4, 40, 41, 46, 51, 60, 67, 86
authoritarian leader 26, 27, 30–32
authoritarian personality XIV, XV, 27, 32, 45, 149
authoritarian populism XI, 3, 5–7, 14, 16, 18, 31, 41, 51, 58, 60, 67, 93, 142
authoritarianism XI–XVII, 2–11, 15, 18, 19, 23, 33, 39–42, 44, 45, 50, 57, 60, 67, 70, 102, 103, 113–115, 121, 122, 138, 139, 153, 154

Benjamin, Walter 10, 138, 139, 152
Bernstein, Basil 151

Campus Reform 149, 150
capitalism
 authoritarian 17, 23, 46, 57
 casino 25, 29
 communicative 46, 54
Capitol
 events 11, 67, 79
 insurrection XIV, 20, 27, 39, 66, 71, 78, 83, 136, 145
Capitol Hill 11, 66, 71
Charlottesville Rally 8, 75, 144, 165
commodity XI, 31, 41, 46, 49, 50, 54, 67, 101
conservative 11, 23, 24, 28, 41, 60, 69, 71, 77–80, 110, 114, 119–121, 132, 134, 136, 137, 139, 140, 145, 148, 149, 155

conspiracy theories 1, 7, 25, 28, 30, 31, 33, 53, 55, 71, 72, 86, 113, 125, 144, 145
conversationalization 48
Coronavirus/COVID-19 XII, XVI, 28, 40, 46, 53, 115, 116, 125, 145
critical consciousness XVI, 10, 47, 107, 123, 124, 132, 141, 142, 147, 153, 154
critical discourse
 analysis 57, 60, 68, 69
 studies XIV, XVI, 18, 53, 57, 58, 67–69
critical pedagogy XVI, 10, 11, 100, 103, 104, 106–113, 115, 119–126, 138
Critical Race Theory (CRT) 11, 112, 132–136, 144
Critical Theory XII, 15, 19, 41, 42, 45–47, 70, 104, 107, 112, 149
cultural diversity 18
culture industry 49, 50, 52

decolonial 124, 145, 146, 151
demagogy 18
Democrats 28, 29, 49, 81–83, 88, 106, 115
dehistoricization 41, 46, 47, 67, 87–89, 94, 101, 126, 150, 155
dehumanization XII, XIII, 49, 145, 146
deplatform 39
dictatorship 20
discourse
 as commodity 41, 49, 50
 extremism 57, 71, 72, 87, 121
 historical approach 11, 68–70
 of amusement 41, 52, 67
 one-dimensional authoritarian 46, 59, 67, 86
 pedagogic 151, 152
digital aggressiveness, language of XIV, 48, 66, 93
digital extremism 57
digital propaganda 33, 86

echo chamber 85, 86
Election 2020 1, 17, 28, 29, 79, 82
Erasebook 78

168 INDEX

Facebook 39, 40, 46, 51–54, 58, 59, 66, 71, 73, 77–79
Fairclough, Norman 48, 68, 83
far right/far-right
  authoritarianism XIV, 3–5, 122, 139, 154
  in Europe 21, 29
  populist authoritarianism 3–5, 10, 11, 70
fascism 5, 10, 11, 14–17, 50, 51, 136, 138, 139
  Europe XIII, 15, 21
  Latin America XIII, 20
  neo- XIII, XIV, 17, 18, 21, 23, 24, 69, 71, 144, 154
  new 14–17, 23, 33
  post- 17
  proto- 17
  United States XIII, 25, 33
fascist ideologies XIV, 10, 24, 25
Frankfurt School XIII, XV, 11, 15, 40, 42, 45, 60, 104, 107, 138, 149
Freire, Paulo 104, 107, 126, 140, 153, 155
Fromm, Erich XII
front stage performance 32, 51, 81, 82

Gab 33, 58, 71, 78, 80, 145
Golden Dawn XIV, 24, 73, 75, 77

hidden curriculum 109
historical narrative 137–151, 145, 150–153
Hitler, Adolf 17–19, 26, 48, 59, 73, 75, 86, 90
Horkheimer, Max 154

ideology
  fascist XIV, 10, 24, 25
  neoliberal 139
ideological confusion 2, 3, 7, 30–32, 45, 83, 134, 144
ideological domination 42
identity 6, 23, 25, 44, 51, 56, 69, 93 143, 146
Iron March XV, 11, 41, 47, 58, 60, 67, 71–77, 79, 85–87, 89, 90, 92, 149
immigrants XI, 8, 11, 21, 25, 28, 30, 49, 77, 82, 83, 93, 118, 119, 143
influencer 50, 58, 59
instrumentalism 41, 47, 89, 94, 140, 154
Islamophobia 15, 16

January 6th, 2021 1, 2, 20, 27, 68, 71, 78–80, 84, 85

Kellner, Douglas 18, 49

language
  of aggressiveness XIV, 48, 66, 93
  of total administration 43, 45, 47, 85

Manichean 135, 141
Marcuse, Herbert 14, 15, 19, 23, 41–48, 52, 55, 56, 60, 86, 88, 147, 150
Mazzoleni, Gianpietro 56
mediatization 3, 4, 41, 55–60, 67
meritocracy 102
militarization XII, 17, 24, 49, 117
militia 2, 4, 25, 27, 28, 30, 79, 93

narrative XI, XIII, 32, 82, 84–86, 94, 111, 125, 126, 133, 137–141, 144–147, 149–155
Nazism 15, 93
neoliberal XII, XVI, XVII, 6, 7, 15, 16, 20, 22, 28, 100, 101, 103, 106, 111, 114, 115, 121, 133, 139, 141
neoliberalism 20, 106, 113–115, 121
neo-Nazi XIII, XIV, 2, 4, 11, 26, 41, 47, 49, 58, 60, 67, 72–78, 88, 139, 149
neo-Nazi party XIV, XV, 22, 24, 77

omniopticon 59
one-dimensional
  discourse 39, 43–46, 60, 85, 86, 143
  historical narrative 150, 153
  man 41, 42
operationalism 41, 47, 48

pandemic XII, XVI, 6, 28, 29, 40, 46, 81, 115, 116, 125, 132
Parler 11, 33, 41, 58, 60, 67, 71, 77–80, 84, 85, 87, 88
pedagogic discourse 151, 152
pedagogy XVI, 3, 7, 9–11, 19, 46, 100, 103, 104, 106–113, 115, 117, 119–126, 138, 140, 151, 153–155
performative politics 32
populism
  authoritarian XI, XIII, 3, 5–7, 14, 16, 18, 31, 41, 51, 58, 60, 67, 93, 142
  far-right XIII, XIV, XV, 4–7, 30, 125, 139, 145
  right-wing 2, 4, 6, 7, 18, 21, 23, 28, 31, 42, 51, 57, 121

INDEX 169

populist
  discourse XIV, 4, 8, 11, 67–69, 83, 89
  leader 22, 23, 29, 32, 33, 51, 81, 82, 143

QAnon 2, 28, 78, 113, 144, 145

racism XI, XII, 2, 3, 7, 16, 18, 22, 24–26, 28,
    31, 32, 40, 92, 105, 109, 112, 113, 122, 123,
    132–139, 145, 146, 148, 154
rally 8, 26, 68, 71, 75, 79–84, 91, 92, 144, 165
recontextualization 148, 150–152
Republican Party 3, 25, 26, 30, 80, 134, 145
Republicans 3, 25–31, 77, 80, 106, 115, 132,
    134, 136, 144, 145
revisionism (historical) 7, 11, 88, 126, 136,
    138, 142–145, 149, 154
right
  extreme 6, 18, 20, 22, 24, 28, 30, 88
  far XI, XIII–XV, 2–8, 10, 11, 14, 22–24,
    27, 29–33, 39, 41, 49, 51, 58, 67–75, 77–79,
    82–84, 88–90, 93, 103, 121, 122, 125, 126,
    135–137, 139, 142–145, 148–150, 154, 155
right-wing 2, 4–8, 11, 18, 19, 21–25, 28, 30, 31,
    41, 42, 51, 57, 58, 69
  populism 2, 4, 6, 7, 18, 21, 23, 28, 31, 42,
    51, 57, 121
Riley, Dylan 17

Save America Rally 68, 71, 80, 83
self 1, 5, 41, 48–51, 53, 59, 69, 78, 79, 81, 93,
    101, 110, 111, 143, 146, 149
social media XIV, 1, 3, 4, 7–11, 28, 33, 39–60,
    66, 67, 69, 71, 74, 77, 79, 80, 82, 83, 85,
    93, 94, 113, 117, 118, 124, 125, 144, 145,
    150, 155
  and self-branding 51

social media-critical discourse studies
    57
speech at Ellipse 68, 71, 79, 80–82, 84, 85
Spencer, Richard 26, 28, 76
synopticon 59

Telegram 11, 33, 58, 60, 67, 71, 78, 79, 85–88
TikTok 125
total administration 43, 45, 47, 85
totalitarian 43, 44, 47, 50
Topos, Topoi 70, 76, 80, 83, 86, 89
trauma XII, XIII, 122, 148
Traverso, Enzo 16, 142, 143
Trump, Donald XIV, 1–4, 6–9, 17, 18, 21,
    23–33, 39, 47–49, 58, 59, 66, 67, 71, 72,
    74–86, 89–93, 110, 119, 121, 122, 134–136,
    142, 144, 145, 161–163, 165
Trumpism XIII, 5, 7–9, 11, 14, 17, 19, 21,
    26–28, 30–33, 57, 67, 79, 82, 83, 86, 90,
    114, 134, 136, 138, 139, 142, 144, 147
  as a far-right populist movement XIV, 2,
    3, 23, 142
Trumpist discourse 3, 11, 80, 82
Twexit 78
Twitter 11, 33, 39–41, 49, 51–55, 58, 59, 66, 67,
    71, 72, 77, 79, 80, 89, 145, 162, 164

us vs. them 83

van Leeuwen, Teo 47, 152

White-supremacy/supremacist 1–3, 18, 24,
    26, 28, 31, 33, 58, 59, 72, 73, 75–77, 85,
    87, 112, 122, 132–134, 137, 144
Wodak, Ruth 4, 6, 11, 18, 22, 32, 33, 45, 51, 68,
    69, 70, 152

Printed in the United States
by Baker & Taylor Publisher Services